# The Market Guys' Five Points for Trading Success

## IDENTIFY, PINPOINT, STRIKE, PROTECT, AND ACT!

A. J. Monte
Rick Swope

BICENTENNIAL
BICENTENNIAL
1807
WILEY
2007
BICENTENNIAL
BICENTENNIAL

John Wiley & Sons, Inc.

Published by John Wiley & Sons, Inc., Hoboken, New Jersey.
Published simultaneously in Canada.

Wiley Bicentennial Logo: Richard J. Pacifico

For general information on our other products and services or for technical
support, please contact our Customer Care Department within the United States at
(800) 762-2974, outside the United States at (317) 572-3993 or fax (317) 572-4002.

Wiley also publishes its books in a variety of electronic formats. Some content that
appears in print may not be available in electronic formats. For more information
about Wiley products, visit our Web site at www.wiley.com.

*Library of Congress Cataloging-in-Publication Data:*

Monte, A. J., 1958-
    The market guys' five points for trading success : identify, pinpoint, strike,
protect, and act! / A. J. Monte And Rick Swope.
        p.   cm.
    Includes index.
    ISBN 978-0-470-13897-7 (cloth)
        1. Stocks.   2. Investments.   3. Speculation.   I. Swope, Rick, 1964-   II. Title.
    HG6041.M653   2008
    332.63'22–dc22

                                                                2007028034

Printed in the United States of America

10 9 8 7 6 5 4 3 2 1

# Contents

**Point II:** Establish a Clear Support Level: Pinpoint Support

**Point III:** Wait for the Pivot Point: Strike with the Buyers

**Chapter 14**    Going to the Dance: Finding
Your Broker

**Point V:** Take Action: Act for Results

**Chapter 15**    The Trade and Beyond:
Wealth Has a Purpose

# Preface

When we stand before a new audience for the first time, we often get some variation of the following question: "Why should I listen to anything you have to tell me?" It's a fair question and one that we would expect you to ask of anyone who offers their advice. Over the years, we have had the privilege of working with hundreds of thousands of investors and traders all around the world. Long before this book was ever considered, The Market Guys were talking to traders in London, teaching beginner options to students in Taipei, and helping investors protect their portfolios in Stockholm. Through all of these experiences, we have observed certain strategies and characteristics that are common to successful traders. We have also observed certain other strategies and characteristics that are common to unsuccessful traders.

We have joined you on the front lines of trading and investing. We did not just read about stocks and options and use that information to build a supposedly better mousetrap. Rather, we have bought and paid for our education through real trades. We know what it feels like to go home with a trade that could ruin your family finances. We have watched helplessly as the market shut down for want of buyers when we desperately needed to sell. We counseled traders who were placing their last dollar on a high-risk speculative trade in the hope that they could possibly escape their failings in the market.

Along the way, we realized that we were uniquely positioned to actually help people protect their assets while building wealth. You see, we didn't create The Market Guys' Five Points for Trading Success as a marketing gimmick to entice you to purchase our version of beating the market. In a sense, this was a book that had to be written. It was born of our passion to teach and truly make a difference in peoples' lives. If we can help one person preserve a retirement account through a simple risk management strategy, our work has been worthwhile. It has been said that teaching is a function of who you are, not what you do. Simply, a teacher must teach. Regardless of our financial lot in life, we would continue to teach because we love to see a life transformed.

We are not so vain as to suggest that ours is the only path to success in the markets. Many well-intentioned traders, financial advisers, and money managers will doubtless take issue with various parts of our presentation. The world of finance and economics leaves that door open. As teachers, we know that we must continue to learn even as we teach. If we find a point that needs to be refined or a strategy that could be improved, we will be the first to incorporate the changes. In the meantime, know that what we have laid out in this book is the best that we have encountered.

The book contains 15 chapters, with each of the five points arriving at every third chapter. We begin by discussing the business of trading and the importance of a trading plan. A key benefit of the trading plan is helping you manage your emotions, which is the subject of Chapter 2. Then we move into the tools of technical analysis and some of the common mistakes that people make in the markets. One of the lighter topics is Chapter 7; the seventh-inning stretch. Here, we touch on the importance of keeping yourself in shape to enjoy the fruits of your labors. More strategies and techniques follow in the next two chapters as we review the best ways to find stocks and where to enter a new trade. From there, we introduce you to the exciting world of options and show you that they are not just for the professional trader. Chapter 12 covers the critical topic of managing risk using Point IV, the 1% Rule. The home stretch takes a light-hearted approach to fictional traders who have not quite reached the pinnacle of success. After a short discussion on how to select a broker, we move to the final Point V, which implores us to take action.

Another feature that you'll find throughout the text is the Chatter Box. We have written this book together, but there are various times when we share personal stories to help explain a point or add some emphasis. These vignettes may talk about people we've worked with, life experiences, or other observations and are noted as either Rick's Chatter Box or AJ's Chatter Box.

*The Market Guys' Five Points for Trading Success* is a compilation of strategies and practices that we trust will empower you to be successful in the markets. But we want it to be much more than a how-to reference book for trading. Throughout the following chapters, you'll read stories and examples of real people in real situations.

You'll learn a bit more about our journey in this world of finances and how we've grown over the years. Of course, you will see that we are laying out for you the accumulated learning and experiences from our minds. More than that, though, we hope you will see that we are also offering you a gift from our hearts.

In the final chapter, which discusses Point V, you will realize that our admonition to you to take action extends beyond the mere act of executing a trade. We want you to understand the reason we continue to reach out to our audience every day. Wealth really does have a purpose. And that purpose dovetails with our purpose. We trust that our faithfulness will leave the path we walk just a little straighter for the ones who follow.

RICK AND AJ
*June 2007*

# Acknowledgments

Through this book, The Market Guys have invested our time, energy, and passion to give you the very best we have. However, there are so many more who have given of themselves to make this project a reality. We wish to recognize some of them for their contributions in this space.

## RICK

*I want to thank my own "Market Kids," Caleb and Tori, for giving up time with Dad to meet writing deadlines and giving me hugs at the critical moments. The support and encouragement of my wife, Dani, kept me going through many late nights and long miles. She is uniquely gifted with tireless enthusiasm and encouragement. Finally, I am grateful to my parents, who not only gave me both roots and wings, but are continuing that legacy with their grandchildren. The foundation of that legacy for our family is 2 Corinthians 8:9: the secret of true riches.*

## AJ

*I am fortunate to be someone who was able to marry his high school sweetheart. Yvonne, I've known you since you were 15 years old. Not only have you been my best friend, whom I trust with my life, but you have also been the rock who grounds me in life. To my two wonderful sons, Greg and Anthony, you give me the energy to continue on. I see greatness in both of you, and I trust you will go out in the world and make a difference. Mom and Dad, I have learned how to be successful from watching you both. Understand that the lessons you have taught me as a child are now changing the lives of millions of people around the world for good.*

We both wish to thank Laura Walsh, Emilie Herman, and the rest of the staff at Wiley Publishing. Their patience and encouragement helped to transform a couple of market guys into authors. Thanks to Bill Johnson for sharing his expertise in options, and finally, we want to thank you, the reader, for considering this book worthy of your hard-earned dollars. We trust you will have found the investment worthwhile.

# About the Authors

## Rick Swope

Rick has presented in many seminars across the United States and around the world for some of the world's top financial firms. Specializing in the areas of technical analysis and risk management, his topics have continually stayed in demand. His passion for teaching is obvious, and his energy is contagious. His teaching experience includes corporate training, seminar speaking, and six years as an adjunct lecturer in probability and statistics for engineers.

Rick was the managing partner of a trading firm in Cincinnati for several years, providing technical analysis, trading strategy, and software training to the firm's traders. Rick worked with many of the pioneers of day trading: the so-called SOES Bandits, who paved the way for millions of retail traders around the world today. Rick created the first active trading field sales team for the Charles Schwab company. Many members of that team are now training and consulting leaders in other firms around the country.

Rick is the co-host of The Market Guys'on-demand radio show, which is consistently rated among the top on-demand business programs in the world. He is the co-host of *Wealth & Wisdom,* a weekly financial show on WXEL PBS television in south Florida. He has been a speaker in many locations including the London IX Show, the Toronto Financial Forum, the International Finance Center Hong Kong, and the Chicago Board Options Exchange. His education through his doctoral studies was in the areas of engineering, mathematics, operations research, and statistics, and he has been a registered securities principal.

## AJ Monte, CMT

AJ Monte began his trading career on the floor of the New York Commodities Exchange (COMEX) in August 1982. Shortly after that, he started his own trading firm and spent over 10 years trading gold, silver, and copper along with coffee, sugar, cocoa, and orange juice. He served for two years as the chairman of the Options Floor Trading Committee for COMEX and is considered to be one of the world's leading authorities in option trading.

Just before leaving the trading floor, to trade as a Nasdaq market maker, he helped with the production of the Hollywood hit film *Trading Places,* starring Dan Aykroyd and Eddie Murphy. Over 20 years later, this movie is still being enjoyed by millions around the world. Even though it was written as a comedy film, it is one of the best educational works about life on the trading floor.

Several years later, AJ pioneered the Trading Analytics Group for Charles Schwab & Co., which is a collection of team professionals who educate both clients and high-profile brokers in the areas of technical and fundamental analysis. As a member of the Market Technicians Association (MTA), he is also a chartered market technician.

AJ now co-hosts a prime-time financial television show called *Wealth & Wisdom,* which airs on PBS through station WXEL in West Palm Beach and is heard through on-demand radio as one of The Market Guys. AJ is still going strong on the seminar circuit, speaking as a master trainer for Anthony Robbins Wealth Mastery and master trainer for the Chicago Board Options Exchange, along with guest appearances at money shows and trading expos around the world.

# Introduction

*T*he Market Guys' Five Points for Trading Success exemplifies our philosophy of Keep It Super Simple (KISS). Before you begin with the first chapter of this book, take a few minutes and review the following overview of the five points. You'll see that the points are easy to grasp and just as easy to follow. Even if you're a new trader, we think you'll appreciate the simplicity of the strategy.

## 1. Follow the Money Trail: Identify the Trend

If you're going to buy a stock, be sure it is in a well-established uptrend. Put your money where the money is going. You don't have enough money to turn the market around, so don't try to buy into a downtrend. We've yet to meet the trader who can consistently buy the bottom and sell the top. Go with the flow.

## 2. Establish a Clear Support Level: Pinpoint Support

For a long stock position, you need to identify a clear support level. This is the level where the buyers step in after a period of selling and push the stock back up. Identifying this price level is critical because it will help you identify when you are wrong and you need to exit the position. Trading without a clearly defined support level will leave you blind in your risk management.

## 3. Wait for the Pivot Point: Strike with the Buyers

The pivot point is created when an uptrending stock has pulled back to support and then started a new leg upward. It looks like a "V" on the line chart. The left side of the "V" is the pullback down to support. The right side of the "V" is formed when the buyers step back in and rally the stock off support. Even though the stock is in an overall uptrend, the rule here is to buy with the buyers.

## 4. The 1% Rule: Protect Your Position

The 1% Rule is your guideline for deliberately and specifically managing risk. Limit your loss on any given trade to 1 percent of your trading account. This is accomplished by identifying your risk per share based on the support identified in Point II and then tying it into your position size. By trading the right position size and exiting the trade when support is broken, you are able to limit a single trade loss to 1 percent of your trading account value.

## 5. Take Action: Act for Results

Taking action brings The Market Guys' Five Points for Trading Success into reality. It involves two steps: actually executing the trade and then recognizing that your wealth has a purpose. Don't be afraid to take some risk and be ready to reap the rewards. When you've achieved success, change your world.

1

# Blueprint for Success

## CREATING YOUR TRADING PLAN

In 490 B.C. the Persian army invaded the plains of Marathon and met the forces of Athens in what was perhaps the single most important battle in Greek history. The Athenian army took the offensive against the vastly larger Persian forces while they were still preparing for battle. Against great odds, the Greeks prevailed. According to legend, a Greek soldier named Pheidippides ran from Marathon to Athens with the message, "Rejoice! We conquer!" He immediately collapsed and died from his efforts. Today, in the United States alone, nearly half a million runners participate every year in the 26.2-mile race that commemorates Pheidippides's valiant feat.

In preparation for this event, runners will lay out a schedule that covers diet, running mileage, hill workouts versus speed training, sleep, recovery days, and hydration. Entire web sites, books, and software packages are devoted to making sure the runner doesn't overlook any detail that could hinder performance when race day finally rolls around. Depending on the experience of the runner, weeks or even months are dedicated to planning and preparation for the marathon. If you scour through all the articles and books written on marathon competition, almost all will include, or at least refer to, some type of training plan. And yet, for all the preparation, most runners will be finished with the event just a few hours after the starting gun fires. Of course, they'll all walk away with a space-age marathon blanket, T-shirt, goody bag, and sore legs that won't be back to normal for at least two weeks.

Why is it that the same person who wouldn't dream of running a marathon without a complete plan will manage their finances without so much as a thought about how they'll achieve their objectives? Take it a step further—many of these same people run through their investments without even defining their objectives! The reason we open this book with a discussion of a trading plan is that it will set the foundation for everything we do. One of the fatal flaws of trading is that it lets us enter the game without a trading plan. Worse, we may even be successful for a time.

It is not at all uncommon for a new trader to place a trade and make a profit. The new trader is especially careful to analyze the trade prior to opening the position. Then they step through the trade with the care that one takes when treading new territory. Before they know it, the trade is profitable and they close the position with a net gain. They start thinking, "Hey, this is easier than I thought!" and they move to the next trade. Before long, they're taking positions with more confidence and the assumed risk increases with each trade. This same trader may have a stretch of profitable trading but then falls into a losing pattern. Or they experience "The Trade"; the single trade that cures them of any remaining vestige of confidence as it falls below every support and drains their account into a maintenance call. The problem is that this trader may not even realize that they have fallen into a period of net losses or, if they do recognize it, they don't understand the reasons for their change in fortune. As a last resort, they'll change their trading style; opening exceptionally large positions to try to exact revenge on the market, trading options without proper training or becoming a long-term investor by holding on to positions that were originally meant to be short-term trades. All of this is the result of not having a trading plan and holding yourself accountable to the objectives that you're trading toward. In this chapter, we'll discuss in detail some of the key components of a trading plan and then conclude with a trading plan checklist.

## Trading Is No Longer a Team Sport

Retail trading really came into its heyday in the mid-1990s with the explosive growth of day trading. In 1997, two guys from Houston, Chris Block and Jeff Burke, made the cover of *Inc.* magazine with the teaser headline "Bad Boys of Wall Street." The article started with this opening line: *Their aim: move fast, make money, have fun. Who knew they would threaten a whole industry in the process?* With talk about fast cars, new offices, and armies of traders who were practically siphoning money from the market in mere seconds, the phenomenon of retail day trading was launched. One example refers to Jeff Burke's biggest day in the market when he made $50,000. $50,000 in one day! People were flocking to the Block Trading headquarters in Houston and dropping $25,000 just for the right to lock down a city for opening a franchise at some point in the future. Block Trading is no longer around, but there are some lessons to be learned from those early days.

First of all, in the mid-1990s the state of technology required that people find a retail trading office to trade. Sure, there were some choices that allowed for trading remotely, but the quality of information and trade execution wasn't nearly as high as what was available in a trading office. These offices created an atmosphere of anticipation and played on the trader's ego. They were often dimly lit with the shades pulled over the windows. Multiple television monitors constantly played CNBC and other networks for immediate market commentary. Other monitors displayed real-time news feeds, which scrolled through headlines too fast to allow for any analysis but served to let the traders know they were still plugged into the action. Banks of trading computers sat side by side, with traders coming and going throughout the day. It wasn't unusual to see a highly respected heart surgeon trading next to a college dropout and the two of them speaking to each other as colleagues. Occasionally, a trader would enter the room with one of the subscription-based split pagers. These creative devices did exactly what the name suggests. Whenever news hit the wires of a company announcing a stock split, the pager would send an alert with the information. For a time, the fortunate trader could take a position before the news was fully digested by the market and then sell into the crowd's buying.

The technology also allowed traders on the floor to access Level 2 data. In addition to the National Best Bid and Offer (NBBO), with Level 2 you could see all of the price and volume levels below the high bid and above the low offer (see Figure 1.1). This was something that most *brokers* hadn't seen at that time. Finally, these traders often traded before the market opened at 9:30 A.M. and traded well past the market's close at 4:00 P.M. Using the new kids on the technology block,

## International Business Machines

| Symbol | IBM   |      | -1.33 |        |           |
|--------|-------|------|-------|--------|-----------|
| Bid    | 94.52 | High | 96.11 |        |           |
| Ask    | 94.55 | Low  | 94.26 | Volume | 4,300,000 |

| MM   | Bid   | Size | MM   | Ask   | Size |
|------|-------|------|------|-------|------|
| NYS  | 94.52 | 1000 | ARCA | 94.55 | 100  |
| ARCA | 94.51 | 300  | ARCA | 94.58 | 400  |
| INET | 94.51 | 500  | NYS  | 94.59 | 1000 |
| PSE  | 94.50 | 500  | PSE  | 94.61 | 500  |

(MM = Market Maker)

**Figure 1.1   Level 2 National Best Bid and Offer (NBBO)**

electronic communication networks (ECNs), retail traders could buy and sell to each other even when the rest of the market was closed. Finally, these rooms were often separated from the lobby area by an attentive gatekeeper, who let only the chosen traders through a door that bore the sign, "Trading Room—Traders Only."

While these retail trading rooms had many faults that are outside both the scope and objective of this book, there was one key benefit that they provided to the trader. An esprit de corps developed between traders because they were trading day after day with the same people. This camaraderie caused traders to help each other through education and accountability. One of the common practices of day traders in these retail offices was to call out fills. Let's say several traders wanted to buy 1,000 shares each of Microsoft. The first trader to get his buy order filled would call out the details of the fill: which market maker filled his order, how many shares they sold, and whether the order was filled on the bid or offer. All of this information would be helpful to the other traders as they managed their orders. For example, if a key market maker (often called the Axe) filled the order very quickly on the bid, that told the other traders that there may be heavy selling pressure and they could lower their buy order or cancel it altogether in anticipation of a price drop. The point to be made here is that the group of traders as a whole had more information than individual traders alone.

The mechanics of a trade were also much easier to learn in the retail trading rooms. There are seemingly endless details that a new trader must learn about the trading software, types of trades, when to place trades, position sizing, and so forth. In the isolation of one's own home office, finding the answers to these questions or learning the nuances of the minor details can be difficult at best, impossible at worst. However, in the retail trading offices, these issues were discussed throughout the day, and a new trader would very quickly pick up the salient points of the game.

Besides the learning environment that trading floors offered, the accountability that naturally resulted from trading elbow to elbow was another significant benefit. If you took a position and called out the fill as we described a moment ago, everyone around you knew what you were trading. That meant they knew if you were making money—or losing money! There was a peer pressure that grew if you stayed in a losing position. Nobody likes to have to admit that they're losing money, so it was easier to close out a position for a small loss than to hold on to a loser and have to continually explain to your fellow traders why you thought this trade was going to be different. In today's trading environment, we trade with almost total anonymity. Often, a trader's own spouse isn't aware of the activity in the trading account. This situation makes it very easy to rationalize bad trades in our heads and continue holding a bad position.

To accommodate these deficiencies in the contemporary trading environment, a trading plan needs to include both points: education and accountability. It's imperative that the trader recognize that while the market is generally simple to enter, there are many facets of trading that require a sequential education plan. For example, any new trader can step in and place a buy order, followed by a sell order. But understanding how to properly analyze chart patterns prior to entering the trade isn't intuitive. Learning to read a chart is very similar to learning a new language. Both require some formal education followed by practice using the new language. The market is also constantly changing, and the education plan should include continuing education. In the past decade we've seen such changes as decimalization of pricing, increasing interest in options trading, and expanded capabilities of trading software platforms. If you hide your head in the sand and fail to advance with the market and technology, you will eventually be left at a disadvantage.

When a trading plan is developed, it becomes the benchmark for accountability. The plan will become the surrogate for the trader who once sat by your side and knew if you were following your defined strategy. Let's assume that your plan is to be a day trader. By definition, a day trader opens the day and closes the day in cash. Long or short positions are opened and closed during market hours, and the price moves are measured in minutes or hours. Because your plan includes a strategy for your time horizon, you'll know when that strategy is broken. We'll take a look at an example of how this would work. After analyzing the opening of the market, you see that the stock price gapped down and dropped to support. You decide to buy the stock on support based on the expectation that it will bounce off support in the next hour and you'll capture a profit from the quick rally. After entering the position, the stock languishes on the support line for the rest of the day. It neither bounces up to new highs nor drops below support to new lows. At this point, you have a decision to make. Based on your trading plan, you should exit the position and close the day in cash. You could always reestablish the long position tomorrow if the stock is still holding on to support. However, you decide to hold the position overnight by rationalizing that it could gap up tomorrow in the same way it gapped down today and you don't want to miss the move. This type of decision is really based on hope rather than any proper analysis. The worst-case scenario occurs the next day when the stock gaps down below support. Having rationalized the first departure from the trading plan, you now continue with reasons why the drop shouldn't continue. Two weeks later you find that you're spending every moment in the market staring at this open position as the stock continues on its downward course, searching for any semblance of support that you can hang your hopes upon. How did you get here? Simple—you broke the rules that you established in your trading plan. Even if the position had not moved into a loss, it didn't reach your objective (a bounce off of support) in the time frame that your strategy requires. Most traders find themselves in this situation because they don't have a trading plan, though, not because they ignored their trading plan. The point here is that a trading plan will highlight for you the proper course of action and help to hold you accountable to your decision.

Before we move on, we should take a closer look at the issue of trading time horizons. When The Market Guys present at trading expos, we'll often jokingly advise people to avoid becoming investors because they're bad traders. But the painful truth is that many people have long-term positions in their portfolio that were originally meant to be short-term trades. In fact, the U.S. Internal Revenue Service recognizes "worthless stock" when a stock price has dropped to the point that there is no reasonable hope of recovery. Isn't it ironic that the IRS will recognize the truth in a trade before we will? Don't raise your hand as you read this paragraph (especially if you're reading this on an airplane or sitting next to your wife at an antiques auction), but how many of you still have Webvan Group (see Figure 1.2) somewhere in your account? At what point should you have recognized that maybe this stock wasn't going to return to its previous highs? At one time, this stock was a popular trading stock among retail day traders. Many of these traders made good profits over time on this stock, too. Somewhere along the way, though, the position they bought didn't behave the way it had in the past. For the unfortunate trader who held the position in the hope that it would recover, the stock never met their expectation. By the end of 2001, the price had dropped below a penny and has rested comfortably there ever since.

The reason we're spending additional time on this point is that it is one of the most common mistakes made by novice and experienced traders alike. As long as the position is open, there is hope for recovery, however remote. Once the position is closed, we've locked in our loss. There is a misleading belief that a loss isn't a loss

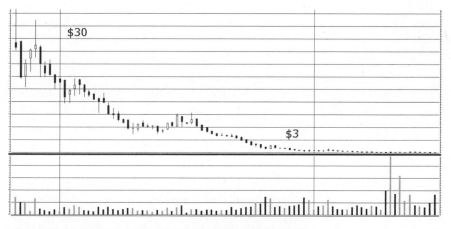

**Figure 1.2   Webvan (Ticker: WBVNQ) 1999–2001**

until the trade is closed. Nonsense! Don't ever use this fool's logic on yourself. Whether a trade is open or closed, if the stock price is lower now than when you bought it, you have a loss! One of the characteristics of trading options is that it forces you to admit your loss by a predetermined date when the option expires. Stock traders can fool themselves ad infinitum because a stock doesn't expire unless the company finally declares bankruptcy and reorganizes. Your trading plan should define your time horizon—whether it's intraday, short-term swing trading over one to two weeks, or position trading over a number of months. Your analysis of the trade should be based on that time horizon, and then you need to be diligent in holding yourself accountable to that plan. If you've opened a position and found that the trade has started to exceed your time horizon, close the trade and find a new position. You may not be losing money in the stock itself, but if you've locked your cash into a nonperformer, you're experiencing a loss of opportunity. Remember, you could always place your cash into a certificate of deposit and get a nominal interest return.

## Beware the Siren Song of Gurus

We'd like to have a dollar for every time someone asked The Market Guys about our opinion on the "winning stock market system du jour." There are some common traits that may be found in the claims of these systems:

- They'll show you how to make money with unrealistically low risk.
- The founder has "discovered" a secret to the market that somehow evaded millions of other traders.
- The system will teach you what only the professionals know and don't want you to know.
- Their disciples will march before a camera with claims of having made thousands or millions in a relatively short time period.
- They'll tell you that you're not making money because you're trading the wrong product—for example, currencies are more profitable than stocks, gold is more profitable than mutual funds, and so on.

We'll assume that we're not surprising you here with anything that you haven't already seen on late-night infomercials or pop-up banners on your favorite search engine. One of the questions that comes to our minds each time we see these is: Why do they always include the caveat "Results Not Typical" when their followers are onscreen making claims of riches? If the system really works, shouldn't the results be typical? Let's be clear about the purpose of *The Market Guys' Five Points for Trading Success*—we're not showing you anything new or revolutionary. We especially don't claim to hold a "secret" that we'll tell you for the right price. We're offering this guide as a collection of best practices that are known to retail and professional traders alike. If you've reached this point in your reading with the belief that by the end of this book you'll have the secret to fast riches, then please stop now and discard those thoughts. The markets reward the patient and disciplined, not the greedy and careless.

Looking at this phenomenon from another angle, consider the following credentials and decide if you would listen to this person as a financial guru. Ben was diligent in attending to his financial plan. At least once a week, he would review the numbers and make the appropriate buy decisions. One thing about Ben, though, is that he never sold. He had been working with the same strategy for years and he stuck to his plan. As Ben would tell it, he didn't get caught up in complex investments. He never touched options, currencies, or futures. He had a single objective and pursued it with unassuming patience. Just a few years ago, Ben had less than $100,000 cash. Last year, Ben decided to retire at 52 years old with over $66 million in his account. Again we'll pose the question: Would you consider this person as a role model for your financial planning? Take it a step further. If you saw the previous biographical description under a sales banner advertising "Ben's Secrets to Wealth and Financial Security," a five-CD set along with accompanying workbooks for only $99, would you drop the $99? Well, it would certainly make sense until we give you the final piece of the profile puzzle. Ben Chason had just won the annuitized $163 million Mega Millions jackpot, a multistate lottery. The $66 million was his after-tax check from his winning numbers. Interestingly, we also see lottery winners in the markets. These are the people who, for example, had stock options loaded into their employee retirement accounts during the 1990s' tech boom and woke up to find seven- or eight-figure account equities. While we can admire them for their good fortune, we need to be careful about setting them on a pedestal as the model of mastering the markets.

---

### Chatter Box—AJ

While Rick and I are traveling around the world, it is not uncommon for us to meet people who are excited about the opportunities in trading the U.S. markets. If you are just starting out with your own trading plan, be sure your excitement doesn't get in the way of making good, sound investment decisions. If you are at the basic levels of trading, everyone you meet at the trade shows will look like an expert. Don't be fooled by the bells and whistles; simply check the resumes of those who claim to be experts and you will have a better chance of avoiding the "noise." We will be talking more about this in the chapters that follow.

---

When you look at others who exhibit the outward appearance of having mastered the markets, you'll be tempted to trade what they're trading. Take a look to your left and you'll see the gold trader and decide that gold is where you need to be. So you load up on gold stock, gold funds, gold futures, and rare coins. But then it hits you that gold can drop in price, too. You then look to the right and hear that options are the way to make consistent money. After all, you've always heard that the most you can lose is the price you pay for the option, right? Because you don't understand how to trade options, you still aren't making money but at least you're losing it more slowly. It may take longer, but the strategy will still deplete your account. It's a bit like getting nibbled to death by a duck; it doesn't really hurt along the way but the end result is the same. Finally, you decide that your real problem is that your analysis isn't comprehensive enough. Having pored through all the trading magazines and books you can find, you realize that you're only using less than 5 percent of the possible technical indicators. If the Fibonacci retracements, fans, and circles aren't important, then why are they discussed by the experienced traders? Surely, that's the reason why your trading isn't profitable. You decide to purchase the complete course on Elliott waves and get yourself to the point where you can discuss Fibonacci as if you'd discovered the Golden Ratio yourself.

Now your pretrade analysis includes a combined convergence of retracements, wave analysis, Bollinger Bands, and three stochastics. But you're still losing money.

Here's where your trading plan comes into play. Your plan includes a definition of what you plan to trade. If you're going to trade stocks, then ignore the calls to chase the riches of gold. If you want to trade gold, fine—then develop a new plan. Don't ignore your existing plan because you stayed up too late in the hotel room and the only entertainment on TV was an infomercial for collectible coins. The Market Guys are great believers in the power of options as a trading product. But if you don't have a plan to learn how to trade them properly and what your strategy looks like, then don't touch them! Your plan should also outline your trading objectives. If you've decided that your goal is to beat the broad market performance by 10 percent, then you should be working toward an 11 percent return when the Dow or S&P 500 is up 10 percent. That's a reasonably conservative goal for a trader who is approaching retirement age and can't sustain large drops in his account value. Now if you see a banner scrolling across your computer screen with claims of 700 percent returns in the market, your response should be to smile and move on. That's not your goal, and you're fooling yourself if you think that those kinds of returns don't come with a corresponding increase in risk.

## Know When to Fold 'Em

We would be remiss in our discussion of a trading plan if we didn't take a few moments to delve into the trader-cum-gambler personality. In 1997, we had a trader who came into our day-trading office with a single trading objective. He had noticed that a particular stock had repeated the same cycle for the previous several years (see Figure 1.3). The stock would dip at the end of the year and then rise through the first part of the following year. Toward the end of the year, the stock would drop downward, only to rise again in the first quarter of the following year. His plan was to short the stock before the dip and ride the falling wave through the end of the year. He didn't have a what-if plan at all. If the stock failed to perform as he expected, there was no risk management. In essence, he was laying his fortune on "Red-One"—the highest payout slot on the roulette wheel.

Since his story made it into this chapter of the book, you've already guessed that the ball didn't land on Red-One. As the year

**Figure 1.3    A Cycling Stock that Failed to Cycle**

came to a close, not only did the stock fail to drop, but it was trending upward, which put him into a maintenance call. That's when
the value of your equity drops to the point that any purchases or
shorts made on margin (borrowed money) must either be covered
or more money must be deposited into the account to protect the
broker against the trader's defaulting on the loan. So the trader
went for the double-or-nothing move. He collected more funds and
shorted more of the same stock. His reasoning was the same that
afflicts many traders who find themselves in losing positions. If the
stock was a good buy a month ago, it's a great buy today. The problem, though, was that he was shoveling funds into shorting a stock
that was on a clear uptrend. Not long afterward, he was in another
maintenance call. What was different about this maintenance call
was that he didn't have any more funds to feed the fire that was
roaring from his positions that had crashed and burned. He was
forced to close his positions at a substantial loss. The saddest part
of the story is that all of this trading was done without his wife's
knowledge. He had made the initial trade and, when the troubles
mounted, he drew funds from his family's other accounts without
telling anyone else. His gambling tendencies were too shameful
to admit, and he hoped that he could recover without anyone's
becoming aware of his follies. Unfortunately, he wasn't the only
trader who came into our trading floor primarily because it was
closer than the riverboats.

How do you know if you or someone close to you has a trading problem? The following behaviors can signal the need for help:

*Preoccupation.* Problem traders spend a lot of mental energy thinking about the next time they will trade, planning their strategy, or thinking of ways to get money for trading. This will begin to impact their health, their ability to sleep, and their ability to focus on other issues. The problem trader will be distracted at work or appear distant to family and friends.

*Inability to stop or control trading.* Problem traders find that they cannot stop trading when they want to. Maybe they decide to quit altogether, but then they still trade anyway. When they trade, they may try to control the amount of time or money they spend, but they are unable to stick to the limits they set. They often trade until their last dollar is gone. These traders will see trades that no one else sees because they need the miracle trade to make up for their losses.

*"Chasing" losses.* Problem traders get a strong urge or idea to win back money that they have lost in the past. They may say, "If only I could win back what I've lost, I wouldn't have to trade anymore." More and more, they feel trapped. They start thinking that the hole they have dug is so deep that only a big trading win can get them out of it. Their best hope is to hit a home run, and they'll keep swinging until they do so.

*Trading to escape negative emotions.* Problem traders may trade in order to feel better temporarily or to change their mood. They may feel angry, lonely, bored, anxious, or depressed, and they trade to escape these emotions. Trading feels like an escape from their problems. After trading, the negative feelings return, as bad as ever. Because the act of trading gives them temporary relief from the negative emotions, they must trade more frequently and assume greater risks with each trade.

*Lying to conceal trading.* The problem trader has lied to his spouse, family, friends, or employer in order to hide or to minimize his trading losses. These lies range from concealment to outright lying. The trader feels a growing shame for his lack of discipline and hopes that if he can win back his losses, he'll be able to avoid confronting the issue altogether.

*Borrowing to pay for trading.* Debts grow because of trading. Bills are unpaid. Money that could be used to pay bills is used for trading. Problem traders may have borrowed money from family or friends because of trading losses. They may have sold possessions, stocks, or bonds; borrowed from retirement accounts or savings; or gotten a second mortgage because of trading losses.

*Allowing trading to jeopardize other parts of life.* Trading can ruin marriages, friendships, careers, school performance, and reputations. Divorce, bankruptcy, or legal problems are all closely associated with compulsive trading. Compulsive traders act very much like someone with a drug habit. Former activities and social gatherings are shunned when the trader is experiencing mounting losses.

*Ambivalence about quitting or controlling trading.* A problem trader may say things like:

"I know I should stop but I love to trade."

"My wife/husband/partner/parents/children want me to quit but I'm not sure I do."

"Maybe I can slow my trading to the point where it is manageable."

"I want to quit but don't think I can."

Now that you've read through the list of symptoms, you should know that this list is a compulsive gambling checklist. The only change that we've made is to replace the word *gambling* with the word *trading*. Nevertheless, you can see the patterns emerge in the trader we described. He was borrowing money to pay for trading, concealing his trading from his family, jeopardizing his entire financial well-being, and he was most certainly preoccupied with his trades. Toward the end of his short-lived trading career, he would enter the trading floor early in the morning and sit and stare at the stock chart all day. He was becoming physically drained from the mental and emotional energy that he was investing daily in a losing account. If we've cut too close to the truth about your trading habits with this discussion, then we encourage you to seek a helping hand. Sure, every trade involves risk and to a certain degree is a gamble. But there is a significant difference between taking a calculated gamble and being an out-of-control gambler. The former knows where the limits are and is disciplined to operate within those limits. The latter may or may not understand the importance of limits but disregards them in any case.

## Shucking Right Down to the Cob

### Chatter Box—Rick

The Deep South has a lot to offer, but one of my favorites is the collection of homespun sayings that captures the essence of a thought better than most. When you're upset, you get your feathers ruffled; if something is hard to find, it's as scarce as hen's teeth; and if you're really worried, someone might say you're as nervous as a long-tailed cat in a room full of rocking chairs. I have a good friend who often talks about "shuckin' right down to the cob." It's his way of saying, "Let's strip the extras off and talk about what's really important."

Now it's time to take a look at the cob of your trading plan. What do you really need to make sure this plan is going to work for you?

### 1. Education

Before you enter the trading waters, you must first prepare yourself through education and training. As we've mentioned, the markets will let anyone onto the playing field, but that doesn't mean you're necessarily qualified. The only requirement for admission is a funded account. There are many willing players to take your account from you, one trade at a time.

The Market Guys have a basic rule: KISS—Keep it Super Simple. That should apply to your education, too. We've watched people who have listened to every podcast show we've produced, read every article we've written, participated in every web seminar we've conducted, and attended as many live events as they could. They've taken copious notes and requested copies of every presentation. Yet they still haven't placed a trade. Don't let yourself get caught in the paralysis-by-analysis trap. You need to be adequately prepared before you begin trading, but there is no virtue or benefit in creating your own trading PhD program. That said, what are the important areas of preparation?

First of all, you should be thoroughly familiar with the software that you plan to use for trading. Almost every brokerage firm offers a basic execution and analysis platform via the web. These are generally the simplest and most foolproof. They are usually designed for the beginner or part-time trader. You should take advantage of opportunities to learn the software, through either online tutorials or customer service assistance. Some of the deeply discounted brokerage firms offer little or no support when it comes to using the software. Stay away from these operations unless you are already familiar with the mechanics of trading and are confident that you're ready to use the software without assistance. We'll discuss the process of selecting a broker and software later in the book. If you decide to trade with one of the advanced trading platforms, make sure that there is a valid reason for moving up the technology chain besides the fact that the advanced systems look great on your computer monitor and draws the attention of your administrative assistant. Advanced trading software has more ways to get you in trouble if you don't know what you're doing. Hopefully, your parents didn't give you the keys to a Ferrari when you first learned to drive. The Ford Fiesta didn't have all the power and speed, but there was a time when that was actually a benefit. The same principle applies to trading software. The Level 2 screen is mesmerizing to a new trader. You can watch as market makers and ECNs jockey for position on the bid and offer, changing their share size and price every few seconds. The numbers stream like the prices on a gas pump when you're filling your car. It makes for fun eye candy, but the distraction often turns out to be pricey entertainment for many traders who use it as the basis for their buy and sell decisions.

You also need a solid initial education on the product that you're trading. If you decide to trade equities first—as many traders do—then ground yourself in the basics. Do you know the difference between a dividend-paying stock and one that doesn't pay dividends? The first time you see your position trading ex-dividend you will! When a company declares a dividend, it sets a record date when you must be on the company's books as a shareholder to receive the dividend. Once the company sets the record date, the stock exchanges assign the ex-dividend date. The ex-dividend date is normally set for stocks two business days before the record date. If you purchase a stock on its ex-dividend date or after, you will not receive the next dividend payment. Instead, the seller gets the dividend. If you purchase before the ex-dividend date, you get the dividend. Here's the kicker: The stock price will often fall by the dollar amount of the dividend if the dividend is significant. If you didn't know this, you might be shocked to see your stock drop several dollars for no apparent reason and, consequently, you exit a good trade due to ignorance. With options, there are many more factors to consider than with stocks. When you trade stocks, you're looking at the trend and making a decision about whether the trend is up, down, or sideways. If you buy stocks, you want the trend to go up. If you short stocks, you want the trend to go down. Sounds easy enough, right? If you're trading options, you may want the trend to go up, but you also need it to go up within a certain time frame (before the option expires!). Of course, you may choose an option strategy that requires that the stock go neither up nor down but continue in a sideways channel in order for you to profit. Futures have a different type of account funding requirement than stocks or options and impact your account equity differently. This isn't the forum for explaining these nuances in detail, but you can start to see how your choice of trading product affects your training and education. Just because you're a successful stock trader doesn't mean you can walk onto the currency field and enjoy the same success.

Your education and training must include a proper foundation for understanding the psychology of trading. We cover this in more detail in Chapter 2, "Are You Out of Your Mind?" Keep in mind that since trading is not a proper science in the sense that there is not a quantifiable cause-and-effect relationship between stock prices and events, you need to understand and control the emotional part of the process. If you don't think that dealing with money is an emotional activity, then you probably have ice water flowing through your veins. For the rest of us mortals, we'll spend the remainder of our lives keeping in check the overwhelming urge to do dumb things when it comes to our money.

Part of your initial education and training may include some form of paper trading. The term *paper trading* comes from the days when you would simulate real trading by writing the trades on a paper trading log and make note of your profits and losses as well as any comments on the trade itself. Today, many trading software packages include a simulation mode, which will look and feel like the real thing with real market data. The only difference is that when you log off and log back on, you start with a clean slate. Paper trading gives you the opportunity to analyze setups and buy and sell without actually putting your money at risk. You can begin to feel the emotional roller coaster that accompanies trading when you first get started. The criticism of paper trading is that it doesn't adequately prepare you for real trading because there is no substitute for actually putting your money on the line. It's like the old joke about a fellow who was asked about the difference between a recession and a depression. "A recession," he replied, "is when my neighbor loses his job. A depression is when I lose my job." We agree that paper trading may not tell you when you're ready to trade but it does a good job of telling you when you're not ready to trade. As we've said many times in our seminars, if you're losing money while you're paper trading, please don't start trading live!

Pilots often use a flight simulator to practice certain maneuvers that they may not want to replicate in actual flying. For instance, you can practice taking off and losing an engine on climbout. These exercises are useful to sharpen your skills and prepare you for the actual event, should it ever occur. However, a flight instructor would never stick a new student in a simulator for 20 hours and then bid him good luck on his first real solo flight. There is a distinct benefit of learning alongside an instructor who can help you through the actual maneuvers in real flight. The same thought applies to paper trading. Use it to refine your skills, learn the basics and prepare for the real thing, but understand that your first trade that places thousands of dollars on the line will affect you quite differently.

Your trading plan should provide at least a basic guide toward your continuing education. Many traders will be drawn toward trading clubs but approach them with care. Some trading clubs will sell you their preferred trading products or require that you pool your money with other club members for club trades. Pooled funds are traded as club trades and are often decided by the membership through a consensus vote. It would be difficult to think of a worse approach for deciding on trades. In our experience, the consensus is usually arrived at by one of two means. The first is the influence exerted by the most outspoken members. This is nothing more than putting your money into a nonregulated mutual fund with amateur managers who get their authority from the silent acquiescence of the rest of the club. The second way to reach club consensus is to take the path of least resistance in order not to offend anyone. Since the goal is to minimize risk, these trades will track the indices or slightly lag. The club thinks the market will be rising so they buy a position in the DIAs (the Dow Jones Industrial Average tracking stock). Do you really need a club to help you decide to invest in the broad market? The better choice is to find reputable education on your own and continue to invest in your personal development.

## 2. Funding

Deciding how much to trade with and where the funds will come from are critical decisions as you start trading. As a general rule, most people should not trade with more than about 20 percent of their overall investment portfolio. This is a very broad statement and should be adjusted for such factors as age, time to retirement, risk tolerance, and total net worth. Most brokerage firms have a minimum account balance that is required for a trading account. However, some of these minimums are as low as $500. It's difficult to assign a threshold for funding your first trading account but $5000 to $10,000 is the minimum that we generally recommend. To apply a baseball analogy, successful trading is about hitting singles and doubles. When a trader starts out with an underfunded account, the tendency is toward either extreme of (1) not swinging at all for fear of striking out or (2) swinging for the home run in order to grow the account as quickly as possible. The first extreme manifests itself in the trader who is afraid to trade. When they finally place a trade, they're unable to take a loss if the trade moves against them. They use the reasoning that they have to hold on and hope the stock recovers, because they can't afford to lose money in the account. The second extreme is the trader who decides to buy 50 out-of-the-money option contracts because they're so cheap. A better choice might be to buy 50 lottery tickets. The odds of making money on a single trade aren't too far apart, but the lottery payout is higher.

Don't take lightly the decision of when to add money to the account or when to transfer money out of the account. The rules for this decision should be clearly started in your trading plan in order to avoid being driven by your emotions. There is a strong temptation for traders to prop up their trading account when they're losing money because they can afford to. This is especially true for high-net-worth traders. They don't experience the same proportional pain of loss that others do, so they'll continually transfer funds into their trading account in order to hold on to a losing trade or to speculate on high-risk trades. In Las Vegas, these characters are referred to as "whales." They're the ones who will continue placing bets, even though they lose money, for the sheer entertainment of the bet. Hoteliers love these people and will provide free rooms, escorts, meals, and entertainment as long as they play. Wall Street provides the same type of venue for masses of traders who feed the market in spite of their inability to profit. And they don't even offer you a good meal in return—go figure.

There comes a time when you've diligently applied yourself to this endeavor called trading and you're making a profit. You should also have rules for transferring funds out of your trading account into other investments. If you're more successful in your trading account than your other investments, your trading account will eventually grow beyond the 20 percent rule we discussed earlier. Does this mean you should trade your entire portfolio? The answer is no, because trading carries a different type and level of risk. You may be outperforming the market and tempted to trade your entire portfolio, but resist the urge. Most traders go through swings between outperforming the broad market and underperforming the broad market. Sometimes this is due to market forces such as a shift into a sideways market when your trading skills work best in a trending market. Other times, this may be due to personal forces such as family stress or health issues. Having a portion of your portfolio in such investments as bonds, index funds, or real estate will serve to balance the risks and returns through various market conditions.

### 3. Goals and Objectives

Why do you trade? This needs to be specifically addressed in your trading plan. There is no right or wrong answer to this question as long as you're honest with yourself. Is your goal to be a full-time trader? What's your plan for transitioning from your current income source to trading? Have you talked to others who trade full time or have made the attempt and failed? You are not the first person to enter this field. Many have tried, with varying degrees of success. Learn as much as you can from the experiences of others. One of the key considerations in trading full time is the need to generate a profit consistently. Many traders are profitable when they trade part-time but begin to lose money when they start trading full-time. The reason is quite simple: The pressure that comes from using your trades as your sole income source often causes you to make bad emotional decisions. It's similar to the underfunded trader. Neither of you believe that you can afford a loss so you do everything you can to avoid it. The part-time trader can afford to go for long periods without placing a trade; preferring to wait for a low-risk, high-reward setup. However, the full-time trader knows that he won't make any money if he's not trading, so he finds trades whether they exist or not.

Many traders simply use trading as a way to outperform the broad market. Their goal is not to be financially independent through trading or to build profits for a specific reward like a new boat or home. They want the ability to use their own research and judgment and direct a portion of their portfolio into opportunities that they've identified. This is one of the most conservative trading strategies and, as such, one of the most attainable goals. The decision rule for when it's time to stop trading becomes easy. You allow yourself a certain amount of time to learn the skills and reach your objective. If after one year, for example, you're still underperforming the broad market, then stop trading. Decide whether you need to learn more or end your trading altogether. If you can't beat the broad market, why not just invest your money in a low-cost index fund? It requires none of your time and attention and you'll pay lower fees.

### 4. Markets and Products

As part of your trading plan, you need to decide what and where you will be trading. Stocks are the easiest products for most people to understand and begin trading. Included in the stock category are exchange-traded funds (ETFs). These are essentially mutual funds that trade just like stocks. Traditional mutual funds are priced and traded once a day at net asset value (NAV). The NAV is calculated after the markets close by benchmarking the closing price of all the constituent stocks within the fund. Any buy or sell orders entered during the day are then executed after the NAV is calculated. ETFs, however, trade throughout the day and may be bought and sold just like stocks. You may be familiar with some ETFs without realizing what they are. For example, the Dow Jones Industrial Average can't be traded directly. However, you can trade the DIA ETF (referred to as the Diamonds), which follows the value of the index (see Figure 1.4). The Nasdaq 100 may be traded through the QQQQ ETF (the Q's) and the S&P 500

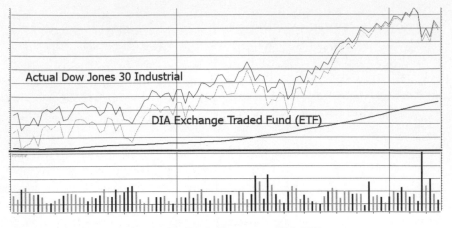

**Figure 1.4    Dow Jones Industrial 30 versus DIA ETF**

Index has the SPYETF (the Spyders). Besides indices, ETFs are often used to trade specific sectors or industries. You can trade the biotech sector, for example, with the ETF ticker symbol BBH.

Traders will often graduate into options after learning the basics of stocks. It's important to understand stock trading before trading options because part of the options pricing model is the price of the underlying stock. If you don't understand the nature of price movement with stocks, you'll only magnify your confusion when you trade options. Having a plan to transition into options will help you avoid making the move too early. As we discussed earlier in this chapter, there are many so-called experts who will try to convince you that options (or gold or currencies or futures—you get the idea) are the path to riches. You'll be sorely tempted to drop your current trading strategy and style and follow their 12-step plan. If you decide to trade various products, then develop a plan for each. Each plan should include the salient points we're covering in this discussion and should stand alone. Your funding requirements for your futures trading will likely be different than the funding requirements for your stock trading. Likewise, if you're highly leveraged through futures trading, you should expect better returns than simply outperforming the broad market. The risk you assume should have a corresponding level of return.

Your trading plan should identify which market you plan to trade. Of course, this is often determined by the product. Some stocks only trade on the Nasdaq exchange while others trade on the New York Stock Exchange (NYSE). Many traders around the world will trade their local exchanges for such products as contracts for difference (CFDs) while also trading the U.S. markets for the liquidity offered. The consideration of which market to trade is not as significant as it once was. There was a time when the execution difference between virtual markets and physical markets was drastic. Technology has created a forced leveling and the historic differences are becoming less of an issue.

### 5. Trade Setup and Execution

It may seem intuitive to define the process by which trades are identified and executed while ignoring the other trading plan components discussed in this chapter. Lest we gloss over this important concept, the following is an outline of the salient points to consider in this section:

*Time horizon.* You must decide in advance how long the trade will be held. Do not change time horizons in the middle of a trade to accommodate a bad trade. This is quite different from riding a profitable trade. Don't exit a winning position just to satisfy your defined holding period, but don't become an investor because you're a bad trader.

*Stock screening.* How are you going to pare down the population of thousands of stocks into a pool that you can reasonably analyze for trading? Are you a trend trader, or will you be trading channels, or both? Are you going to attempt to pick reversals? Will you screen stocks for large-capitalization companies, or will you be speculating with penny stocks?

*Pretrade analysis.* Charts are the primary tool of technical analysis, but there are many variations to charts and techniques for using them. Candlestick charts are the personal favorite of many traders, but some people will swear by point-and-figure charts because they remove the time scale from the analysis. Once you choose a charting style, what indicators and entry/ exit rules will you apply?

*Risk analysis.* Knowing when to exit a losing trade is one of the most important skills that a trader develops from experience. However, the beginning trader must define risk management rules from the first trade. Are you going to use The Market

Guys' 1% Rule or do you have another risk tolerance level that you'll apply? You need to decide how you'll protect an open position. For example, a long stock position could be protected with a long put option or a sell stop order.

*Position sizing.* Some traders answer this question by looking at how much they can afford. We recommend tying your position size into your risk tolerance and have provided guidance to accomplish that later in the book. Your trading plan should include rules for your position size, including adding to the position as well as exiting the position. Remember, if you buy 1,000 shares, there's no requirement that you sell all 1,000 shares at the same time.

*Trade execution.* Finally, consider how your trade will be executed. You may have different rules for different market conditions. For example, some traders will use limit orders only in the first and last half hour of trading to help protect against the higher volatility found during these periods. Some traders enter a position with a market order and exit with limit orders.

### 6. Trade Diary

Knowing exactly how profitable you are through trading is critical for improving. The best way to keep tabs on your profits and growth is through a detailed trading diary. The trading diary will help you identify what works and what doesn't. Along with that, it will quickly show you when your trading strategy is starting to break down. Some traders employ a strategy that performs remarkably well in a bull market but underperforms in a sideways or bear market. Your trading diary will be the first to flag you when conditions are changing and you need to adjust your strategy.

There is no limit to the information that you choose to log into your trading diary, although it is possible to overanalyze your performance and spend more time with your spreadsheets and less time with the markets. Whatever your predisposition may be toward self-analysis, the following is a suggested minimum list of information that your diary should contain:

- Product traded
- Entry price, date, and time

- Reason for entry
- Position size
- Stop price
- Exit price, date, and time
- Reason for exit
- Net profit or loss
- Market conditions
- Miscellaneous notes

## Grow with Your Plan

As we wrap up this discussion of the trading plan, there is one more important point that needs to be made. The trading plan should serve to make you a better trader and guide you through your growth. It is by no means a malevolent dictator that, once created, must be served without question. You'll find that your trading plan will evolve over time, reflecting your increase of both knowledge and experience. It represents your best effort at a set of rules that you believe will help you reach maximum profitability. However, it is a snapshot frozen in time. As you continue trading, you may find products that are more profitable for you. Some traders are most profitable in sideways markets when they learn to trade options. They don't enjoy the same success with stocks, which may be what they started trading. There's no problem with making the change as long as you develop a new plan. We've known many traders who were lured into the markets by the promise of quick riches that were supposedly available to anyone willing to commit to day trading full time. Reality set in very quickly, and these same traders discovered that trading was more profitable for them if they lengthened their time horizon from minutes to weeks. Once again, it is perfectly acceptable to switch from being a day trader to a swing trader if you've developed a plan to do so.

Your trading diary will be your feedback loop for changes that you'll make to your trading approach. Look for the patterns that tell you what time of day is best to enter an opening trade, which products produce the best returns, or when it's just time to take a break and regroup. The markets will always be changing; be sure you change with them.

# 2

# Are You Out of Your Mind?

## HOW TO WORK WITH YOUR EMOTIONS

Without question, the biggest challenge for any new trader is learning how to remove emotions from the decision-making process when it comes time to make a trade. It really doesn't matter how much experience you have; you will find that this will be your biggest battle when trading the markets. If you were to ask a seasoned trader if they are able to completely remove the emotions associated with risk positions they've taken in the market, and they answered "yes," then they would be lying to you. We have seen it time after time, over many years in the market, people coming to us with the same story . . . "I don't believe it. I was up 50 percent on this stock last week and now I'm down. I can't take a loss now. I'll just hold on a little bit more and see what happens." Throughout this chapter, we'll discuss ways to keep our emotions in check and follow our trading plan. As you'll see, in the trading business you may actually profit from being out of your mind!

## Avoiding Pain, Seeking Pleasure

It is well documented among many scientific studies that our brains are designed to direct us away from pain and toward pleasure. So one of the reasons people hold on to a losing trade is that it's the brain's way of avoiding pain. Hoping for a breakeven point is an idea people have that gives them pleasure when they think that "one day" they will not have to take the loss. If this is the way you have been thinking, then rest assured you are in good company. It doesn't mean you are doing the right thing, but you are in good company.

Since your brain is wired to avoid the pain, it will look for ways to get around having to take the loss. I'm sure you have heard of how, when we feel threatened, our survival instincts tell us to fight when we're in danger in order to defend ourselves, or run from a situation that could result in our being harmed. Blood moves from the extremities of our bodies to the critical organs and muscles that bring us to "fight-or-flight" mode. The fight-or-flight response, also known as the acute stress response, was first discovered by Walter Cannon back in 1929. His theory talked about how animals react to threats with a general discharge of the sympathetic nervous system, priming the animal for fighting or fleeing. In extremely dangerous situations, our bodies go into shock and adrenaline is released into our bloodstream, giving us extraordinary strength that helps us in our defense. You don't even have to think about it. When we are threatened, our bodies naturally adjust and our minds quickly throw us into autopilot. Over time, we have learned that our quick reactions help guide us to safety. However, while in fight mode, we will naturally take a stance to defend ourselves when our backs are against the wall.

But what happens when our financial lives are in danger? If you have ever found yourself in a losing position in the market, and in financial danger, you may have noticed the physical changes that take place in your body. Your heartbeat increases, your blood pressure goes up, you perspire uncontrollably, and your stomach muscles tighten up, not to mention the loss of sleep from the added stress. Sound familiar? These symptoms are very close to what you would experience in a fight-or-flight response.

When faced with having to take a loss, you would rather flee from the threat of having to take a financial loss and go with something that sounds better like "dollar cost averaging." Yeah, that's a great idea. Let's buy more of the stock that's been beating the pants off of us. Then you think, "If I cost average down, then I'll only have to climb up half the distance to get back to my breakeven point." What happens next? The market takes another turn for the worse, and you realize that you can't run from this situation, so you go into fight mode. This is when you decide once again to buy more, at new lows, because you absolutely refuse to take a loss at this point. You begin to think that what started out as a short-term trade is now better suited for a long-term investment, and you start looking for good things about this company to justify reasons why you should hold on to it for a couple of years. You have just committed one of the great mortal sins of trading, which is changing your strategy to justify a loss.

As you can see, our survival instincts don't really help us in the financial markets. First, we are not able to flee from big losses when we are under attack. Secondly, the market is just too big for us to fight. So the next best thing we can do is learn as much as we can about this beast we call The Market. Once we understand what the market is capable of and how it can hurt us, then we can approach it with caution in order to better defend ourselves against an attack before it happens.

## Piloting Your Trades

The first step toward avoiding a catastrophic loss is learning how to deal with the emotions associated with trading. One of the best ways to understand how important it is to remove our emotions from the decision-making process is to compare trading with flying an airplane. We've found that there are a large number of pilots who show up in The Market Guys' audience, and both of the authors are pilots, so it's easy for us to use this analogy.

When flying a plane, safety is the pilot's paramount consideration. Let's face it, if you take off from the ground only to find later that you didn't have enough fuel in your plane, you're going to be in trouble. So every pilot is required to go through a preflight checklist: fuel, brakes, seat belts, and so on. Making sure that your engines are running properly and that you have a backup plan in case you have engine failure is part of every pilot's checklist. One of the reasons checklists are so important is that our minds will play tricks on us from time to time. If we rely solely on our memories, then it will only be a matter of time before one of life's distractions gets in the way and causes us to forget a minor little detail like making sure the landing gear is down before touchdown.

Now let's compare this to trading. How often do you use a checklist before putting your money at risk? Do you check to see if the stock is going up before you buy it or are you busy trying to pick a bottom in order to get a bargain price? If you regularly try to pick bottoms as a strategy, then you are letting your emotions get in the way of the decision-making process, because what you are really saying is, "I think this stock has hit its low and I believe it will go higher from here." In this case, it's your opinion that you are trusting and not the actual facts of what's happening with the stock. That's like a pilot saying, "I am going to head north even though I should be heading west because I think the wind is going to change direction after I get in the air. Let's take off and see what happens." Who is going to get in a plane with this kind of pilot? We're not, and neither should you.

Another dangerous condition that pilots are challenged with from time to time is when the body plays tricks on the mind. Naturally, our body senses when gravity is pulling us to the ground. If you were in an elevator, you could generally discern, even with your eyes closed, whether you were going up or down. Going up, you would feel your body getting heavier; going down you would feel lighter. Your ears would pop and your senses would tell you that there is a change in your altitude. The same thing happens in a plane. If you were to close your eyes in a plane and then initiate a slight turn to the left or right, your body would tell your mind that you were gaining altitude. The forces acting on your body from being in a turn push you down in the seat and trick your mind into thinking that this added weight, like in an elevator, is the result of gaining altitude. This, of course, would be a lie. Night flying or flying in overcast conditions can be a very dangerous place for a pilot who is not aware that her body is lying to her. Experienced pilots are fully aware of this, and when they sense that their bodies are tricking their minds, they immediately force themselves to refer to their instrument panel to get the truth. The instruments will tell pilots if they are in a turn or in a climb. Instruments also tell them what direction they are heading.

We can apply this analogy to the trader who is taking risk in the market because of the similarities in how our minds interpret the data. If you, a trader, decided to go with a feeling instead of looking at the truth seen in price trends, you may be fooled into thinking that your money is in a safe place when, in fact, you are heading in the wrong direction. We have seen many people crash and burn in the market because they bought a stock on a broker recommendation or because an analyst upgraded a particular company. Then, when the stock drops 30, 40, 50 percent or more, they hold on because they believe in the story of the company. How many times have you seen a person buy a stock just before an earnings announcement because they heard an analyst say that they expected the company to report stronger-than-expected earnings? After the stock beats the earnings estimate like the analyst expected, the stock plunges to a new 52-week low.

This happens more often than you would imagine, and the reason people lose money in situations like this is that they are trading on a feeling. Like the pilot, we need to focus on the instrument panel to get the truth and not rely on what our minds are telling us. For the trader, our instrument panel is the price chart.

## Technical Analysis or Tea Leaves?

For many years technical analysts were met with resistance from the diehard fundamental analysts who labeled them as fortune-tellers who might as well use tea leaves to predict the market. Price charts were looked upon as crystal balls that added little value to the world of money managers. However, in July 2000 a financial earthquake shook up the financial world. Fundamental analysts ran for the hills as Lucent Technology news hit the market, causing this former Bell Labs gem of a stock to drop its share price by more than 91 percent in less than a year. Not too long after that, in October 2001, a company called Enron announced more than $600 million in quarterly losses, sparking a national investigation of its leadership team. That triggered the beginning of the end for employees and shareholders alike. Then, when you thought it couldn't get any worse, it did. WorldCom, the world's second largest long distance carrier, filed the largest bankruptcy in U.S. history in July 2002.

For the first time in history, fundamental analysis came under attack as senators and government officials questioned the validity of company reports and analyst forecasts. Investigators started holding up price charts during investigative hearings, asking analysts and company executives why they did not see this coming. They held these price charts up to the cameras, showing significant downward trends. "Would you buy a stock like this?" was the oft-repeated question.

From that point on, technical analysis became less of a forecasting tool and more of a risk management tool. We will be covering the basic ideas behind technical analysis in Chapter 4. For now, understand that it helps us remove our emotions from the decision-making process. This is especially crucial when we have money on the line.

## Fundamental Seduction

Whether we are in the United States, Europe, or Asia speaking at trade shows or expositions, someone always steps up during one of these events to ask, "What about the fundamentals? Don't you guys even look at the company reports?" Our answer is always the same. Yes, we look at the fundamentals to see if our stock candidate has earnings and we check to see how much debt they are carrying on the books. Many times, the company reports tell us which stocks to trade, but the fundamentals never give us the signals that tell us when to get into a position. More importantly, the fundamentals don't tell us when to get out when the position is turning against us. By the time the accountants update the reports that go to the analysts, the price move will have already taken place. Are you really going to wait until the end of the quarter to make the decision to get out when a stock is moving against you? Of course not, and this is why we focus so much of our attention on the price action.

The other reason we put less weight into the fundamentals is that there is too much information out there. You will see that once you have an opinion about a stock, your mind will search for information in order to support your opinion. For example, you think the stock is going to go higher and you've read the opinions of the Wall Street analysts who also think this stock is going higher. So, you buy it. Next week, you look at the stock only to see that it is now trading at a lower price than where you bought it. At this point you are not too worried because you have faith in the report you've read and you see that the company had very strong sales numbers last quarter. The next week, the stock price continues to fall. In desperation, you reach for the company report. Once again you take another look at the price-to-earnings ratio (P/E) and see that its earnings continue to be strong. In fact, it has a lower P/E than the rest of the stocks in that sector. So you make the decision to hold on.

Do you see what has just happened? Your opinion caused you to search for more data to justify your reasons to hold on. This information overload, combined with your getting involved with the product or service of this company, has caused you to fall in love with this stock. Don't marry your stock positions because they usually won't remain faithful. The longer you hold on to them when they are going down, the harder it will be for you to separate yourself from the losers when you are wrong.

## Chatter Box—AJ

Learning how to take small losses along the way is a great way to avoid getting attached to your portfolio. True traders look at the numbers with the realization that they are going to be wrong every once in a while. In fact, there may be times when they are wrong multiple times in a row. However, accepting this ahead of time makes it easier for the trader to take the loss, knowing that the goal is to keep the losses small along the way. We will be talking more about this in Chapter 12 when we cover the 1% Rule for risk management. Learning to take small losses along the way is something many people are challenged with because they have associated realized loss with pain. Remember what we said about how the mind moves away from pain and toward things of pleasure? To fix this you must learn how to find pleasure in taking a small loss. Refusing to take a loss is like a fighter getting into the ring with his opponent, thinking he is never going to get punched in the face. A good fighter learns how to absorb a blow by moving with the punch, and this allows him to continue on with the fight. A trader learns how to take small losses, which allows him to hold on to his trading capital so he can get back into the market without getting knocked out. Reward yourself after you have taken a small loss, and don't look back at the trade to see what might have happened had you held on.

There will be times when you sell a stock at a loss, and immediately after you sell it, the stock rallies. However, looking back at your stocks to see if you made the right decision will only condition you to hold on to the losers. There may be occasions when the stock will drop in price and 12 months later it will be higher than where you sold it. But would you have really held on to it for a year to get back into the positive side of the trade? This is not what a professional trader would do, so you shouldn't do this either.

## Using Best Practices

One of the things that we've found most helpful for our students is having them put a trading plan together. As we covered in the first chapter, you should have a trading plan in place before you execute your first trade. Your trading plan should be written down, clearly articulated, with no gray areas. When you have identified your exit points, make sure you post them in a place that is clearly visible, preferably somewhere near your trading computer, and be sure to stick with the plan.

Another good idea that will help you hold steady in your mind-set as a trader is to ask for the help of a close friend or spouse. You may be surprised to know that husband-and-wife teams work very well. Right about now, all of the husbands are thinking, "There is no way I'm going to have my wife on this account with me—she'd kill me if she knew how much money I lost last month." This may come as a surprise to a lot of the male traders out there, but women often make better traders than men because most women will not ride a loss as far as a man would. Men have a greater tendency to fight the market when things turn against us. The next time you feel the urge to ride a loss in an effort to fight your way back to the breakeven point, try to remember that the market is too big for you to fight. If you still find that you are challenged in this area, then have a friend, partner, or trading buddy hold you accountable for your actions.

In other words, if you say you are going to get out of a position at a certain price level, then stick to it and have your partner hold you to it. Professional floor traders and market makers report to head traders who hold them accountable, so why shouldn't you have someone you can check in with? The fact is that many trading firms around the world will not allow their traders to take large positions home with them overnight because it adds too much risk to the firm.

## The Business of Trading

If you plan on taking your trading strategy seriously, then you must think of this as if you were starting a new business. If you are fortunate enough to know someone who is a professional trader, ask him if you can visit his office. Take a look with your own eyes at how the trading floors operate. If you get the opportunity to meet the head traders, make sure you ask them how they monitor risk. These people pay for their salaries over and over again each month when they do what's expected of them. That job, once again, is to limit losses.

Every entrepreneur knows that there are start-up costs involved in any new venture, and it is highly unlikely that a new business will make a profit right away. In fact, most new businesses only begin to see profits a year or two after their doors are opened. As you are starting out in your new trading business, you should have the same mind-set as other entrepreneurs. The price of a new computer system, the books and tapes you add to your library, the seminars you attend—these are all part of the start-up costs. Just be careful you are not spending too much money on the seminar circuit. On that note, make sure you are getting your information only from experts who are walking the walk and not just talking the talk. The Market Guys spend many months on the road each and every year attending trade shows and money expos. It's shocking to see just how many snake oil salesmen are out there. In fact, we were once in a show in Frankfurt, Germany, where one of the trade show booths had a vodka bar set up right in the middle of the floor with tables all around it. We walked around the bar to peek our heads in to see just how many cases of booze there were in their inventory. While this was a business model we would never endorse, the fact is there are many companies out there who are in the seminar business just to get your money.

We make it a point to tell everyone in our audience to make sure they vet their source before buying any material that shows you how to make a profit. Before you take trading advice from someone, please do yourself a favor and make sure you are dealing with individuals who are putting their money on the line when they are trading the market. Also, make sure they are willing to share the bad trades as well as the good trades with you. How many times have you seen an ad in a magazine or a commercial on television proclaiming that you can make 200 to 300 percent profits by using their system? Or the infomercials given by someone who was once homeless and living on a park bench but now makes millions of dollars trading spreads in the options markets overnight? Can you make millions trading options? Yes, you can. But let's get real—relying on television commercials that play on your emotions is not the way to go.

We'll assume that if you are reading this book right now you have checked out the credibility of The Market Guys and our Keep It Super Simple (KISS) method of trading. We are very proud to say that our approach to risk management has resulted in many success stories around the world. Our favorite stories are not the ones that talk about fabulous profits but the stories that talk about the end of losses. When a trader comes to us and tells us that they are no longer losing money, we know they're now on the path to profits.

## Overcoming Fear and Greed

We have already addressed how pain and pleasure motivate us to make certain decisions, so now let's talk about two cousins: fear and greed. We fear the pain that we want to avoid, and we become greedy for the pleasure that attends to a winning trade. Let's explore how these emotions work in our trading and how we can overcome them.

The more powerful of the two is fear. Fear is one reason why most people will avoid buying a stock on its high. The large majority of amateur traders would feel more comfortable buying a stock on a 52-week low rather than a 52-week high. The reason for this behavior is that the trader has a mind-set that says, "If I buy this stock on its high, it could fall. So, I'll wait for it to drop some before I buy it." This is the fear emotion working against you. If you think about what you are doing when you wait for a stock to drop before you buy it, you will see that you're really waiting for the sellers to control the stock. In order for a stock price to drop, the sellers have to take control of the price. Conversely, if the buyers were in control, the stock price would rise. Therefore, you are buying a stock that is weakening.

When you compare this way of thinking to that of a professional trader, you will see that a seasoned trader would feel very comfortable buying a stock on its high because their mind-set is to Buy High and Sell Higher. In other words, buy the stock when it is being controlled by the buyers, and you will be getting into a stock that is strengthening. Stocks that are in growth mode will continue to set new highs. If a stock is going to move from a low point to a higher point, it will set new highs all along the way! If a professional trader sees a stock that has been going up in a nice steady trend, they are confident in their own decisions because there is a good chance that the stock will continue up. If they make a bad choice and the stock drops in price after they buy it, then they simply get out with a small loss and move on to the next stock. Successful traders have a simple strategy: Buy strength and sell weakness. You can't make it any simpler than that.

Another characteristic we often observe in new traders is how fear leads to overanalysis. When you are unsure of your knowledge, strategy, or ability to pick a good stock, you will continue to question yourself. This type of fear will cause you to go back and check out the company a little bit more. You might find yourself digging into the company report to verify earnings once again, or you might hammer away at a few more analyst reports to see if there is anything that would negate your reasons for buying this company. Before you know it, you have spent so much time analyzing and probing that the stock has already made its move up. Then you wind up saying to yourself, "It's too high now. Let me wait and see what happens."

Have you ever heard the old saying, "Overanalysis equals paralysis?" It's true, and the underlying cause of this paralysis is fear. You may have lost money in the past after you bought a stock on a high and you are fearful that it will happen again, so you refrain from looking at any stock that's on a 52-week high. You respond quite like a child who once got burned on a stove. Any child who burns himself on a stove will most likely not want to get close to that stove again. This is a natural response part of a self-defense system. It teaches us lessons when we experience pain. Every time we feel pain, the mind remembers the event that caused the pain and then transforms that memory into a fear that shapes our behavior patterns. This is nothing more than a conditioned response.

Greed also conditions our behavior in harmful ways. If you have ever tasted the sweetness of a profit after buying a stock and shortly after you sell, it rallies to even higher levels, you will know what we're taking about here. Once you've tasted it, you want it over and over again. Unfortunately, those home-run trades only come once in a while. But as a result of your tasting this sweetness, you will find that a pattern forms where you wind up holding on to those losing stocks longer than you should.

Another reason people hold on to losing trades is that greed has caused them to believe that this losing stock is going to come back soon and launch just like that winning stock did. If you're not careful, this risky behavior pattern will wind up costing you money like a one-armed bandit in a Las Vegas casino. We often travel to Las Vegas to speak at financial and trading shows, and it never ceases to amaze us how those slot machines captivate people. We assume that most people know that the odds are stacked heavily on the side of the casino, yet thousands of people sit there for hours as they put in their coins, waiting for big payoffs.

If you took a psychology course in college, you may remember the name Ivan Pavlov. In 1904, Ivan Pavlov won the Nobel Prize in physiology/medicine for his research on digestion. The work he did with his dogs made him a household name as he documented how our nervous systems trigger certain reflexes. The similarity between Pavlov's dogs and the Las Vegas gambler is uncanny, and it's a short trip from trader to gambler. Before you reject the connection between the behavior patterns of the Vegas gambler and the market trader, remember that pleasure and greed are akin to one another. Both emotions drive us toward behavior that may ultimately harm us more than help us. It's important that you know this; if you ignore this fact, you may wind up unexpectedly gambling your financial future away.

Pavlov's work involved a metronome and dog food. He would sound the metronome at the same time he gave food to the experimental dogs. After a short while, the dogs, which previously salivated only when they saw and ate their food, would begin to salivate when the metronome sounded. He also found that the dogs would salivate after he rang the bell even if there were no food present. He published these results in 1903, calling it a conditioned reflex. This is different than an innate reflex, which is what a child would do if he touched a hot stove. This pain again teaches the child and a valuable lesson is learned. Pavlov called this learning process conditioning, and he also found that the conditioned reflex will be repressed if the positive stimulus, in the metronome sounding, proved wrong too often. In other words, if the metronome sounded repeatedly without any food appearing, the dogs would eventually stop salivating at the sound.

Can you see the similarity between Pavlov's dogs and the Las Vegas gambler sitting at the slot machine? The casino is playing with the gambler like Pavlov experimented with his dogs. The behavior exhibited by the gambler of putting dollars into the slot is rewarded with a treat that amounts to a small payoff of coins from the machine. As coins fall into the coin tray, the bells ring and the behavior continues. After a while, another small payoff arrives and more bells sound, but this time the gambler has less money.

As time goes on, these small payoffs result in our sample gambler believing that she will continue to be rewarded and she starts to salivate with greed. Like Pavlov's dogs, she salivates even if there was no reward. This is the same reason why a trader will hold on to a losing trade even if there is no reward. Greed drives us to hold on to our losses, and if we continue to let greed take over, we will get to a point where one of two things will happen. Either the pain will get too great to hold on any longer or you will run out of money and blow up your trading account.

So how does one break out of this vicious circle? The first step is to admit when you are wrong and pull away from the stocks that are costing you money time after time. This will be very difficult at first because most people don't like to admit when they are wrong. In fact, many traders feel that they have to go back and defeat the stock that cost them their profit, and it becomes some sort of duel they play with the market. Their new goal is not to make a profit but rather to get back what they lost. Then, if they are lucky enough to get back to the breakeven point, they walk away feeling like a winner. Once you come to the realization that you are on the wrong side of a losing position, you can start fresh with a new list of stocks.

## Filtering Your Emotion

If you are looking for ways to help remove the emotions associated with trading, you must first make sure to filter your thoughts. Make sure you are analyzing your stocks for their trend value. Rate your stocks from 1 to 5, giving your stock a score of 1 if the trend is nice and steady with a long history of consistency. If the trend is too extreme, meaning you are a buyer and the price chart is going up vertically, then give it a 3. If you are a buyer and the stock is going down, you may throw that one off your list or give it a 5.

Then you would measure the emotional value of that same stock on a scale from 1 to 5, with 5 representing a very high emotional charge. If you are picking up a stock because you heard Slim Trainer mention it on that stock show *Crazy Money*, we would rate that at the top of the emotional scorecard by giving it a 5. On the other hand, if you got a hot stock tip from your brother-in-law Pete, we would rate that with a 3 because, although your brother-in-law knows a lot about the market, chances are he has already bought into the story of the company without even checking a price chart to see if the trend of the stock was up.

Once you have these two numbers, total them up for each stock. The stocks with the lowest numbers are your best choices. The best score you can get for a stock is a 2. This represents a stock with a great trend (score of 1) and no emotional charge (score of 1). Using filters like this will gradually help you develop the mind-set you need to become a highly successful trader.

# Case Studies

*Dan*

Over the years we have helped many people reach their ultimate financial goals. Nothing makes us happier than when we meet people like Dan.

Dan was a house painter in the Washington, D.C., area who had a goal to make a million dollars in the stock market. Like a lot of people who are new to the market, Dan was hoping to get advice from the broker he had his account with. He assumed that his broker would be able to tell him how to trade and invest in the markets, and he was excited about the opportunities. One day, Dan made an appointment to visit a representative who worked for a so-called full-service brokerage firm. This company claimed to be one of the world's leading financial management and advisory companies, so Dan thought he had found the right place. However, when he told this particular representative what his plan was, the representative laughed when he saw Dan's check for $2,000. "Sir," he said, "if this is what you plan on opening your account with, then we would suggest you take your $2,000 and go to Las Vegas with it. You'll have a better chance reaching your goal there." Outraged, Dan stormed out of the office and down the road to a broker who would take his money.

Fortunately, Dan did not give up so easily. He spent time learning how to trade options and the importance of having a good risk management plan in place. He had early success in the first six months of trading, and this allowed him to put a plan together to build his dream house. His plan was to make money each month in the option markets, and each month he would take some of his profits and put it toward the construction of his new home. He didn't want a mortgage in the end, so he decided to buy the land first. The next month, he made enough in the markets to build a foundation, and each month after that, he would add something to the house. One day, he called to tell us the roof was on. This was a big deal for him because the rain was no longer beating down on the frame of his new home. He referred to his new status simply as "dry." Later in the same year, he called to give us an update and said that he was ready to put on the front door. He said, "I want a big double wooden door—one that is warm and beautiful, a door that makes people feel welcomed when they knock on it."

Dan's plan forced him to stay disciplined, and his mind-set kept him from getting too attached to his stock position. He was in love with the idea of building his dream house, instead of being in love with his stock positions. He didn't want to marry his stocks because then he would not be able to sell them to raise enough money to build his house. He also knew that he could not ride a loss in any one position because if he did this, he would jeopardize the construction of this dream home and all would be lost. Dan was able to finish his home, and after making over $700,000 in the market in less than three years, he called to inform us of his final purchase. To complete his ultimate dream he took some of his profits and purchased a brand new Mercedes Benz to park in his new garage. The last part of his plan was the icing on the cake, and that was to drive over to the broker who told him to go to Las Vegas in order to show him what he had done with his $2,000.

### Lesley

Another success story is Lesley Fontaine. Lesley started with a relatively small account and turned it into a million dollars by focusing on price charts to help her make those all-important trading decisions. For years, Lesley, by her own admission, would get emotionally tied up in the companies she invested in. Whether it was the product that she fell in love with or the service the company provided, her problem was that she found herself holding on too long. She believed strongly in the company, and it was this faith in the company's leadership team that caused Lesley to hold on when these stocks would drop in price. Once we showed her how to remove these emotional chains from her decision-making process, she quickly learned how to properly enter a new position and, more importantly, how to exit a stock when key support levels were being broken. Amazingly, this newly acquired skill was the key that helped her reach the million-dollar mark. We will never forget the day she achieved this milestone because she called to play a song written by Barenaked Ladies. It was their hit single "If I Had $1,000,000." Her success has spread around the world, as she is now one of our featured guests on The Market Guys' on-demand radio program. Her new title is the Emotional Trader Lady!

## Steve

Over the years, we have seen and heard many success stories about people who have overcome the emotional challenges in order to reach the pinnacle of success with regard to trading the markets. However, with every success story we see the tragedies as well. One such person, whom we will call Steve, comes to mind. Steve had a high-level sales position with Siebel Systems (Nasdaq ticker symbol: SEBL). The company provided businesses with customer relationship management software and was considered to be one of the technology darlings in the mid- to late 1990s. Seibel rewarded Steve with large bonuses over the years, as well as stock options. Many companies pay their sales force in stock options because it takes time for these stock options to vest, and during this vesting period companies like Siebel Systems are able to hold on to key producers like Steve. Should the employee decide to leave the company, they could lose the options that were awarded to them. So you can see how there was an incentive to stay in the ranks.

As Siebel Systems continued to grow, so did Steve's investment account. In fact, his account balance grew to over $152 million dollars. Each day, we would speak with Steve to discuss ideas of how to grow this large sum of money until one day the price of the stock started breaking down below key support levels. We would talk about risk management ideas such as diversification, protective puts, stop loss orders, and other things that would protect this nest egg of an account. However, Steve was so attached to his company that he abandoned all ideas that had anything to do with selling his stock. In fact, his words to us still ring clear. He said, "I know there is a chance this stock could drop, but I am willing to pay for the growth." You see, Steve's optimism about the company and its products blinded him to the fact that this stock was breaking down technically. The sad part of this story is that Steve wound up losing over $100 million dollars as a result of wanting to hang on.

We ran into Steve at a seminar we were doing in Washington, D.C., a few years later and he came over to thank us for all of the lessons we taught him over the years. But what amazes us the most is how he was able to cope with such a loss. There were still many millions of dollars left in his account after that devastating loss but no matter how you look at it, $100 million dollars was lost because of an emotional attachment to the company he worked for.

*Diane*

These stories are not made up to make for an interesting book. These are very real people, in very real situations, with very real emotions. One of the most interesting stories of all is about a woman who lived in Syosset, Long Island. We will call her Diane to protect her identity. For many years, Diane and her husband owned a hardware store not far from the Long Island Rail Road. They eventually decided to sell their business in a plan to phase into retirement. Shortly after they began this new chapter in their lives, her husband passed away and she was left widowed. After careful consideration, she decided to take some of the money she received from the sale of their hardware store and invest it in a new plan for the long term. She opened an account with a discount broker down the street and deposited $200,000 with them to get things started.

Diane shopped around for a good stock to buy. She had always heard that you should buy companies that you are familiar with, or at least a company that has products or services that you like yourself. Well, she always remembered liking a certain chocolate drink. It came in a glass bottle with a yellow label, and printed in blue ink was the word *Yoo-hoo*. This is the same drink that famous baseball player Yogi Berra enjoyed, and if it was good enough for Yogi, it was good enough for Diane, too. This is the stock that Diane wanted, so she called up her broker and placed an order to buy $200,000 worth of this one stock. Her instructions to her broker were to buy as many shares as possible of ticker symbol YHOO with the money she had in her account. The next day she looked at her account and saw that the stock was up. The second and third day were the same, and after a week of this excitement she discovered that what she thought was Yoo-hoo, the chocolate drink, was in fact an Internet company called Yahoo!. There was no reason to sell the stock now because even though it was not the company she thought is was in the first place, she was making money with this fortunate mistake. In fact, she was making a lot of money, so she held on. Three years and a series of stock splits later, this $200,000 investment turned into a $23 million dollar windfall. This was the good part of this unusual story, but it didn't stay good for Diane because her emotional attachment later caused her to ignore sound risk management advice.

We discussed with Diane the possibility of moving out of this Yahoo! position and into a more diverse bond portfolio. When she turned down that idea, we discussed protecting the position with stop loss orders and protective puts to lock in this massive profit. The stock started to show signs of weakness as Internet stocks across the board starting breaking down below key support levels. Does this story sound familiar? Instead of removing herself from the emotional bond she developed with this company, Diane decided to go on a world cruise instead. To make matters even worse, Diane borrowed money from the margin side of her account to purchase land in Boca Raton, Florida, before leaving on her extended vacation. Upon coming back from her cruise around the world, Diane was welcomed by the news of the Internet bubble bursting and a letter from her broker informing her that she was in a margin call. This meant that the money she had in her account, which was pure profit when she left on her cruise, turned into a huge debt owed to her broker for the land that she purchased in south Florida. We can't say that this story had a tragic ending because Diane was still able to hold onto $2 million of her $23 million. If you consider that she started by investing $200,000, she still did better than if she had bought Yoo-hoo.

Why do so many people decide to hold on when things get tough? This goes back to what we talked about in Pavlov's dogs. Greed does a funny thing to us without us even realizing it, and if you are not careful, the same things can happen to you. In the examples of the people we've talked about, these individuals were able to pull their financial lives together and live happily ever after. But what about those individuals who have suffered and continue to suffer real heartache because greed got the best of them?

After years in this business, we find that the stories are endless. Like Andrew in Michigan, who lost all of his mother's life insurance benefit because he decided to hold on to a stock even though the stock was losing money year after year in a steady downward spiral. Robert, in New York, sold a Wonder Bread route that he spent 25 years building for retirement only to cash in and put all of his $600,000 life savings in the market so he could turn it into millions. Not only did he lose all of it, but he lost his marriage, his children abandoned him, and later his health suffered greatly because of the stress of having to deal with this financial catastrophe. We tell these stories as often as possible so that others like you don't fall into the same trap.

## Mind Your Emotions

Removing your emotions when it comes time to invest or trade in the market can be as easy as learning how to read a price chart. The Market Guys have embraced the idea of simplicity, and in the next chapter we will talk about the first and most important point of the Five Points for Trading Success: *Follow the Money Trail.* This means putting your money where the money is going. If you learn how to do this well, then the decisions will be easier and a lot of stress will be avoided. Learn how to profit by moving with the momentum, like Dan and Lesley. But also learn from people like Steve, Diane, Andrew, and Robert, who let greed get the best of them. It's all a matter you of how you develop your trader's mind-set.

POINT

# FOLLOW THE MONEY TRAIL
## Identify the Trend

# It Pays to Be Trendy

## PUTTING YOUR MONEY WITH THE MONEY

The debate has raged for years about the validity of trends in the markets. In 1973, Burton Malkiel published his classic tome, *A Random Walk Down Wall Street* (New York: W. W. Norton), which essentially makes the case that past stock prices have no bearing on future price direction. He makes the claim that at any given point in time, a stock price has equal probability of rising or falling; therefore, any in-depth analysis is fruitless. The prevailing long-term trend is upward, but short-term movements within the broad trend are random. Over 20 years later, Andrew Lo and A. Craig MacKinlay began presenting statistical evidence to the contrary and eventually published their own counter title, *A Non-Random Walk Down Wall Street* (Princeton, NJ: Princeton University Press, 1999). Indeed, certain correlations may be found and the possibility of outperforming the broad market due to factors other than luck exists.

We want to clearly state at this point that we will not be presenting statistical models as the basis for this, the first point in *The Market Guys' Five Points for Trading Success*. Having seen that statistics will tend to sing any desired song when the underlying data have been sufficiently tortured, we are offering this chapter based on our empirical observations rather than a comprehensive financial theory. In the simplest terms, this is how we've traded on and off the trading floor for over a quarter century and it's worked for us. As far as we've been able to discern, any proof of random markets or weaknesses in technical analysis will not require us to return any of our profits from trading the markets.

## The Crowd May Be Wrong, but They're Still the Crowd

Before we talk about trends, including how they're formed and why they persist, let's take a micro view of a single trade. In its most basic form, a trade is simply the pairing of a buyer and a seller. It's been said that the buyer buys because he expects the price to rise while the seller sells because he expects the price to fall. Therefore, the conclusion is that one party or the other is always wrong. This doesn't take into account the reasons behind a trade, though. Take, for example, a situation where a trader has 10,000 shares of stock that was purchased at a price that was 50 percent of the current level. This trader owns stock that has doubled in value. After reviewing the technical indicators on a chart, it appears that the stock is highly extended from its moving average support line. However, the stock is still showing strength as each day's close is higher than the previous day's close. If this trader truly believed that the price was going to drop in the next trading session, it would be reasonable to expect him to sell his entire position. Instead, the trader sells a portion of his position and keeps the remainder open to take advantage of any move higher in the stock price.

In this example, the trader is not necessarily expecting the price to fall. Rather, he is managing risk by locking in some of his profits. He started as a speculator by assuming risk in the market and he is now lowering his risk by lowering his exposure to loss of profits in the event the price should fall. It's important to make this distinction because the reasons people buy and sell are more complex than just watching two sides make a wild guess at the direction of the next trade price. The swings between traders assuming risk and traders transferring risk are at the heart of trends in the market. Now multiply this single trade by many thousands or millions of transactions and we see the trend wave forming. Note that we're not advocating always looking for the reasons behind the trend in technical analysis, but rather attempting to understand why trends rise and fall.

## Dow Theory

Charles Dow introduced his theory of the markets back in the early 1900s, but more than a hundred years passed before investors and money managers alike realized how important technical analysis was for managing risk in the marketplace. Charts are what we rely on to help remove the emotions from the decision-making process, and these are the tools The Market Guys use to trade the markets.

Whether you are a seasoned investor who has spent many years taking risk in the market or one who is just starting out on a journey into the world of trading, you should make it a point to review Mr. Dow's ideas as often as possible. We do our best to discuss the tenets of Dow Theory whenever we can. Although there are many who argue the relevance of Dow Theory, we believe that following the trends will give you the highest probability of making money in the markets. In every seminar we give, you can count on the fact that we will be looking at charts. Trend analysis is the basis of how we pick stocks, and analyzing these trends helps us establish our risk points. There is a lot of truth to the old saying, "Repetition is the best teacher." If you apply these simple concepts to every chart you look at, you will eventually become a master technician yourself.

Charles Dow made a simple observation that eventually propelled him to be one of the greatest analysts of all time. He recognized that there were certain companies in the United States that were the driving forces behind the U.S. economy. He believed that if he measured the progress of the companies that were responsible for stimulating the overall growth, he would have a leading indicator for investors. So, on July 3, 1884, the Dow Jones Company, which published the *Wall Street Journal,* introduced 12 companies and the Dow Jones Industrial Average was born. Twelve years later, the editors got together and added more stocks to the index in order to get better insight into the driving forces of the economy at the time. The index is reassessed every few years to ensure that the average reflects the blue-chip sector of the market. Following is a list of the original Dow stocks that made up the Industrial Average in July 1884.

**The Original Dow Jones Industrial Average, July 3, 1884**

Chicago & North Western
Union Pacific
Delaware, Lackawanna & Western

Missouri Pacific

Lake Shore

Louisville & Nashville

New York Central

Pacific Mail

St. Paul

Western Union

Northern Pacific preferred

You can see by looking at these companies what the nature of the economy was at the time, and although today's index looks a lot different, you will still see in it the "blue chips" that are the driving our present-day economy.

Today the Dow Jones Industrial Average (DJIA) is a price-weighted average of 30 stocks traded on the New York Stock Exchange (NYSE) and the Nasdaq. Often referred to as "the Dow," the DJIA is the oldest and single most watched index in the world. Many times, you will hear financial commentators say "the market" is up today, or "the market' is down, and most of the time they are referring to the Dow. The Dow is so popular that many investors believe this index represents the whole of the U.S. markets. This, of course, is not true, but it is amazing to see how many other markets around the world react to the Dow when it is the highlight of the day. The current Dow 30 is listed below.

### The Current Dow Jones Industrial Average

3M Company (MMM)

Alcoa Inc. (AA)

Altria Group, Inc. (MO)

American Express Co. (AXP)

American International Group (AIG)

AT&T Inc. (T)

Boeing Co. (BA)

Caterpillar, Inc. (CAT)

Citigroup Inc. (C)

Coca-Cola Co. (KO)

DuPont (E. I.) deNemours (DD)

Exxon Mobil Corp. (XOM)

General Electric Co. (GE)

General Motors (GM)

Hewlett-Packard Co. (HPQ)

Home Depot, Inc. (HD)

Honeywell International, Inc. (HON)

Intel Corp. (INTC)

International Business Machines (IBM)

JPMorgan Chase & Co. (JPM)

Johnson & Johnson (JNJ)

McDonalds Corp. (MCD)

Merck & Co., Inc. (MRK)

Microsoft Corp. (MSFT)

Pfizer Inc. (PFE)

Procter & Gamble Co. (PG)

United Technologies Corp. (UTX)

Verizon Communications Inc. (VZ)

Wal-Mart Stores, Inc. (WMT)

Walt Disney Co. (DIS)

In 1916 the number of stocks making up the Dow increased to 20, and in 1928 the number increased once again to a total of 30 stocks. General Electric is the only original member left in the index, although it was dropped a couple of times, then reinstated between 1898 and 1907. The Dow is the oldest continuing U.S. index and remains with us as a constant reminder of the man who brought us technical analysis, Charles Dow.

One of the tenets discussed in Dow Theory is that the markets have three trends: up, down, and sideways. We find this to be the most important of the six tenets because it helps us position our money in the direction of the money flow. In other words, if you want to make money in the market, then make sure you are putting your money where the money is going. Going with the money flow means we should be buying in the direction of the trend.

This shouldn't be too hard to understand, yet you would be surprised to see just how many people buy stocks that are in downtrends. People all over the world try to buy stocks that are at bottom prices because we are all programmed, from a very young age, to think that buying anything at a lower price is good. If you have ever gone shopping at a department store, you may have noticed that shoppers everywhere are attracted to the word *sale*. Many who have bought a new car tell us that they've spent long hours learning how to negotiate a good price before they've even entered the car dealership. If you have ever bought a new car for yourself, you know exactly what we are talking about here. If you are planning to purchase a car, this usually means you are going to experience sales pressure, and if you are not a good negotiator, you will most likely pay a higher price for that automobile than a buyer who is prepared and knows how to deal with the salesperson. Either way, we know that we are going to try to talk the salesperson down on the price, and when we finally do manage to negotiate a price that feels good, we think we've gotten a bargain. As a result of these behavior patterns, we are conditioned to buy low.

After many years of this conditioning, we assume that this is the way we should shop for stocks. But when we apply these same buying strategies to the stock market, we lose money and wonder why. Changing a thought process like this is a lot like trying to break a bad habit. It's not as easy as it sounds, and although buying stocks that are trading at 52-week lows sounds like a good idea, it is not. The better idea is to buy stocks that are on 52-week highs. It almost seems unnatural to prefer paying a higher price for anything, yet we must convince ourselves to think this way when we are trading because we are not shopping—we are trading for profit. If you want to make money in the market, you will have to understand that growth companies and growth stocks are most likely going to set new highs each and every week. So buying a stock like this shouldn't be too scary, especially if you know there is a good chance that it will go higher. Another way to look at this is to realize that stocks on their 52-week lows will most likely reach another new low, so buying a stock in this condition will most likely cost you money. Let's face it, is your buy order really going to change the minds of all those people who have been selling this stock throughout the year? Instead of trying to buy low and sell high, which is what most people think of as a good plan, go ahead and tell yourself that you are going to buy high to sell higher. Thinking this way will put you on the right side of the trend.

## Uptrends

In order to understand what it means to position yourself ahead of the money flow, we need to look at what defines the three types of trends. Let's start with the *uptrend*. Charles Dow defined an uptrend as a time when successive rallies in a security price close at levels higher than those achieved in previous rallies and when lows occur at levels higher than previous lows. When you see a chart that looks like Figure 3.1, it should be obvious to you that the buyers are controlling price. The story of an uptrend tells us that the buyers are willing to support the stock at higher levels while at the same time the sellers are moving their sell limits higher in order to get the best sale price. If you had a crowd of people rushing over to buy stock from you, wouldn't you want to raise your sale price to get the highest possible profit? Of course you would. Our strategy on the buy side is to position ourselves alongside the other buyers who are busy pushing the stock up. Recognizing an uptrend allows us to put our money in the direction of the money flow. If your strategy is to find stocks that are in upward trends, then try looking at companies that are trading on their 52-week highs.

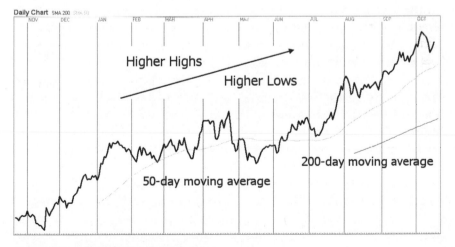

**Figure 3.1    Defining an Uptrend**

Another way is to scan headlines for companies that are in the news, and if the trend is going up with a nice steady slope, you can add them to your watch list. We prefer you qualify a stock for your watch list by looking at the moving averages. As you can see in Figure 3.1, this stock's 50-day *simple moving average (SMA)* is above the 200-day simple moving average. When the moving averages are running up and parallel to one another, we know that the stock has been in an uptrend for some time. This is just one easy way to sort for stocks that are being bought up by the buyers. We have had great success in using this method, which is why we will be expanding on the use of moving averages throughout this book.

In the real world, not all stocks are going to look like the one in our example. Some will have uptrends that are more extreme, meaning the price action will be more vertical, while other stocks may show a more erratic footprint that might reflect a more volatile price history. This, of course, would make it harder for us to identify the actual trend of the stock. Although using the 50- and 200-day moving averages makes it easier for us to identify the overall trend, it is important for you to know how to draw a trend line. As we mentioned earlier in the definition of an upward trend, lows occur at levels higher than previous lows, which means it's the buyers who are more motivated to push the stock higher. This also means that the sellers are less willing to push the stock lower; therefore, it only makes sense that we monitor the behavior pattern of the buyers when looking at stocks that are trending higher. If the buyers decide to give up on the stock, we will see this in the price action because these lows, also known as *troughs,* will no longer be successively higher. If we notice that the lows or troughs are moving successively lower, then that would be our signal to get out of the stock.

When constructing a trend line in a stock that is going up, we would measure the lows because we want to keep our eyes on the buyers. In Figure 3.2, points A, B, and C are lows that are successively higher. This tells us that during the time these points were established, the buyers were willing to pay higher prices. The aggressive action of the buyers causes the sellers to back off to higher levels and the footprint is seen with higher highs following the higher lows. Drawing the trend line begins with your connecting the dots. Before you do this, you would scan the price chart to see if there are any other low points that fall in line with the ones you have already identified as established lows (see Figure 3.3).

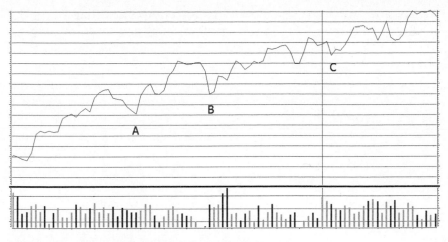

**Figure 3.2    Identifying the Lows in an Uptrend**

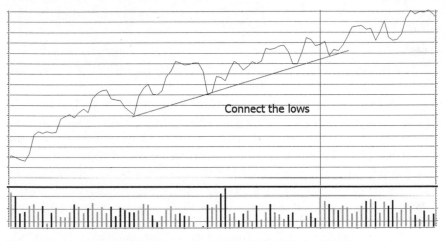

**Figure 3.3    Connecting the Lows to Form the Uptrend Line**

In Figure 3.4 you will see that we have connected points A, B, and C while extending the line further to the right. Notice how successive lows reach the trend line and then will occasionally dip below. Drawing a trend line takes minimal artistic talent, but it's important to know that you don't have to get the points to match up exactly in a row. There may be points on the chart where the price will dip slightly below your line or rise before touching the line. Just remember that you are using your trend line to gauge the intensity of the buying activity.

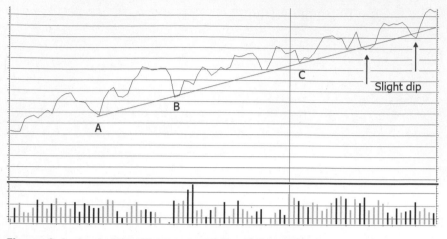

**Figure 3.4   Lows May Vary around the Uptrend Line**

### Looking at the Angle of the Trend Line

Measuring the angle of the trend line will also help you develop a feel for the market or stock you are trading. If you see a stock that has been gradually going up in price over time with a nice steady 30- to 40-degree slope in the trend line, chances are the trend will continue. This means we would stay in a long position for as long as this trend continues in an upward direction. However, if we see prices start to drop and stay below the trend line, this would be our signal to get out of the stock entirely, defend our profits, or, more importantly, protect our account from a potential loss. Just understand that it is the buyers who are controlling the price in an uptrend, and focusing on the price will help us control the emotional side of the trading plan, as we discussed in Chapter 2.

Buying pressure can also be measured by the steepness of the trend, relative to recent trend angles. Assume you're looking at a stock with an uptrend angle of 20 degrees. If the slope of the trend line begins to accelerate to 50 to 70 degrees or more, this means the buyers are becoming more aggressive. When you see this happen, make sure you are ready to exit the position as the chances of a pullback in price becomes greater as the angle of the slope increases. It should make sense to you that, although we see vertical price moves in stocks from time to time, vertical price moves do not last forever. Of course, understand that the angle of the trend is a function of the scale that you're using on your chart. Therefore, the angles that we discuss are relative to each other, not absolute.

Another way to think about this is to remember that the steeper the trend, the less reliable the trend line becomes. Figure 3.5 shows an example of a stock that started out with a nice steady trend, but over time the angle of the trend line increases. Adjusting our trend lines to account for the increase in angle is called *fanning the lines*. Trend line A is where we connected a series of low points, giving us a nice steady slope. There is nothing out of the ordinary here, but if you look at the angle of trend line B, you will see that the increase in slope tells us the buying pressure is increasing. This is a signal that the buyers are getting more aggressive. As time passes, we can once again see the angle of the trend continuing to increase. If you were in this stock and found your trend line looking like the one at point D, it would be time to take action. Your call to action would require selling out of all or at least some of the position. If you are unsure of the exit point, then another good idea would be to place a sell stop order just below the trend line at point D. Let the buyers tell you when it's time to get out. If they ease up on the buying pressure, then the stock will naturally pull back in price and your stop order will trigger automatically. This will move you to cash, and once again you'll have enough buying power in your account for the next trade.

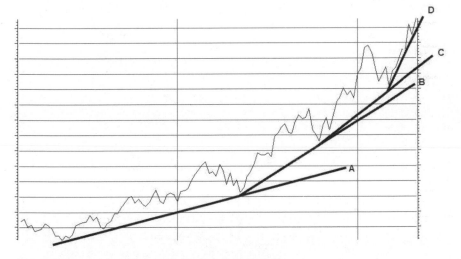

**Figure 3.5 Increasing Relative Trend Angles**

### Volume Confirms the Trend

One of the other important tenets of Dow Theory has to do with volume analysis, and it states that trends are confirmed by volume. What this means is that if you see the trading volume of a stock increasing in the direction of the trend, you have supporting evidence that the trend is a strong one (see Figure 3.6). If you see a stock going up in price but notice that the volume is steadily decreasing, this would tell us that we wouldn't want to rely on that trend as much.

Imagine you are flying a kite. The kite represents the stock price, while the daily trading volume represents the wind needed to get the kite to fly. Hopefully, you have happy childhood memories that will help you picture this in your mind. If not, then by all means go out there and fly a kite. It is a great stress reliever, and if you have any friends or family members that you can invite, bring them along, pack a nice picnic basket, and make a day out of it. It will be fun.

Flying this kite will absolutely help you learn how to read volume on a price chart. In order for your kite to fly, you will need wind under it. The stronger the wind, the faster the kite will climb.

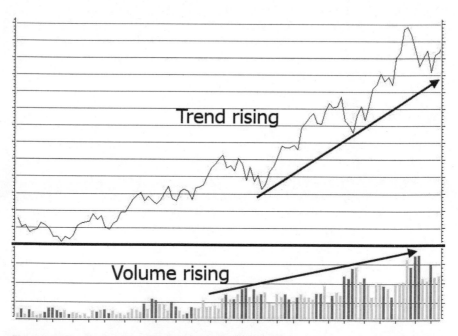

**Figure 3.6   Uptrend with Supporting Volume**

The same applies for the stocks you will be trading. For a stock to sustain an upward trend, you need volume under it (the stronger the volume, the steeper the trend). But what would happen to your kite if all of a sudden the wind started to die down? If you have had this happen to you as a child you might remember having to run a little bit in order to create your own wind, right? If you didn't run, the kite would start to flounder in the sky and you knew that if the wind didn't pick up soon, the kite would fall.

You will see the same thing happen to the price of a stock. If the volume starts to drop and you see that your stock is starting to flounder in price, then there is a good chance your stock is going to drop. If you see a steep trend line and you notice that the volume is dramatically falling off, then you will often see the stock price break the trend line or fall below an established support level and you are now in a freefall. This is why we are so focused on encouraging you to use trailing stops. You don't have to look at your stocks every minute of every day; just make it a point to keep tabs on the price, and if you see these signs, then you know it's time to take action. The worst thing you could do is just sit there and hope that the stock is going to go higher. If you feel that something is changing but you're not quite sure if you see a clear signal, then your first move should always be to protect the position. You can never go wrong by being defensive. We are usually caught off guard when we are in our most relaxed position.

## Downtrends

*Downtrends* are price patterns that show a negative slope. The highs are getting lower and the lows are also moving successively lower. Downtrend lines are drawn from high to high because we want to track the path of the sellers who are, during this time, controlling the price. You can also think of a downtrend line as a signal that tells us supply is greater than the demand. It is not a good idea to be a buyer while the downtrend is in force, yet there are many people who take this advice lightly. If this is the only thing you get out of this chapter, then the price you paid for this book will pay for itself over and over again.

To construct a downtrend line, scan the chart with your eyes to see if you can pick out any noticeable highs or peaks in the price action.

We did this for you in Figure 3.7 where you can see our high points at A, B, and C. From there, it's just a matter of you connecting the dots. In Figure 3.8 you can see how we have drawn our line through the tops. You do not have to be precise when connecting these points, so don't worry about being exactly on the mark. Many times, you will cross through some of the peaks, but the main goal is to identify a general area where the sellers have displayed a history of selling. This selling action eventually pushes the price to lower lows, and the downtrend is identified. You will also see that downtrend lines act as resistance. In Figure 3.8 lower lows follow lower highs because the

**Figure 3.7   Identifying the Highs in a Downtrend**

**Figure 3.8   Connecting the Highs to Form the Downtrend Line**

buyers continue to fade the market and move to the sidelines. Any move over this downtrend line confirmed by an increase in volume tells us that demand is increasing; therefore, a change in trend could be coming.

## Sideways Trend

The third type of trend is one of our favorites. The *sideways trend* frustrates most investors, but it's a price trend that many traders, especially option traders, look for. Simply put, it is a period of time on a chart where prices lay flat or move within a well-defined trading range. Also known as a consolidation pattern or price channel, buyers and sellers reach a stalemate where each side establishes boundaries that represent support and resistance.

Another way to look at a sideways trend is to think of it as a time when supply and demand are in balance. Figure 3.9 is an example of a sideways trend where the stock is basically stuck in a price range. As mentioned before, option traders favor such price ranges because there are many different trading strategies they can initiate within this channel. They can profit from such trades because there are clear lines of support and resistance, which allows them to manage their risk.

## Support and Resistance

We've covered the ideas behind building a trend line and how important it is to gauge the motivation level of the buyers and sellers. In doing so, we've referred to the support and resistance. Let's

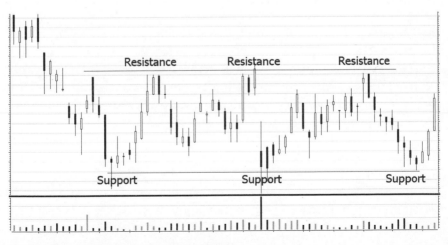

**Figure 3.9   Sideways Trending Stock**

develop those concepts a little more. *Support* is the level at which demand for the stock is strong enough to keep the stock from dropping any further. Support levels are usually identified somewhere below where the stock is actually trading, and although it is not an exact price point, we look at support as a general area. You could also think of support as a floor where the buyers are more motivated than the sellers. Understand that technical analysis is not an exact science, so many times the support level may not seem clear to you. However, practice will hone your skills, and over time your eye will easily be able to pick out support levels.

On the other side is *resistance*. Resistance is the price level at which the selling pressure is strong enough to prevent the stock from rising further. You can think of this as a ceiling where the sellers have convinced the buyers that they are outnumbered and the buyers move to the sidelines. Like support, this is not an exact price level. It's best to think of resistance as a price area where supply in the stock has overcome the demand. These resistance areas are found above where the stock is currently trading, and every buyer should be aware of the price points where overhead supply exists. It's good practice to know where the sellers are stacking up before you ever consider taking a long position.

Looking back at Figure 3.9 you see an example of a stock that has been trading in a horizontal price channel. Notice the support level, which connects the lows of the channel. Remember, we are looking for general areas where there has been a history of buying activity. We know that this is an area of demand because the buyers were able to rally the stock from these points. Should the price drop and stay below the lows, this would tell us that the buyers are losing their ability to hold up the stock and the sellers are taking charge of the price action.

The resistance line is drawn horizontally by connecting the channel highs. If there were any highs that crossed slightly over this line, it would be okay because once again we are looking for general areas as opposed to exact price points. Should we see a strong move over resistance on high volume, this would be called a *breakout*. Breakouts are footprints that tell us the buyers are getting aggressive. When the sellers see this aggression, they will "fade the market" by raising their sell prices in an effort to see how far the buyers will chase the market.

## Moving Averages

We would be missing a big piece of the trend story if we didn't discuss *moving averages*. We'll discuss the details of constructing and using the moving average more in the next chapter. For now, recognize that they are one of the most valuable tools we have when it comes to identifying and analyzing price trends. Many times, you will find that the trend lines you draw will run parallel or even on top of one of the major moving averages.

You may have heard it said that a moving average is a lazy man's trend line. With that said, let us point out that we are always in favor of simplifying the process, so think of this as our way of helping you keep things super simple. The other point to consider is that you are not the only person in the world using moving averages to identify trends in the market. Therefore, when a stock is breaking below a major moving average, the general trading population is put on alert. Once the traders are in defense mode, you will see a drop in the buying pressure. From there, the natural progression is an increase in supply and the sell off begins. The fact that many millions of investors and traders use moving averages as a signal to get in or out of a stock tells us that we cannot ignore the power these simple lines have with regard to affecting the price action of a stock or index. In Figure 3.10 you will see how closely the 50-day moving average

**Figure 3.10   Trend Line Closely Following the 50-Day Moving Average**

correlates to the intermediate trend line. Notice how the stock shows a pattern of price rallies near these support levels. Many people follow moving averages, so it's not unusual to see the major moving averages act as support for the stock.

Unfortunately, not enough investors have realized the value in using moving averages. Most charts include a basic selection of moving averages. Not only will they help you determine the trend of the market, but they also serve as tools to manage risk. Learning how to minimize loss when you pick the wrong stock is critical to your success. If you have never used moving averages before, then we strongly recommend you start using them now. After a while, you may eliminate the need to draw trend lines altogether. Your trained eye will eventually be able to see the trend in a flash. This not only saves you time in selecting a good stock, but it also removes any doubt when it comes time to exit a stock or option position.

## Back on Track

After reading this chapter, you may have recognized that you have been fighting the trend. You try to buy the next low because you just know that the rally is coming. Or you short the stock that is pushing new heights because there is no good reason for the price to be at such high levels. Our hope is that you will get back on the track of following the money trail. Maybe the company isn't worthy of the lofty stock price it happens to possess, but you need to understand that your short sale won't bring the market back in balance. Put your money where the money is flowing. If the money is flowing into a stock, go ahead and buy it. When the money is flowing out of a stock, join the sellers. Your profits and sanity will both reap the rewards of moving with the market rather than against it.

# CHAPTER 4

# The Trader's Toolbox

## HOW TO PICK A HAMMER WHEN THE MARKET GIVES YOU A NAIL

There are many choices in analysis tools and strategies for traders and investors. One of the biggest challenges facing the trader is which tool to use for a given market condition. And once you've selected a tool, when should you switch to a different tool? You need to properly apply the right technical or fundamental strategy, or you'll find yourself making the wrong move at the right time.

### Chatter Box—Rick

Several years after purchasing my first new home, I decided to finish the basement. The space was a walk-out basement (now cleverly described as "terrace-level" by creative real estate marketers) with three sides that were poured concrete walls. Since my construction expertise falls at the lower end of the skill spectrum, I consulted several friends about the best way to finish the walls. They told me that the simplest approach would be to install furring strips along the entire length of the poured walls. Furring strips are nothing more than slats of treated lumber that run perpendicular to the floor. The drywall panels

*(Continued)*

could then be attached to the furring strips and the wall finished the same as a typical framed wall.

The challenge was figuring out the best way to attach the furring strips to the concrete wall. The two most common methods are drilling into the wall and installing masonry screws or using a powder-actuated nail gun to drive the nails into the wall. For those of you who aren't familiar with a powder-actuated nail gun, I can explain it very easily. The tool looks like a small weapon. One end is loaded with a powder cartridge, quite similar to a rifle shell. The other end is loaded with a nail wrapped in a rubber seat. In order to set the nail, you simply place the nail tip against the wall and pull the trigger. The powder in the cartridge explodes, firing the nail into the wall with a single shot. Now let's review the options. First, I could do a lot of work manhandling a drill against a solid wall followed by more work setting the screw. Or I could fire a gun at the wall. In my book, this was a classic no-brainer.

So I went to my local home improvement store and purchased a nail gun with plenty of cartridges and nails. I dutifully loaded the gun per the instructions and carefully set the nail tip against the wall. Taking care to ensure that everything was in order, I pulled the trigger. There was a loud crack, a bit of recoil, and a puff of smoke where the nail was firmly set through the furring strip into the wall. It would be an understatement to say that the nail gun became my favorite tool that day. Furring strips only require several anchors to attach them to a wall but I had an excuse to set a dozen nails into each strip. Eventually, I ran out of furring strips. There I was with a perfectly good nail gun and nothing to nail! Now I was trying to figure out alternative uses for this tool. Sure, a handsaw was specifically designed for cutting lengths of board but a properly aligned nail gun just might be able to accomplish the task with a single shot.

Many traders find themselves armed with the equivalent of a powder-actuated nail gun when they approach the market. It's been said that if the only tool you know how to use is a hammer, everything starts to look an awful lot like a nail. An interesting twist to this phenomenon is that it becomes more frequent with the more arcane technical indicators. A trader who uses a simple moving average, for example, generally has no problem with using the indicator when appropriate and disregarding it when not appropriate. However, we've met more than just a few traders who, upon learning about Fibonacci retracement levels, wouldn't dream of entering the markets if you took away their Fibonacci lines. Why is this? Perhaps it's an extension of the nail gun story. The trader finds a tool that not only looks good but is also a lot of fun to apply. Eventually, they convince themselves that they have their hands on the best tool in the toolbox.

The difference between finishing out a basement and the market is this: If you try to use your nail gun to cut lengths of board in the basement project, your folly will be readily apparent. If you attempt to apply Fibonacci lines to every chart you read, the charts will let you. In fact, the chart data will be more than sufficient to allow you to "see" the pattern in just about every application, thereby reinforcing your belief that you're using the best tool. When the trade moves against you and you start to lose money, there are a multitude of other factors to which you can attribute the loss. Then when the next trade opportunity arises, out comes the nail gun.

This chapter is designed to give you a solid understanding of some of the more common tools that you have at your disposal, including their strengths and limitations. Each technical indicator that we cover will follow this format:

1. Overview
2. Calculation
3. Application
4. Example

Remember that the goal is to keep everything simple. Calculations are included to enhance your understanding of how the indicator is derived, but if you want to skip past them, you won't lose anything in your ability to learn the application. One more point to note is that the charts shown are black and white. Therefore, when we refer to candlesticks on the charts, a white candlestick is an up day where the closing price is higher than the opening price. A black candle is a down day where the closing price is lower than the opening price. Most charting programs allow for color charting, and green is up while red is down. In our discussions, green and white are interchangeable while red and black are interchangeable.

## Trend Lines

### Overview

Trend lines are not much more than the adult version of connect-the-dots. We introduced these handy tools in the previous chapter. They are used to create a smooth picture of the prevailing direction of the stock price movement. Of course, as the name suggests, trend lines are drawn when we identify a trend, either an uptrend or a downtrend. The simplest definition of an uptrend is higher highs and higher lows. Along with that, a downtrend is identified as lower highs and lower lows. Both parts of the definition must hold for the trend to be in effect. For example, if a stock is making higher highs and lower lows, it is not an uptrend. The picture that is created from higher highs and lower lows is an expanding fan resulting from the widening range over where the stock is trading.

Another important consideration of the trend line is that it may change frequently. As we learned from Dow Theory, prices tend to exhibit different trends over various time horizons. When we switch our view from intraday charting to weekly charting, we may see different trends in effect. Over the previous few hours, we see the prices trending down, but they suddenly stop and begin to rise into an uptrend. A short-term downtrend may be halted by a longer-term uptrend. Along with this, the shorter-term trends will, by definition, fluctuate between uptrends and downtrends. That's what makes them short term.

### Calculation

One of the nice features of the trend line is that there is no calculation per se. As such, it is appealing because it is so easily understood by even a beginner. The trend line is drawn as a best-fit line based on a subjective review of the chart. By definition, a line is defined by any two points. Therefore, we can initially create a trend line by identifying two price points on the chart and connecting them with a straight line.

For an uptrend, we want to connect the lows of the trend. As we mentioned in the overview, the uptrend will exhibit higher lows along the trend. The trader needs to find these lows and draw a line that best crosses through these lows. A downtrend is marked by lower highs, and it is this level that defines the downtrend line. Therefore, we want to draw a straight line that best captures the falling highs along the downtrend.

The question often arises as to which price point to use in connecting the higher lows in an uptrend. Should you connect the lowest low for the day? What about the closing price of the day? Some traders suggest that you use the bottom of the candlestick body, regardless of whether that happens to be the open or the close. In practice, you may actually incorporate multiple price points as you view the trend and decide where to strike the trend line. Dr. Richard M. Wyskida, associate dean of the College of Engineering at the University of Alabama in Huntsville, often advised his students to plot a data set and then step back and "let the data talk to you." The point he was making is that it is helpful to get a picture of the data before rushing into various analyses. The fact is, our eye will usually see pictures and patterns emerge from the price chart before the technical indicators reveal them quantitatively. So how does this help us with drawing a trend line? As we look at the chart, we will see the pattern of cycles along the trend. We'll identify the price swinging to new highs, stalling and dropping to the next higher low. The low will reverse and the stock will rally to the next higher high. Sometimes, the reversal points will fit nicely to the candlestick bodies; sometimes it will fit better to the shadows (highs and lows). This is illustrated in Figure 4.1. Notice at point A that the three points that the trend line

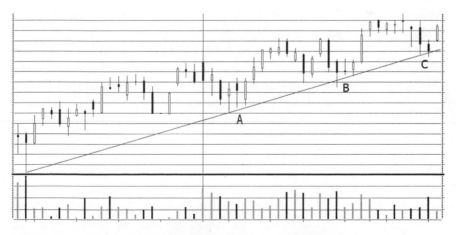

**Figure 4.1    Connecting the Higher Lows in an Uptrend**

crosses are all the lows for the trading days. The candlestick bodies of the first two days are much higher than the trend line itself. At point B, the first day's low penetrates below the trend line, the second day is slightly above and the third day rests quite close to the line. At point C, the first day's low is on the trend line while the second day's candlestick body sits on the trend line with the low dropping below. If we were to set rigid rules regarding which price point to use, you can see how this would create trouble for us. However, a glance at the chart shows that we've drawn a trend line that captures the higher lows quite well because we've given ourselves a little flexibility in where the line is placed.

### Application

The trend line will help us define support in an uptrend and resistance in a downtrend. Since we're connecting the higher lows in an uptrend, we expect that the price will trade above the trend line. As the price rises, each pullback will drop down to the trend line. We consider that to be normal and expected movement as long as the trend holds. Support, by definition, is the price level at which the buying pressure overcomes the selling pressure and the stock begins to move higher. Since we've created the trend line based on just this activity occurring, our expectation is that it will continue. If the stock price should drop significantly below our trend line, then it has moved into an area that is not normal and expected in the uptrend. Notice that we say "significantly" because as we saw in Figure 4.1, occasional and minor drops below the trend line are not unusual. They are the result of the subjective placement of the trend line itself.

We already mentioned that a line is defined by two points but it becomes more robust as we add more points. Figure 4.1 shows three distinct reversals where the lows are successively higher at points A, B and C. Once the trend line is established, it becomes the basis for entering a trade as well as exiting a trade. Since we expect the price to rise off of support as long as the trend holds, we look for buying opportunities shortly after the stock hits the trend line and begins to move back up. We then protect ourselves by placing a sell stop order below the trend line. Based on our expectation, if the stock should drop below the support indicated by the trend line, we assume that the trade is moving against us and we exit the position. As you can see, the trend line got us into the trade and will tell us when it's time to move on.

*Example*

Look at Figure 4.2 and see if you can quickly identify the higher lows that define the trend line. Of course, we've already drawn the line for you, but you should still observe the upswings that were used to place the line. The first low is at the extreme lower left side of the chart. The second point, which initially defines the line, is at the center of the chart. Point A is the third point and confirms the trend line that was established by the first two points.

In our example in Figure 4.2, we could enter a long trade at point A based on the fact that we have already established the trend line, and now we see the stock moving up and away from the line. Notice that immediately before the very long up day, the stock price dipped slightly. It even penetrated the trend line before closing back above the line. This is why we place the stop order below the trend line. It allows for minor intraday dips without stopping the position prematurely.

Let's look at what happened at point B. The stock price dropped hard to the trend line, as evidenced by the long black candle. On that day the sellers were clearly in control. That's the very reason why we wouldn't buy the stock on that day, even though the trend line still appeared to be holding as support. We want to buy when the buyers are buying, not when the sellers are selling. The next day would have been the day we would have expected to enter the trade, but instead of holding support, the price dropped hard below the

**Figure 4.2   Uptrend Example**

trend line support. Once that trend line support was broken, the sellers established control and moved the stock progressively lower from that point.

Any trader with a long position would likely have exited the week or two before point B based on a trailing stop after the quick rally or perhaps the warning signs given by the side-by-side long black candles. However, if you were still holding on to a long position after point B, the first drop where the stock closed below the trend line support would have been the must-exit point. Sure, you would have allowed the stock to drop quite a bit from the high, but holding and hoping would clearly have compounded the loss.

## Channel Lines

### Overview

Many times, we observe prices bouncing between cyclical highs and lows, where the peaks seem to be running parallel to the valleys. The price may be slightly trending or simply running sideways, but the highs can be connected by a line, and the lows can be connected by another, parallel line. When this occurs, we consider the price to be channeling, and the lines we draw are the channel lines.

Channeling goes by various names, including oscillating, channeling, sideways, and consolidating. If the channel occurs without an underlying trend—that is, the price moves sideways without a change in the highs or lows—many traders will look for a breakout from the channel before taking on a new position. Channels often continue for long stretches, which confirms the channel lines with multiple points. These long channels allow us to clearly see the support and resistance, which makes it easier to identify the level at which we would exit the trade.

### Calculation

As with the trend line, once again there is no calculation in drawing the channel lines. What we look for is a best-fit line that connects the highs of the channel range. A second best-fit line is then drawn, which connects the lows. The upper and lower channel lines should run approximately parallel to each other. Look at the upper channel line in Figure 4.3. Notice how the high of the first candle almost touches the line, while the highs of the second cycle are a bit lower. Several points actually penetrate above the line during the day but

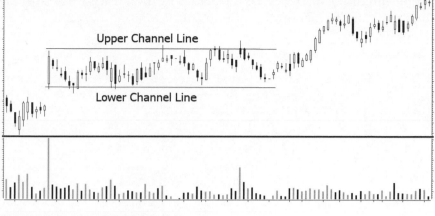

**Figure 4.3    Channeling Stock**

close at or below the line. The same picture can be seen along the lower channel line. Some points are above, some dip slightly below, and others are right at the line. This is what we mean by a best-fit line. It is the rare chart that will let you draw a line with all points sitting squarely along the line with no variations.

In Figure 4.4 the price is channeling but with an upward trend. The upper and lower channel lines are drawn with a best-fit line and run parallel to each other. However, both channel lines run upward at the same angle. Notice that if we omit the

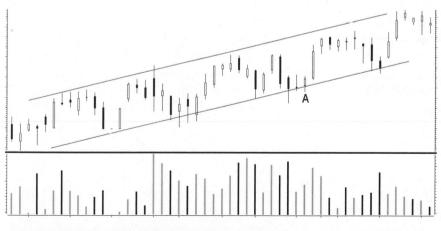

**Figure 4.4    Channeling Stock with an Uptrend**

upper channel line, we are left with simply an uptrend support line since we're connecting the higher lows.

### Application

Channeling stocks may be traded either within the channel to capture short-term moves along the cycles or as breakouts when the price finally penetrates one of the channel lines. If you choose to trade within the channel, you want to ensure that the channel is wide enough to allow for a reasonable profit from the trade. Some prices move within a well-defined channel but with so little distance between the highs and lows as to make it hardly worth the effort.

When trading within the channel, the goal is to buy as close to the lower channel line support as possible. Keep in mind that you still need to buy with the buyers, which means that a long trade should only be entered following a green (or white) candle. The target for a long trade is the upper channel line resistance. It takes some practice to recognize when the trade may not reach the target and profits need to be taken early. As we saw from drawing the lines, sometimes the cycles don't reach the channel lines, so you shouldn't tenaciously hold a position until it absolutely reaches the target line. For a long trade that was entered at the lower channel support line, the sell stop order should be placed slightly below the lower channel line. If the channel fails and the price drops, you want to exit the trade.

Channels with a downward trend may be traded in the same way, except you'll be looking for short trade opportunities. Always trade a trending channel in the direction of the overall trend. If the channel has a downward trend, the best trade is when you can enter a short position close to the upper channel resistance. Again, remember to wait until the sellers are in control, as evidenced by a red (or black) candle as the price drops off the resistance. A short trade would be protected with a market buy stop placed slightly above the upper channel resistance line.

A channel breakout is the alternative approach to trading channels and is the favorite of many traders. With a channel breakout, we're not going to predict which way the price will break out; we just want to pounce on the opportunity when it arises. A channel breakout to the top occurs when the price reaches the upper channel resistance line and rallies to close decisively above the line. This trade is especially significant when the volume rises on the breakout day. A breakout with very low volume relative to recent volume has to be approached with caution. That's not to say you can't trade a breakout with low volume but it is not the preferred setup.

Sometimes the price within the channel will give early warning signs that a breakout may be imminent. For example, if the price rises up toward the upper channel line and then hovers at the line instead of falling back into the channel, the buyers are not backing down in the face of expected selling. Don't buy yet, but be on the lookout for the buyers making the next push, which would result in a breakout.

There are two entry points for a breakout. The first is to buy the stock on the initial breakout. If the breakout is strong, however, you may not be able to buy close to the upper channel line. Alternatively, you could wait for the stock to pull back to the upper channel line and retest it as a support level. When this happens, enter the long trade on the pullback following a green candle. The only danger with waiting for a pullback to the upper channel line following a breakout is that it may not happen. Some breakouts are so strong that the breakout is followed by a rally that never again reaches the upper channel line.

### Example

Point A in Figure 4.4 is an example of where to enter a long trade within an upward trending channel. Notice that although point A is the third day that the price was at the lower channel line support, it was the first day with a green candle. The green candle was not so long that you would be entering the trade well into the channel. It is close enough to the lower channel support line that we still have plenty of room within the channel from which to profit. The following day was a sharp rally, and it was followed by five days of sideways trading. Since the price wasn't making new highs, the trade should be closed even though it had not quite reached the upper channel line. In this case, close was good enough!

Figure 4.5 shows us a channel breakout with both options for entering a long trade. Notice that the price hovered close to the upper channel line for about a week before it finally broke above. At point A, you would have been able to enter a long trade on the initial breakout. While the volume associated with the breakout wasn't as strong as the ideal, it wasn't weak, so the trade could be taken. Upon entering the trade at point A, you would place your sell stop slightly

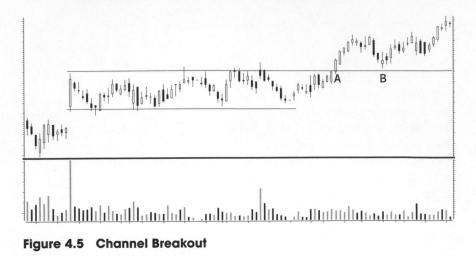

**Figure 4.5    Channel Breakout**

below the upper channel resistance line. Once the breakout occurs, we expect the upper channel line to become support.

As we can see at point B, we're given a second opportunity to enter a long trade when the price falls back to test the support line. If you had entered the long position at point A, you may have taken a profit with a trailing stop when the price started to fall. If not, you would still be in the trade at point B, because the price didn't dip below the support line. Either entry would have allowed you to profit from the subsequent rally that followed point B.

## Moving Averages

### Overview

Moving averages are perhaps the most commonly used technical indicator for a variety of reasons. First, they are easily understood by most traders. The concept of an average is one that is applied in everyday life. We talk about average salary, average height, and average fuel economy in a new vehicle. The moving average updates the average value each time a new data point appears on the chart. Second, moving averages have always shown their utility as a support level when the price is above the average and as a resistance level when the price is trading below the average. Third, moving averages may be calculated over multiple periods, which gives the trader great flexibility in applying them as single indicators or combining them together as multiple indicators.

## Calculation

We'll focus this discussion on the two most popular moving averages: the simple moving average (SMA) and the exponential moving average (EMA). There are a number of other moving averages available, including weighted moving average and linear displaced moving average. We've found through practice that the SMA and EMA capture the utility of moving averages very well.

The SMA is the arithmetic mean of the data set. The equation for the SMA is as follows:

$$SMA = (X1 + X2 + \cdots + Xn)/n$$

Where
　　$Xi$ = closing price of period i
　　$n$ = number of data points

Therefore, the 20-day SMA would have 20 data points consisting of the closing price of the most recent 20 days. The 20 points are totaled and divided by 20 to arrive at the average value. When a new trading day is complete, the new closing price is added into the total while the oldest is dropped. In this way, the average "moves" with the progression of time.

The exponential moving average differs from the SMA in that the data is weighted to give the most recent price more significance than the older price data. Since the most recent price is factored more heavily in the calculation, it follows that the EMA signals price changes more quickly than the SMA.

The equation for the exponential moving average is as follows:

**1.** The exponential smoothing factor is calculated as

$$ESF = 2/(n + 1)$$

Where $n$ = number of data points
　　So for a 20-day EMA, the ESF is 2/21 or 0.095.

**2.** Next, the EMA is calculated as

$$EMA = (\text{Today's closing price} \times ESF) \\ + (\text{Previous EMA value} \times (1 - ESF))$$

We want to emphasize that the calculations are provided here for your reference. Understanding the mathematics behind the indicator is not required for your successful application to trading.

### Application

SMA and EMA are most commonly used as support and resistance levels that follow the action of the price. Trend lines and channel lines, as we've discussed, are straight lines that must be manually adjusted as the movement of the price changes. Moving averages, however, follow the change in price movement because they are calculated indicators rather than subjectively drawn. Therefore, while various traders will interpret trend lines and channel lines differently, an EMA or SMA will be exactly the same for different traders who are examining the same chart.

As we mentioned in the calculation, EMAs will respond more quickly to changes in the price movement. Therefore, the EMA will follow the price more closely than the SMA, resulting in more instances of price touching or crossing the moving average. While this yields more buy and sell signals, it will also tend to yield more false signals. That is, it may tell us to sell when we really shouldn't be selling. There is no right or wrong when it comes to deciding whether to use the EMA or SMA; it is simply a question of how sensitive you want your indicator to be when generating buy and sell signals.

Another question to answer besides which moving average to use is how many periods to include in the moving average. Should you use a 20-day or 50-day moving average? What about a 21-day versus a 20-day? In general, we recommend three basic periods for traders who are just starting to use moving averages. First, the 20-day moving average is a good short-term indicator since it approximates the number of trading days in a month. You could refine the number to 21, but we've observed in practice that 20 is more easily understood, and the extra day doesn't buy a significant improvement in performance. Second, the 50-day moving average is a good intermediate-term indicator since it approaches the number of trading days in a quarter. Once again, purists may gravitate toward the 63-day moving average, but we believe the 50-day is sufficient for beginners. Finally, the 200-day moving average is widely recognized as the best long-term indicator. Many money managers, traders, and others follow the 200-day moving average as a measure of the overall trend. We've seen cases where a stock has rallied for a long time and finally breaks down below short-term support. The fall is fast and furious, yet the price will inexplicably stop as if it were a ball hitting a concrete floor. When the 200-day SMA is overlaid onto the chart, the price stops almost to the penny at the 200-day moving average.

Another common application of the moving averages is to select two different time periods and use both moving averages as crossover indicators. A simple example would be to use the 20-day SMA and the 50-day SMA. The 20-day SMA is called the fast moving average, and the 50-day SMA is the slow moving average. They are referred to as fast and slow due to their speed in responding to changes in price. If the 20-day SMA is below the 50-day SMA and the stock is trading below both, the stock is in a short- intermediate-term downtrend. For a buying signal, we would look for the price to first break above the moving average resistance lines. Next, we would look for the 20-day SMA to cross above the 50-day SMA. This is referred to as a bullish moving average crossover. At the point that the fast moving average is above the slow moving average, we would enter a long position and place our sell stop below the slow moving average. As the price establishes the uptrend, we could tighten the stop by bringing it up to just below the fast moving average.

A word of caution is in order when using moving averages. Because the moving average is specifically intended to identify trends and reversals, they become much less reliable when the price is moving sideways. Even if the price has a wide range, the moving average will go flat for a sideways stock. When this happens, there will be numerous buy and sell signals, but they won't have much validity. Be sure that the chart you're looking at has a trend in either direction before applying the moving average as a technical indicator. In Figure 4.6, the stock has been in a sideways trading range and the 200-day SMA flattens out. While there are a couple of points where the moving average appears to be holding as support or resistance, there are many more where the price simply ignores the line and bounces to either side.

### Example

Figure 4.7 shows an example of a stock that was trading above the 50-day SMA for the latter part of 2006 and into January 2007. We can

**Figure 4.6    200-Day Moving Average in a Sideways Stock**

**Figure 4.7    50-Day Simple Moving Average as Support**

clearly see the price bounce off the 50-day SMA with little to no dip below that support level. The first part of February shows a decisive break below the support, and the price remains below for the rest of the chart. In this example, any long position would have been exited based on a sell stop below the 50-day SMA.

As the stock is trading above the 50-day SMA level, there are several points where the price dips to the moving average and starts to rally. These would all be good entry points for a new long position because the price is above support and the buyers are regaining control as they push the price back up from the moving average. Short-term profits would be recognized by using a trailing stop on each of the minor cycles. Longer-term profits would require placing your stop below the moving average and raising the stop price as the moving average rises.

Figure 4.8 includes both the 20-day SMA (thin gray line) and the 50-day SMA (bold black line). Notice how the 20-day SMA is much more volatile due to the fact that it is faster than the 50-day SMA. In this chart, we observe the moving average crossover. At point A, we can see where the price has started to trade above both moving averages and the 20-day SMA crosses above the 50-day SMA. A long trade would be entered at point A, based on the bullish crossover. We would manage this trade by placing a sell stop below the 50-day moving average if we're looking to capture the intermediate-term profit. As an alternative, some traders will wait until they see a bearish moving average crossover before exiting a trade that was entered on a bullish crossover. Notice that the bearish crossover, where the 20-day SMA drops back below the 50-day SMA, occurs at point B. This is just a few trading days past the drop below the 50-day SMA support. Either exit from the long position would have generated a handsome profit from the extended rally that followed the initial moving average crossover.

**Figure 4.8   Moving Average Crossover**

## Fibonacci Retracement Lines

*Overview*

Fibonacci retracement lines are perhaps the most elegant of the technical indicators, if not the most reliable, because of their origin and ubiquity in nature. Named after the famous twelfth-century mathematician, the Fibonacci retracement lines are based on the Fibonacci number sequence. The sequence is as follows:

1, 2, 3, 5, 8, 13, 21, 34, 55, 89, etc.

Notice that each number is the sum of the previous two numbers. Every two successive numbers in the sequence approaches the Golden Ratio when their quotient is calculated. As the sequence gets higher, the ratio is more closely followed. The Golden Ratio is 1.618 and is observed as follows:

$$3/2 \ = 1.5$$
$$5/3 \ = 1.67$$
$$8/5 \ = 1.6$$
$$13/8 \ = 1.625$$
$$21/13 = 1.615$$
$$34/21 = 1.619$$
$$55/34 = 1.618$$
$$89/55 = 1.618$$

An interesting characteristic of the Golden Ratio is that its inverse is equal to the Golden Ratio minus one. This is shown as

$$(1/1.618) = (1.618 - 1) = .618$$

Finally, as if all this weren't enough to entertain the puzzle fanatic within us, the Fibonacci sequence is evident throughout all of nature. The Golden Ratio has been observed in such diverse natural phenomena as the spiral of a nautilus shell, the petals on a flower, the formation of a pine cone, and the height of your belly button (your total height $\times$ .618!).

*Calculation*

The standard Fibonacci retracement lines used in most trading software packages are 23.6 percent, 38.2 percent, 50 percent and

61.8 percent. We see from the overview that 61.8 percent is derived directly from the Golden Ratio of .618. 100 percent less 61.8 percent yields 38.2 percent and 61.8 percent less 38.2 percent yields 23.6 percent. We see that 50 percent is not a standard number in the Fibonacci sequence, but it is generally included because 50 percent is considered a common retracement for stock prices.

Trading software packages will draw these common retracement levels after you have identified the low and high points along a trading range. For example, if a stock has moved from a low price of $20 to a high price of $30, you would select these two price extremes and the software would draw the appropriate retracement levels at $27.64, $26.18, $25.00, and $23.82.

### Application

The objective of using Fibonacci retracement lines is to identify levels of support when a stock pulls back following a rally or, alternately, to identify levels of resistance when a stock rallies following a drop.

Care must be taken to not enter a trade based solely on the Fibonacci retracement level. As with any support or resistance line, whether drawn such as the trend line or calculated such as the moving average, it is best to confirm the level. An illustration of how you might confirm the level is with the example in the previous calculation paragraph. Let's assume that over the last few weeks the stock has moved from $20 to $30 and is now starting to pull back. You want to enter a long position at some point in the pullback. What would you look for as an entry opportunity? You watch as the stock drops to the first retracement level at $27.64, but you don't see any signs of the price drop slowing. However, as the price approaches $26.18, you notice two things occurring. First, the trading volume, which started strong, has tapered off significantly. Second, the price dipped to $26.00 for a brief time during the day but has since closed above $26.18. Upon examining the daily candlestick chart, you see that today's candle pattern is a hammer reversal. In this instance, you have the Fibonacci retracement level confirmed by both volume and the chart pattern. If the buyers start to step in tomorrow, you may enter a long trade and protect yourself with a sell stop just below the $26.18 level.

### Example

When we look at the range of trading for the uptrend in Figure 4.9, we see the low and high ends of the range identified. Since we're

**Figure 4.9    Fibonacci Retracement Levels in an Uptrend**

starting with an uptrend, we're interested in which price levels will act as support based on the Fibonacci retracements. As we can see at the far right side of the chart, the long black candle indicates a sharp price drop on heavy volume. The following day showed that the selling had halted, at least temporarily, and the volume was much lighter than the initial sell-off. Notice how closely the price reached to the first support line at 38.2 percent. The lower shadow on the long black candle came very close to this level, which was identified by the Fibonacci retracement of the overall trend range.

In this example, we would watch to see if the candle patterns give us any more confirmation of a pending reversal. Simply taking a breather, as is the case here, is not sufficient for a new long position. However, if the price trades close to this support level over the coming few days without falling below, we could buy into a new position and place our sell stop slightly below the 38.2 percent retracement line.

## Stochastic Oscillator

### Overview

The stochastic oscillator, also referred to simply as the stochastic, is an indicator that measures a stock's buying and selling strength relative to its own past performance. By this, we mean that we're not comparing the stock to any market or sector benchmark to determine when it may be time to buy or sell. The Stochastic is generally comprised of two lines: the fast line (called %K) and the slow line (called %D).

As we'll observe in the calculations, the stochastic indicator ranges in value between 0 and 1 (or 0 to 100 percent). As a rule, any value below about 25 percent is considered oversold. The thinking is that the stock is too weak relative to its own past performance and, therefore, should correct with rising prices. Any value above about 75 percent is considered overbought and should correct with falling prices. As an oscillator, the stochastic tends to work better in channels. When a stock moves into a strong uptrend, for example, the stochastic will reach overbought levels without the price correcting downward. Conversely, in a strong downtrend the stochastic will reach the oversold levels without a correction upward.

### Calculation

The first stochastic line is called the fast line because it is calculated directly from the price data. The indicator is based on the current closing price as measured against the highest high and the lowest low in the period over which the stochastic is calculated. The equation is as follows:

$$\%K = (\text{Today's close} - \text{Lowest low})/(\text{Highest high} - \text{Lowest low})$$

If we're using a period of 10 days, then we would identify the highest trade price over the 10-day period and the lowest trade price over the 10-day period for our calculation.

The second stochastic line is referred to as the slow line since it is smoothed through a moving average calculation. As we saw in the section on moving averages, a moving average smooths the volatility of the price data. With the slow stochastic, or %D, the volatility of the %K is smoothed in the same manner. The equation for the slow stochastic is as follows:

$$\%D = N\text{-period moving average of } \%K$$

where N is the number of periods over which the %K is smoothed. %D often uses three periods as a common smoothing factor. As with the moving average on price, the %D may use either a simple, exponential, or weighted moving average calculation. The SMA and EMA are the most common moving averages used in the %D calculation.

### Application

There are three primary ways in which the stochastic is used to identify trading opportunities. The first is as a threshold indicator. As we previously mentioned, the stochastic helps to identify when a stock is overbought or oversold as compared to its own recent past performance. The overbought region is around 70 to 80 percent, while the oversold region is around 20 to 30 percent. There isn't a right or wrong threshold to use with the stochastic. Rather, you need to decide how sensitive you want the indicator to be in generating signals. As you widen the range, the number of signals will decrease. However, the signals that are generated should be stronger. For example, if you decide to use 10 percent and 90 percent as your thresholds, it is apparent that the stochastic will hit these levels fewer times than if you use 30 percent and 70 percent. As a threshold indicator, most traders look for the stochastic to pass the threshold, and then they'll enter a trade when the indicator crosses the threshold in the other direction. Looking at Figure 4.10, we see at point A where the stochastic initially crossed below the 20 percent line, telling us that the stock was oversold. A few days later at point B, the stock crossed back up above the 20 percent line. It is here that we would enter into a new long position based on the stochastic as a threshold indicator.

The second application of the stochastic is to use both the %K and %D together as crossover indicators. Figure 4.11 is the same chart we see in Figure 4.10, except we're using both the %K (black

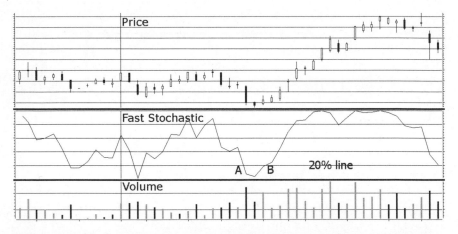

**Figure 4.10   Using the Stochastic Oscillator as a Threshold Indicator**

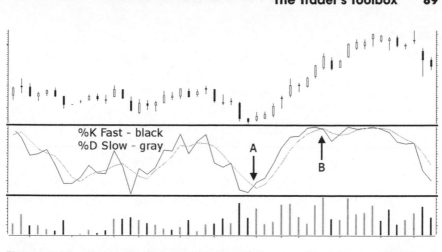

**Figure 4.11  Using the Stochastic Oscillator as a Crossover Indicator**

line) and the %D (gray line). At point A, %K initially crosses up above %D near the 20 percent threshold. We would consider this a bullish crossover and we'd buy the stock. We would hold the position open until %K crosses back below %D near the upper threshold. This occurs at point B in Figure 4.11. As we can see, while this doesn't let us buy the low and sell the high, it does allow us to take a nice bite out of the uptrend.

The third application of the stochastic is to look for a divergence between the price trend and the stochastic trend. Figure 4.12 shows

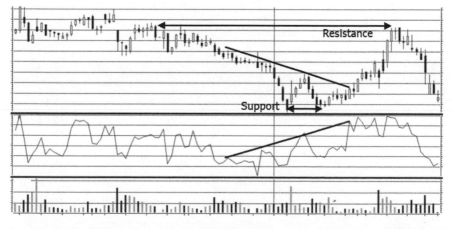

**Figure 4.12  Using the Stochastic Oscillator as a Divergence Indicator**

a daily candlestick chart with %K in the middle window and volume in the lower window. As we can see in the chart, the price highs are getting lower while the highs on the %K are getting higher. This is a divergence between the price and the stochastic, and it is expected that price will correct to follow the stochastic indication. As we can see, the price did rally toward the end of the divergence. Notice how the rally began when the price was approaching a support level and ended as it reached the resistance level. This is an important point: Stochastic divergences tend to be highly subjective and should be used as a confirming indicator, rather than as a stand-alone signal.

### Example

We'll use the stochastic as a crossover indicator for our example in Figure 4.13. We've drawn the %K (black) with a 14-day period and the %D (gray) with a three-day simple smoothing. In this example, we see a region prior to point A where both stochastic lines are below the 20 percent threshold, indicating an oversold condition. In order to enter the long trade, we want to see the %K cross above both the %D line and the 20 percent threshold line. We also want both %K and %D to be rising, which will be further confirmation of the expected price rally. These conditions occur at point A, which is where we would enter the long position. The reverse conditions are the reason for exiting the trade. After moving into the overbought territory above 80 percent, we look for

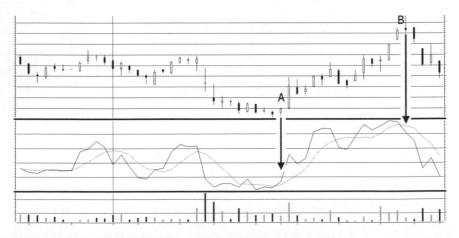

**Figure 4.13   Stochastic Oscillator Crossover Example**

%K to cross below %D and the 80 percent mark. We'll further confirm this by waiting until both stochastics are trending downward. These conditions are met at point B, and it is here that the position is sold.

## Moving Average Convergence Divergence (MACD)

### Overview

The moving average convergence divergence (MACD) indicator is a trend-following indicator that combines two exponential moving averages into an MACD line. It is used with a second line, the signal line, which is an exponential moving average of the MACD line. The MACD tends to work best when the stock price has long, wide swings. Buy and sell signals are generated based on the relationship of the MACD line to the signal line.

It is also common to use an MACD histogram, which is a graphical representation of the difference between the MACD line and the signal line. Many traders find it easier to identify crossovers and trends with the histogram than with the crisscrossing nature of the MACD and signal lines.

### Calculation

The MACD line is a combination of two EMAs. The most common EMAs used in constructing the MACD line are the 12-period EMA and the 26-period EMA. Recall from the calculation of the EMA that a 12-period EMA has an exponential smoothing factor of 15 percent (ESF $= 2/(12 + 1) = 0.154$) and the 26-period EMA has an exponential smoothing factor of 7 percent (ESF $= 2/(26 + 1) = 0.074$). For this reason, the 12-day EMA and the 26-day EMA are also referred to as the 15 percent EMA and the 7 percent EMA. The equation for the MACD line is as follows:

$$MACD = 12\text{-period EMA} - 26\text{-period EMA}$$

The second line used in the MACD indicator is the signal line. The signal line is an exponential moving average of the MACD. As we've seen from previous discussions, when we smooth data through a moving average calculation, the new line is slower to respond than the original line. For that reason, the MACD is considered the fast line and the signal line is considered the slow line. Notice how this mirrors the fast and slow lines in the moving average and stochastic sections of this chapter. The equation for the signal line is:

$$\text{Signal line} = \text{9-period EMA of the MACD}$$

Bear in mind that we're using the common values for the MACD calculation (12, 26, and 9); however, these values may be adjusted to create more or less sensitivity in the indicator. Don't get caught up in the minutia of tweaking these values, thinking that if you use the 10 and 33 MACD line, for example, you'll unlock the secret door to the market. It's fine to increase or decrease the sensitivity of the MACD, but you still want to confirm your trading against the price and volume, as we discuss through this book.

The MACD histogram is plotted as the difference between the MACD line and the signal line or

$$\text{Histogram value} = \text{MACD} - \text{signal}$$

The histogram can assume a positive or negative value, depending on whether the MACD is above or below the signal line.

### Application

There are two primary applications of the MACD indicator. The first is as a crossover indicator. Once again, we look for the crossing between the fast and slow lines. When the MACD line has been trending below the signal line and then crosses up above the signal line, we would consider this to be a bullish sign. This signal would be especially strong if the bullish crossover occurred when the price started to rally off a strong support level. The opposite holds true for a bearish crossover. Here we would look for the MACD line to drop below the signal line, preferably as the price is falling off a strong resistance level.

Figure 4.14 shows an example of a bullish and bearish MACD crossover. At point A, we see that the MACD line has crossed above the signal line. Notice that the histogram is positive, however slightly. Based on the crossover, you would buy the stock at point A. The bearish crossover occurs at point B, where the histogram first drops into negative territory. This tells us that the MACD line has crossed below the signal line, and it is here that you would exit the trade. If we look

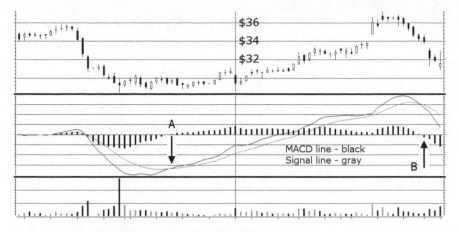

**Figure 4.14    MACD as a Crossover Indicator**

more closely at the price, it's apparent that the stock had dropped around $3 from its high before the MACD crossover generated a sell signal. While we didn't sell at the peak, we see that the MACD still got us out of the trade before the stock fell another $3 the next day.

The second application of the MACD is to use the histogram as an overbought and oversold indicator. Since the MACD may assume any range of values, as opposed to the stochastic, which ranges from 0 to 1, we cannot assign an absolute threshold for overbought and oversold. With the MACD, we're interested in looking at extreme levels of the histogram as compared to recent past performance. If we observe that the histogram suddenly rises significantly higher than it has at any other time in our chart range, then that tells us that the MACD line is rapidly accelerating past the signal line. The interpretation is that the price is too strong relative to its own past performance and, therefore, should correct to the downside.

In Figure 4.15, the histogram peak identified is much more extreme than the previous peaks in the chart. This indicates that the MACD is separating from the signal line more than usual. As such, we would expect the price to correct downward. In order to profit from this, we could enter a short trade when the histogram first begins to descend and then manage the trade with a trailing stop or when the next bullish crossover occurs. It is instructive to see how the histogram generated the sell signal almost two weeks earlier than the bearish crossover signal.

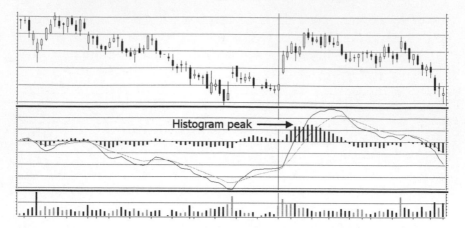

**Figure 4.15   MACD as an Overbought/Oversold Indicator**

*Example*

We can see our first sell signal in Figure 4.16 at point A. The stock had been trading at a resistance level for two to three weeks when the MACD line dropped below the signal line and the histogram went negative. You could enter a short trade at point A and place your buy stop above the resistance level shown. At point B, we get the bullish crossover when the histogram turns positive, indicating that the MACD line has crossed above the signal line. Since the recent price lows were very close to the lows we see on the left side of the chart, we would consider this to be our support level. It wouldn't be

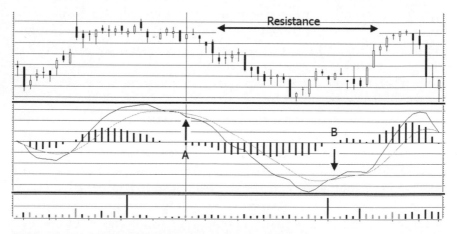

**Figure 4.16   Using MACD for Buy and Sell Signals**

a bad idea to not only close the short trade but reverse the position and buy additional stock for a new long position.

A good question to consider regarding managing the long position that we took at point B is this: Should we wait for the bearish crossover, or do we sell the position earlier? Look at the price at the right side of the chart. Even though the MACD didn't actually drop below the signal line until the last trading day shown, there are two flags that should cause us to consider selling the position before the bearish crossover. First, the histogram rises much more steeply about a week after point B than what we've observed previously on this chart. Second, the price rapidly rises to the resistance level and then starts to show us potential reversal candle patterns. Given the nice profit we realized in about two weeks, it would be prudent to exit the position or at least bring your trailing stop up tighter.

## Bollinger Bands

### Overview

Bollinger Bands are moving average envelopes that surround the price and become wider or narrower as the price volatility increases or decreases. There are two bands, referred to as the upper Bollinger Band and lower Bollinger Band, respectively. Because the bands change with volatility, the price doesn't often break through the bands, although it will on occasion. Bollinger Bands must be compared directly to the stock price; therefore, the bands are overlaid into the price window and not in a separate window.

### Calculation

Although there are only two bands shown, the first calculation is actually a simple moving average of the price. The most common SMA used in the construction of the Bollinger Bands is the 20-period. While the 20-period SMA isn't drawn, the upper Bollinger Band and the lower Bollinger Band are then drawn a specified distance above and below the 20-period SMA. The distance from the 20-period SMA from which the bands are drawn is based on a standard deviation of the data. A standard deviation is a statistical measure of volatility, or data scatter. The equation for the sample standard deviation, used in the calculation of the Bollinger Bands, is as follows:

$$\text{Standard deviation} = \text{Square root } (\text{Sum } (Xi - Xavg)^2/n))$$

Where
   $X_i$ = closing price of period i
   $X_{avg}$ = average of n closing prices
      n = number of periods

Most calculations use (n) in the denominator of the standard deviation while others may use (n − 1). The reason for the difference is that (n − 1) subtracts one (degree of freedom, in statistical terms) to account for sampling error when the average is an estimate. This point is included only for statistical accuracy for those who might otherwise take us to task for this minor item. From a trading standpoint, this is a nonissue.

Given the standard deviation, the upper Bollinger Band is then drawn at two standard deviations above the 20-period SMA. Likewise, the lower Bollinger Band is drawn at two standard deviations below the 20-period SMA. Of course, two standard deviations is a common distance but, once again, this value may be adjusted. If the bands are tightened to one standard deviation, for example, the bands will be very narrow and will tend to generate buy and sell signals that won't be very useful. However, widening the bands by using three or four standard deviations will capture almost all of the price data but won't generate signals very often. This is a balance between too tight and too wide, which you'll refine with practice.

### Application

There are a number of ways to use the Bollinger Bands, including identifying trend continuation when the price presses a band and as a reversal indicator when price oscillates within the band. We'll focus this discussion on one of our favorites—as a breakout indicator following a period of consolidation.

As we've discussed, the Bollinger Bands will alternate between wide and narrow as the price volatility changes. Occasionally, the bands will tighten much more than normal based on the stock's historical behavior. When this happens, we see a squeeze occurring because neither the buyers nor the sellers are taking control. Often, this squeeze is accompanied by a decrease in volume. Think of this situation as a pressure cooker. When the lid is placed on the buyers and sellers, there is an increasing anticipation of who will ultimately win the battle. Once the victor is identified, traders start moving in the direction of the winner. A squeeze, then, is often followed by a strong breakout with increasing volume. The big question for you as the trader is this: Which direction will the breakout go? Don't try to predict the future because if you get caught on the wrong side of the breakout, your loss could be fast and furious. Rather, wait until there is a clear indication of the move and then join the trade. Often, the long and narrow squeezes generate the sharpest breakouts. Use whatever memory jogger you want, but here's one of ours: "The longer the fight, the sharper the flight."

### Example

Figure 4.17 clearly illustrates the Bollinger Band squeeze. Look at how the bands narrow dramatically in the center of the chart. What we look for is not a subtle narrowing that may or may not be considered a squeeze. The ideal tightening is one that jumps out at you when you glance at the chart. In this example, it is possible that you may have been fooled into taking a short position when the stock started to push at the lower band. Without a trailing stop, you may have then been stopped out for a small loss when the price moved back into the band. That's not a problem; that's exactly why we use stops. However, the true breakout is seen a short time later, and the profit generated from your long position on the breakout more than paid for the initial loss from the false start.

**Figure 4.17  Trading a Breakout from a Bollinger Band Squeeze**

## Don't Plow a Field with Your Mercedes

Hopefully, we've opened the horizon for you in understanding how many technical tools there are available to the trader. While we've spent a few pages on the technical aspect of these tools, we want to emphasize two important points as we wrap up this chapter.

First, make sure the tool matches the task. When your stock is trending, don't use an oscillating indicator. As much as you enjoy seeing where the Fibonacci lines fall, don't use them in isolation without confirming your trade with price and volume. We've given you tips and ideas throughout this discussion but we don't claim to have laid out a comprehensive list for these indicators. If you find a couple of indicators that you like to use, take a look at some of the many great technical analysis references that are available and learn more about each indicator's strengths and limitations.

Second, always make sure you follow The Market Guys' Keep It Super Simple rule. After you do your study and decide which indicators to use, don't get mired in adjusting the various parameters. Certainly, find the level of sensitivity in each indicator that works for your trading style. Just remember, though, that trading doesn't lend itself to a black box approach. That is, you'll never have a program that lets you input market data and it will spew forth profitable trades so that you can lie on the beach and collect checks from your broker. Reading charts is a language. Take the time to learn the nuances of the language, and you'll find the conversation much more profitable.

# 10 Common Mistakes Made by Traders (And How to Avoid Them!)

*"Nobody is worthless. Anyone can serve as a bad example."*

It's interesting how our ingrained behavior repeats itself in many areas of our life. Trading the markets is no exception. There are behaviors and habits that we have developed ourselves or copied from others. However they may have been acquired, we perpetuate these habits because we've been using them for so long. We may recognize that our habits and behavior aren't helpful to our trading success, but they've become a comfortable part of our routine. Thomas Jefferson recognized this propensity in individuals when he authored the following phrase from the American Declaration of Independence in 1776:

> . . . all experience hath shewn, that mankind are more disposed to suffer, while evils are sufferable, than to right themselves by abolishing the forms to which they are accustomed.

In the following pages, we want to walk you through 10 of the most common mistakes that we've observed in many thousands of traders. While this is by no means a comprehensive list, we hope to give you an advantage through the Pareto principle. If you recall from high school statistics, Pareto taught us about the 80/20 rule.

That is, most of the results come from fixing the significant few problems. If you apply yourself toward understanding and avoiding these 10 mistakes, you'll reap the benefits of the experiences of the thousands of traders walking the path in front of you.

## Mistake 1: Marrying Your Stock and Finding Trades that Aren't There

As much as you may like trading your favorite stock, never lose sight of the fact that it is a fickle partner to build a trading business around. Just about the time you think that the two of you have an agreement whereby you place the trade and the stock gives you the profit, an event will strike that brings reality to your agreement. Sometimes the event will give you advance warning; other times, it will strike with the swiftness and surprise of a rattlesnake. Either way, if you haven't taken the necessary steps to manage risk, you'll pay a handsome price for your fidelity.

There are many reasons why traders gravitate toward one or several stocks and trade them repeatedly. From our observation, probably the most common reason is that the trader has spent her career with that company or within that industry and there is a comfort level that comes from understanding the fundamentals. We often travel to the beautiful country to our north, Canada, and speak to many traders at various seminars and expositions. Canada has a rich industry in mining and energy, and many of our trading friends have worked some portion of their careers in those fields. So we're not surprised when we start talking about uranium mining, for example, when we're presenting at a seminar. Often, a trader will ask us for our opinion on how to manage a position that they have open. Upon reviewing the charts, we see warning signs that the technical situation is pretty weak. The stock may be in a downtrend, with various indicators signaling her to sell. We start to get concerned when this same trader explains the various fundamental reasons why the stock should be going up. The comments take some form of "I know this company and they're overdue for a break," "The industry has been stagnant for a while and this is the season for good news," or "This company has never been in a downtrend this long before—they'll rally."

All of these comments reflect a belief in the company or industry that stems from familiarity. Of course, as we've seen many times in the markets, the stock price does not always move in tandem with the company performance. Good companies have weak stocks and lousy companies have high-flying stocks. If you try to justify a stock price in the face of technical evidence to the contrary, you might still find yourself liquidating your position to cover a maintenance call. Markets in general and stocks in particular have no requirement to behave rationally. The economist John Maynard Keynes is said to have warned investors that although markets do tend toward rational positions in the long run, "the market can stay irrational longer than you can stay solvent."

Besides coming up with great fundamental arguments about why a stock price should move in the direction you think is right, a trader who is married to a stock can just as easily construct a technical argument. Chart reading, as we've described throughout, is subjective. If it were completely objective, then with enough time and effort, we would be able to program a black box trading system that takes the market data and gives us our lineup of high-profit trades. We know that the reality is much different. Ten traders may see 10 different signs in the exact same chart. We would certainly expect all 10 to identify key features such as the overall price trend and volume trend. But there will always be a little variation in where these traders identify support and resistance (unless they're all using the same moving averages) or which candlestick pattern is the prevailing signal.

In our example, we're assuming that each trader is reading the same chart. The fact is, charts almost become like trader fingerprints. Each trader has a unique layout that they've tailored to their liking. I prefer to analyze daily candlestick charts with a 20-day SMA and a 50-day SMA. You like the daily bar chart with the 50-day EMA and the 200-day EMA. Neither of us is right or wrong and the difference in our charts will result in differences in our interpretation, however great or slight. It's like the story of the blind men and the elephant. One grabbed the elephant's tail and proclaimed the beast to be like a rope. Another grabbed the elephant's trunk and said the animal was a great snake. A third reached for the leg and declared that the creature was most like a tree. By this point, I'm thinking that one more grab and they'll collectively figure the elephant to be a giant waffle iron.

The mistake that the loyal trader makes here is that a chart can be tweaked enough to tell the story that you want to hear. If you think a stock should go higher, you can almost always find a chart style, time horizon, and technical indicator combination to bolster your belief. An unbiased observer may recognize the machinations that you went through to "prove" your claim, but you'll be blind to it yourself. As we covered in Chapter 1, a trading plan will help you remain as objective as possible. If you need to pull out the Chaikin volatility indicator to support your bias when you've never used that indicator before, your trading plan should help to highlight the deviation. At that point, evaluate whether you're analyzing your chart or looking for the warm fuzzies for a conclusion that you've already reached.

Figure 5.1 shows a chart with three separate trends identified. Is this stock in a downtrend, an uptrend, or channeling? The short-term trend is upward, but it's reaching a resistance level marked by the downtrend and channel lines. You can start to see how you can make a good case for whatever decision you reach in advance. The goal of chart reading should be to create the chart and let the data speak to you. You should be doing the listening here, not the talking.

Finally, and this is where the marriage analogy strays from a true marriage, why would you want to hold yourself to a few stocks when there's a world of opportunity out there? Simply put, you can have a lot more fun and reap greater rewards if you don't limit yourself to the one or two stocks that you've always traded. Sometimes even the best stocks go flat or become highly volatile (we guess this is where

**Figure 5.1   Using a Chart to Support a Bias**

the marriage analogy comes back to real life!) and you'd do well to just leave them alone. In the U.S. markets alone, there are over 10,000 stocks to trade. Add to that the options markets and international markets and the choices are practically endless. In down markets, there are stocks making new highs and vice versa. Our experience has taught us that most traders find it difficult to sit on their hands for extended periods without placing a trade. Without the buffet of stocks that the full market offers, these traders will find a trade in their favorite stock, even if it's not there.

## Mistake 2: Failing to Accept a Loss

One of the key differences between a seasoned trader and a novice is their attitude toward a loss. A seasoned trader doesn't hesitate to take a loss when the trade starts to move against him. In fact, we would go so far as to say that the sign of a mature trader is an attitude of welcoming a loss. We suggest celebrating a loss if the loss is small and within the defined risk plan. As a trader, logging small losses into your trading diary is the surest evidence that you have a plan that is working to protect your positions. It is far better to accept a small loss than to take careless risks that expose you to a significant loss.

It's not surprising that this tendency to avoid a loss exists since most of us come to trading from other professions. Due to the technical nature of financial markets and the challenge of pitting oneself against the ranks of highly intelligent and worthy traders, the trading profession especially attracts successful individuals from such fields as engineering and the sciences. For an example, let's look at the case of a medical doctor specializing in the field of obstetrics. Throughout his education, internship, and practice, he's taught to exercise his profession at a level that permits no failures. It is beyond consideration to accept a "loss" in the sense that we're describing. To reason that there is an acceptable loss level and that the successes will offset the losses on balance doesn't even enter into his thinking. Furthermore, by continued study and practice, this doctor will only raise his expertise and the likelihood of a "loss" diminishes to virtually zero. Now this same doctor, after years of practicing medicine, decides to take his accumulated earnings and trade his personal portfolio. His experience has taught him that a loss is unacceptable, and now he begins to apply that logic to his trading. In short order, he realizes that his self-imposed requirement of a zero-loss strategy is the very recipe for his failure. When he discovers that it is possible to lose on 7 out of 10 trades and still be a successful trader, he has to shed the mind-set that brought him to his initial level of success. If his first profession accepted only a 30 percent success rate, he would certainly not be welcome in the delivery room!

We can't mention this point enough: It takes only one loss to wipe out months or years of profitable trading. If you have $100,000 in your trading account and you take a 50 percent loss, you end up with $50,000. To return to breakeven, you need to get a 100 percent return, though! You took a 50 percent hit but you must double your balance to get back to where you started. That's why you must protect yourself against the single catastrophic loss. The best way to do that is to take small losses along the way when your trade moves against you.

Figure 5.2 is a picture of the classic dilemma facing a trader when it comes time to sell a position. Notice that the moving average is trending downward. Also, look at the fact that the stock price is no longer making new highs. It seems to have settled into a trading range, so the trader who refuses to accept a loss begins to get comfortable holding the position. The problem here is that if you buy a stock, the only way you make money is if the stock price rises. Not going down is not the same as going up! Since we don't have a crystal ball that lets us see behind the black curtain to the right of the chart, we'll assume that this trader holds the position open.

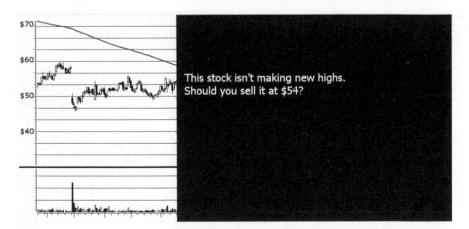

**Figure 5.2  Deciding When to Take a Loss—View 1**

Now we have a little more information on what the stock has done. After deciding to hold the trade in spite of the fact that the stock wasn't making new highs, we see in Figure 5.3 that the stock dipped hard shortly afterward to below $45. Following the dip, the stock inched its way back up to $51. In retrospect, this trader should have taken his loss at $54, but $51 isn't looking so bad, considering that it was about $6 lower just a couple of weeks earlier. Here's where the trader starts to justify his actions. "Aha," he says to himself, "it's a good thing I didn't sell the stock. Look, it's coming back, and I'll soon have a profit."

Of course, this rationalizing flies in the face of good trading practice since the stock is still in a downtrend. Worse, the stock has risen right up to the moving average resistance line. It is at this price level that we expect the sellers to start moving in with enthusiasm. But the trader who refuses to accept a loss holds on. The driving force behind his trading has become hope.

Figure 5.4 shows us the point at which the pain really starts to set in. Having passed on the opportunity to close the trade for a minor loss when the stock was trading at $54, the trader now faces a gap-down sell-off on extremely high volume. This trader only dreams of the chance to close the position at $50 now that the stock has collapsed to $34. Understand in this example that the stock didn't drop out of the blue. There were warning signs galore: a downward trending moving average, failure to make new highs, and climbing to resistance and failing,

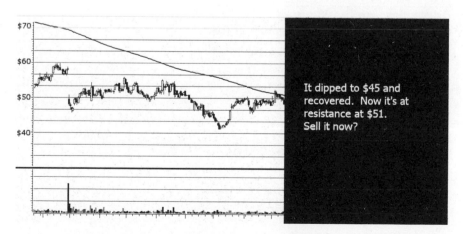

**Figure 5.3    Deciding When to Take a Loss—View 2**

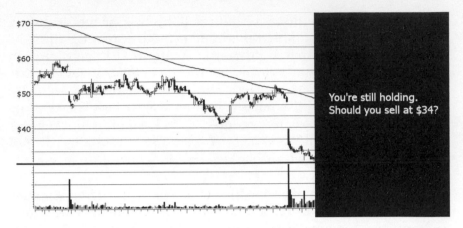

You're still holding.
Should you sell at $34?

**Figure 5.4   Deciding When to Take a Loss—View 3**

just to name a few. We've had traders come to us in situations just like this and ask us how they can protect themselves against strong gap-downs like this. Our first question to them is, "Why in the world were you still in this trade in the first place?!"

It is the rare case where a stock will collapse without any warning signs of weakness. Whether it be a failed support, a shift in volume to the sellers, or simply the end of the uptrend, if your stock isn't going up, get out!

## Mistake 3: Doubling Down on a Losing Position

We'll actually delve into this topic in detail in Chapter 7, but since it's one of our 10 Common Mistakes, we'll briefly introduce it here. Doubling down is a strategy that seeks to gamble a loss away. It's nothing more than a contemporary market variation of a double-or-nothing bet. This mistake is the logical next step for the trader who made Mistake 2 (Failing to Accept a Loss). If we pick up where we left off from Figure 5.4, we see that the stock is now trading at $34. Let's assume that the trader initially purchased 1,000 shares of the stock at $60. At this point, the trade is $26 per share out-of-the-money. In order for the trader to simply break even, the stock price has to rise $26. We've seen from the chart that the stock doesn't appear to have any intention of gaining $26 anytime soon. So the trader starts to think to himself, "Hmmm, this stock probably won't pick up $26 but it may pick up $13. After all, $13 higher is only $47, and that's below where it fell from the resistance line."

Now, if the trader just sits back and holds his position, he needs a $26 rally to break even. However, he begins to reason that the $13 rally is possible. The only way to break even from a $13 rally is to buy another 1,000 shares at $34. You see, he spent $60,000 for the first trade and $34,000 for the second. That's a total of $94,000 for 2,000 shares or $47 per share. Therefore, when the stock moves back up to $47, he breaks even. No loss, no gain.

The problem with this strategy is that *nothing* has changed in the dynamic of the stock. That's fine that the trader wants to break even at $47, but the stock is still in a downtrend and the sellers are still in control. The most likely outcome from this approach is that the stock will continue moving down and the trader is now losing money at twice the rate. Sometimes, traders will apply this strategy again, hoping against hope for a rally that will save them from self-destruction. By the time the pain becomes too great to bear, this trader may be holding on to 4,000 or more shares that are all losing money.

Figure 5.5 shows a stock that started over $800 per share! It's hard to imagine that such a strong stock could fall far. People who bought the stock at these levels didn't think in terms of the stock's losing 90 percent of its value. It's easy to convince yourself that this stock is a bargain at $700 because it was just recently trading at $800. But if you haven't seen an example like this in your own trading, learn the lesson from others who have. Every stock has only one support level that will never be broken—zero. Anything above that is subject to the sellers pushing it further down.

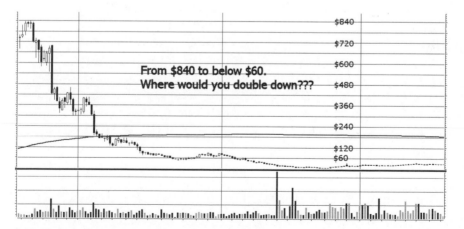

**Figure 5.5   Where Would You Double Down?**

## Mistake 4: Lack of Training and Preparation

Think for a minute about a mutual fund. You send your money to a fund and it is pooled with every other investor's funds. The management team then makes the buy and sell decisions, guided by the fund prospectus. For the privilege of having a professional management team, you pay a fund expense each year. Some funds may be as little as ½ percent or less. Others may charge fees of 2 to 3 percent or more. The point here is that you're relinquishing your right to make the trading decisions to the fund managers. Obviously, they have a fiduciary responsibility to use their skills and judgment to maximize the growth of your assets. If they are able to increase the value of your assets by 10 percent, they will receive their management fee. If they increase the value of your assets by only 2 percent, they will receive their management fee. If they fail and the value of your assets declines, they will receive their management fee. You see where we're going? Most traders and investors hold some type of mutual fund or funds and give no thought to the fund expense. We suspect that the reason it isn't considered is that you never actually write a check for the expense—it simply reduces the value of your investment. Perhaps it's like the direct withdrawal of income taxes. It would be a lot more painful if you received your full wages and then had to return a portion to the government to settle your tax liability.

Now the reason you're reading this book is quite likely because you have decided to make your own buy and sell decisions for at least some portion of your portfolio. An alternative reason is that you have absolutely no interest in trading but yet you suffer from congenital insomnia and previous remedies have fallen short. For the former, we're going to suggest that you implement your own management fees. Instead of paying the fees to a team of outside managers, create your own education account. This account should be used to help you become a better manager of your own money. Set aside 1 percent of the amount of money that you're personally managing and use that as your training and preparation account. If you have a $100,000 portfolio and you're actively managing $20,000, then each year you have $200 to spend on becoming a better investor and trader. We're always amazed at how many people are willing to lose many thousands of dollars due to bad trading decisions or practices, but they refuse to invest even a minimal amount in their education. Look at your trading history and see if you can identify a trade or two that could have been avoided if you knew a bit more about technical analysis. How much did you lose on those trades?

In Chapter 1 we talked about the importance of including education as a component of your trading plan. We want to emphasize again that we subscribe to the Keep It Super Simple philosophy when it comes to market training and education. There are many trainers and teachers out there who will try to convince you that you have to study deep and wide in various aspects of technical analysis before you can unlock the secrets of the market. Just last night, we received an e-mail with the title, "Profits Keep Pouring In!!!" The marketer went on to describe how a particular options sage had generated massive profits from a little-known six-legged option spread. How easy would it be to think that the reason you're not profiting in a particular market is that you don't know how to create this complicated multileg option trade?

The fact is that the ingredients necessary for trading and investing success are pretty simple. Like learning a language, though, the best foundation is laid when you take the time to learn a piece at a time and spend plenty of time practicing. For example, it is possible to attend a crash course and learn charting, technical indicators, and stock strategies all at the same time. But it becomes a bit overwhelming when you try to put it all into practice at the same time. A better approach would be to learn how to read a candlestick chart. Then go out and start reading many candlestick charts to see how the patterns develop. Something will just not click, perhaps identifying certain reversal patterns. So you take another course, read another book, or attend another seminar and learn a bit more. Gradually, you develop the recognition skills that will allow you to find the patterns more quickly and easily.

As in any other area of life, you should never stop learning. Trading and investing is no exception. How long does it take to be a master of the basics? The Market Guys will freely admit that we continue to learn every day. Sometimes it's a tip or trick that we once knew but have forgotten to apply at the right time. Sometimes it's more fundamental in order to keep up with the ever-changing tide of the markets. This is especially important with the changes that we see every year in technology and shifts in how the markets operate. What will the impact on your trading be when all of the markets move to 24-hour trading? If you rely on a gap trading strategy, will you be prepared when there are no more gaps?

You need to make sure that you never lose sight of the other participants in the market. Even though you may be trading alone in the isolation of your home office, there are many traders out there who are striving for every advantage in the markets. Do you really want to enter that arena without adequate training and preparation? We can assure you that there are many traders who will be trading the same stocks as you who have done their homework and have properly equipped themselves.

Picture yourself getting ready to walk on to the field of play at an NFL football game. Across the line from you is the defensive team. The tackles have spent the entire preseason in the weight room building up muscle mass and strength. They've done countless drills on the field, maximizing their cardio fitness and endurance. They've sat through hours of tapes in order to understand the strategies that could be employed against them in any given situation. Finally, they've taped their joints, donned the pads, and slipped on the helmet for action. Now it's time for you to stroll onto the field with the singular objective of getting the ball across the line for a goal. You're feeling pretty comfortable in your loafers and khaki shorts. No cumbersome pads for you; you're well appointed in a light button-up shirt. Your preseason was spent in air-conditioned comfort, munching on a bag of chips. You've heard about some of the defense plays that could be coming your way, but you haven't learned how to recognize them or counter the moves. How reasonable is it to expect that you'll be able to outmaneuver the defense and actually score? Why is it that so many traders and investors enter the field of play in the markets with the same level of training and preparation and yet still somehow expect that they'll be able to score? The markets will occasionally reward the lucky, but only the well-trained and prepared investor or trader will be in it for the long run.

## Mistake 5: Trading with Scared Money

Mistake 5 often is the direct result of having made Mistake 2 (Failing to Accept a Loss) or Mistake 4 (Lack of Training and Preparation). You trade with scared money when you've had a bad trade and now you're gun shy. The term *gun shy* refers to hunting dogs who have developed a fear of guns. Sometimes this occurs through an accident of some sort, like getting hit with a spent shell casing. Sometimes, it's just the loud report that creates a fear within the dog. However it starts, the dog is incapable of working near a hunter, often running at the mere sight of a gun. Unless the dog was born gun shy, it takes much patience and retraining to get the dog back to where she can point and retrieve without trembling in fear. You have to start small and easy and gradually build the dog's confidence.

A gun-shy trader is the same way. You took a trade that started in your direction, and so you decided to relax your risk management discipline. Perhaps you canceled your stop order protection and went away for a few days. After all, the trade was moving in a profitable direction, so you felt as though you didn't need to manage it. When you came back, the stock had dropped 40 percent on a bad earnings announcement. For a day or so, you walk around zombie-like, incredulous at the turn in fortune. When you regain your senses and close the position, you've suffered a catastrophic loss. If you have the funds remaining to continue trading, you will certainly not enter the next trade with the same level of confidence that you had on the last trade. Like the shaking, gun-shy dog, the mere hint of a drop in price will cause you to tremble and close the position at market.

Another type of gun-shy trader is the person who doesn't yet understand the mechanics and strategies of trading, but starts to trade anyway. This trader is the football player we described in Mistake 4 (Lack of Training and Preparation). Oblivious to the defensive team staring him down, he struts onto the playing field. The whistle blows, the play starts, and our khaki-clad trader is stomped into the turf. Chances are very good that on the next play, he'll be running toward his own goal line in an attempt to avoid getting stomped twice.

Scared money results in the trader's taking one of two courses of action. The first course of action is that the trader will attempt to gamble his way out of his mistakes. This is the trader who failed to accept a loss, took a 40 percent hit on a single trade, and figured that it's time for him to double his money on the next trade. This trader allows the scared money to turn him into a Wild West gambler. The initial trade may have been a sound initial entry, purchasing 800 shares of a stock trading at $50. The scared money trade, however, is 5,000 shares of a $3 stock. The trader hopes that his stock will rally to $10 and he'll walk away with a handsome $35,000 profit. More times than not, the $3 stock becomes a $1 stock as the gamble fails to pay off. To reinforce this point, go back to Chapter 1 and review the section on the trader-versus-gambler personality.

The second course of action that may be taken by the gun-shy trader who is trading with scared money is more common. Rather than going for broke and trying to make up the loss in one fell swoop, the trader will hold the trade very close to the vest in order to avoid any more pain. In this scenario, the trader buys a stock at $50 and immediately places a sell stop order at $49.99. After losing her penny, she looks for the next trade. She finds a stock in an uptrend and buys it at $44. She immediately places her sell stop at $43.99. Do you see what's happening? This trader is terrified of taking a loss of the magnitude that created her fear in the first place. She knows better than to think that she can recover her losses in a single trade but she doesn't have the confidence to allow the market to breathe. As such, each trade is choked with a small loss that slowly but surely creates the very loss she was trying to avoid.

A common mistake in trader thinking is that tightening the stop will result in reduced loss. While the loss per trade may be smaller, the frequency of losses will increase. This offsets any advantage that the smaller loss may yield. Remember, you should always let the chart tell you where to place the stop, based on support or resistance. If you approach a trade with an acceptable loss amount already in mind, you're attempting to tell the market what you want. Unfortunately, the market doesn't care what you want.

## Mistake 6: Buying Cheap Options

While we touch on the subject of options throughout this book, our intent isn't for this to serve as a comprehensive options trading guide. Nevertheless, since we present 10 Common Mistakes Made by Traders, we didn't want to discount the list by 10 percent and only list 9 Common Mistakes Made by Traders. With options, you usually get what you pay for. Cheap options generally have only time value in their price. There isn't any intrinsic value that's reflected in the premium. The salient point is this: The value of the option lies in the speculative worth based on where the underlying stock could move. That is, the premium price is grounded on what might happen, not on any intrinsic value at the present time.

Interestingly, the same principle applies to many penny stocks. We could just as easily label this mistake "Buying Cheap Stocks." Sure, it is possible to find value stocks where the company's fundamental worth is discounted through the stock price. Some measures of the underlying worth of a company may be the dividend yield, the price-to-book ratio, or many other varieties of accounting metrics. However, just because a stock price is cheap doesn't mean that the company is discounted. The stock price can be manipulated many ways. Often, when a stock price falls too far, a company will announce a reverse stock split. That accounting maneuver alone may cause the price to move from $5 per share to $15 per share in a three-for-one reverse split. It's the same company but with a new stock price. Has anything changed? Of course not, but now the perception of cheap and expensive is shifted.

One of the reasons that traders flock to cheap stocks and options is the number of shares that can be purchased for a fixed amount of buying power. If you have $50,000, you can choose between 1,000 shares of a $50 stock or 25,000 shares of a $2 stock. Traders start fantasizing about the $2 stock gaining another $2, and they tally up the $50,000 profit. If the $50 stock moves up $2, they're only looking at banking a $2,000 profit. Could the $2 stock double? Yes, but it could also drop to $1. Now that cheap little stock just swallowed $25,000 from your account.

You should take the time to burn the image of Figure 5.6 into your mind. Notice the price scale on the vertical axis of the chart. This stock is trading at around $3 on the left side of the chart. Without the benefit of being able to see into the future on the right side of the chart, it would be easy to rationalize how this should be a $10 stock.

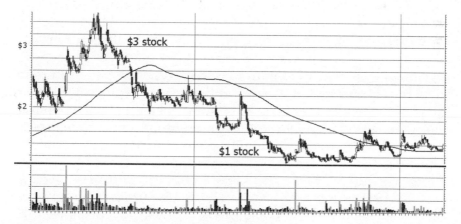

**Figure 5.6   A Cheap Stock Getting Cheaper**

It's especially easy to do that if the stock has recently dropped down from that level. The thinking is that if it were trading at $10 or $20 just six months ago, surely it could jump back up to $8, $10, or more! Instead, the stock continued its downward spiral until it became a $1 stock. Cheap stocks don't always go up; sometimes they go bankrupt.

## Mistake 7: Overcomplicating the Analysis

If you think Fibonacci was a pianist, you're probably not making this mistake. For the rest of you, we have these words of advice: "Lighten up!" We'll repeat our philosophy many times over throughout this book. Keep It Super Simple. The reason we have to drill this thinking into our minds is that at every turn we're programmed by marketing messages that convince us that we'll succeed in the market if we only take the time to learn that which we don't currently know. It's a little like the guy who was asked how much money it would take to make him happy. His response was, "A little more." A little more knowledge is not always a good thing if the knowledge takes you down a rabbit hole of useless information. As we write this section, we're looking at the front cover advertisement in a popular trading magazine. The software provider (who shall remain anonymous) is proclaiming that they provide over 100 free and proprietary technical analysis studies. For crying out loud! If you need to cherry pick from 100 proprietary studies before you can identify a trading opportunity, then we strongly suggest that you consider switching to decaf.

In engineering, we discuss a concept known as signal-to-noise ratio. Essentially, this is a measure of the useful information (signal) to the useless or irrelevant information (noise). The goal is to maximize the signal while minimizing the amount and effect of the noise. It's ironic that engineers, who must understand this concept in order to qualify as a professional engineer, are some of the most egregious transgressors when it comes to the markets. Traders who come from more technical backgrounds have spent their careers learning more advanced methodologies for solving problems. The disconnect between an engineering or scientific endeavor and the stock markets is that the former is generally deterministic while the latter is probabilistic. We'll appeal to the purists who will take us to task for failing to recognize the probabilistic nature of quantum physics. You'll appreciate that such a discussion would certainly qualify as an extreme tangent for this book.

Nevertheless, the sciences have given us firm rules regarding the world around us. The energy of a body in motion, kinetic energy, is one half the body's mass times the velocity squared. It has always been such and will continue to be. It doesn't even matter where you're located in the world. But the markets, being probabilistic, do not always give us a falling stock price when a shooting star candle pattern occurs at the top of an uptrend. It's important that the trader understand this because this is the reason why you cannot create a black box trading system. As far as we know, there isn't anyone sitting on the beach in the Caribbean collecting checks from her broker while her trading system automatically executes winning trades.

Since we recognize that maximizing the signal while minimizing the noise is important, we have to ensure that we're not adding to the noise by layering on scanners, tickers, screens, charts, and lists. Success in the market is not dependent on the one technical tool that you haven't yet acquired. When we meet traders who have fallen into this trap, we like to walk them through a very basic process. First, clear everything off the chart except price and volume. The price may be in your favorite form: candlestick, line, bar, and so on. Second, identify support and resistance role reversal levels. This is explained in much more detail in the following chapter. Third, add confirming indicators as appropriate for the market. In other words, if you're trading a trend, use a moving average. If your stock is channeling, consider adding a Bollinger Band or other oscillating indicator. Whatever you choose for the third step, be judicious in the application. If you get to step three and then add your top 10 technical indicators, you've defeated the purpose of the exercise. Stop and ask yourself if the chart in Figure 5.7 is really the best layout to help you find trading opportunities.

Finally, the trader who is constantly overanalyzing a trade setup is usually the last one to actually place the trade. We refer to this condition as Paralysis by Analysis. By the time he's convinced himself that he found a good trade, he's missed the better part of the move. We don't think it's a coincidence that the first four letters of "analysis" describe this personality completely. It is true that the perfect trade will occasionally present itself. Much more often, though, is the arrival of the imperfect trade that requires a combination of technical analysis paired with the judgment born from many previous trades.

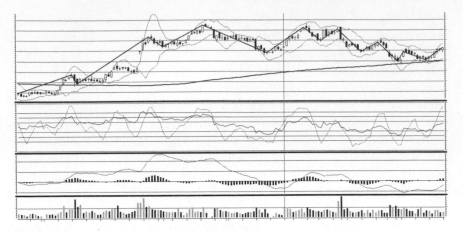

**Figure 5.7    Technical Indicator Overload**

## Mistake 8: Unrealistic Expectations

Use your imagination for a moment with us. Let's assume that you went to Wal-Mart and purchased enough 12-inch rulers to lay end to end along the equator. That's right—you've just set down a line of rulers measuring 24,900 miles long. On the back of one of these rulers, you place a red dot and then you turn the ruler back over. Your friend comes along and starts at any point on the equator and begins to walk. His objective is to select a stopping point, bend down, and turn over the ruler. Is it realistic to expect that he will walk 1, 100, 1,000, or 10,000 miles along the ruler path and happen to reach for the very ruler that you marked with a red dot? If this picture sounds absurd to you, then why do thousands of people each day play the lottery? The Mega Millions lottery, played in 12 U.S. states, has a jackpot with lower odds of winning than finding our marked ruler.

In the trading world, unrealistic expectations don't take the form of expecting to get $100 million from a $1 investment. That stretches the believability factor too much for us. But 700 percent returns each month start to enter our thinking. We once had a trader come to us with a $2,000 trading account. He wanted to know which strategies he could employ that would let him live off of his trading account. We first questioned him about how much he needed to live. Based on the size of his trading account, we were intrigued that he thought he could live on $50 per month. Instead, he told us that he needed at least $5,000 each month for his living expenses. He actually thought he could cash flow $5,000 each month from his $2,000 trading capital. That's $60,000 annually for a whopping 3,000 percent return. We told him that if he could figure out how to consistently draw a 3,000 percent return, he should immediately open a hedge fund and we'd be the first investors.

The first and most realistic expectation from trading the markets is simply to outperform the broad market. If the Dow Jones Industrial Average is up 10 percent, your trading should be up more than 10 percent after commissions and expenses. If the Nasdaq 100 is down 5 percent, your trading should be up or at least down less than 5 percent. The bottom line is: If you can't outperform the broad market, stop trading! It's much easier and profitable for you to place your money in a broad market exchange-traded fund (DIA, SPY, QQQQ) or an index mutual fund. These, at least, will track the market and you don't have to make any buy and sell decisions.

Remember this rule: If you want to get rich quickly, go somewhere else. If you want to get poor quickly, keep trading with the belief that you can get rich quickly. Even the ancient King Solomon recognized this fact of building wealth when he wrote, "The plans of the diligent lead to profit as surely as haste leads to poverty" (Proverbs 21:5).

## Mistake 9: Using Software Crutches

Software can be a great tool, or it can be a monumental waste of time. We've watched countless traders fiddle with their trading software in a classic case of going nowhere fast. Activity should not be confused with productivity in the markets. Traders who are using software as a crutch would be completely lost if they were handed a printed copy of a chart. They couldn't tack on their favorite indicator, toggle between time frames, or pull up the latest news on the stock. There are many great software packages available to traders. As we warned in Mistake 7 (Overcomplicating the Analysis), you don't have to use all of the available tools.

Software can also become a crutch when a trader ceases to learn the language of technical analysis and instead attempts to program his own trading robot. Countless hours are spent refining a trading system and back-testing it against historical market data. This trader is not developing any useful trading skills; rather, he's spinning his wheels in pursuit of the black box, which doesn't exist. For him, the software has become the goal. His every effort and motivation is mastering the software, and he rarely, if ever, actually trades.

Software should never be a substitute for learning, either. Unfortunately, technical analysis is sometimes too quick and easy on contemporary trading platforms. We can easily trick ourselves into thinking that we have an advantage in the market simply because we have the latest and greatest charting/programming/scanning package. If all of trading boiled down to the software, we wouldn't have charts, indicators, screens, and the like. We would turn on the computer, launch the software, and select one of two buttons that appear on the screen: "Buy the Stock" or "Sell the Stock for a Profit." The more advanced software platforms would be equipped with two more buttons: "Buy the Option" and "Sell the Option for a Profit." Ah, that the world of trading were that easy.

## Mistake 10: Trading without a Plan

We covered the importance of a trading plan in detail in Chapter 1, but we want to add just a couple more thoughts to this point. Be sure that you learn from your successes and failures. If you record both as part of your trading plan, you'll be able to adjust your actions and strategies twice as effectively. Remember, also, to occasionally ask yourself the question, "Why am I trading?" Your trading plan is built around the answer to this fundamental question. For most traders, the answer to this question will evolve or completely change over time. It will follow the shifting of goals and priorities that occur throughout life. Be sure that your plan lives and breathes with you. Your plan should serve your purposes rather than your becoming a slave to your plan. Sometimes walking the well-worn path is not the best. Learn from the mistakes made by others before you, and grow on your journey toward trading success.

# ESTABLISH A CLEAR SUPPORT LEVEL

## Pinpoint Support

# 6

# The Role Reversal

## WORKING THE BUYER/SELLER BATTLE LINE

Chapter 3 covered the mechanics behind the steps in drawing a support level on a price chart, which is nothing more than identifying areas where buyers have displayed a history of buying. Here, we will be discussing the reasons why buyers buy when they do. You will see that as you continue to hone your technical analysis skills, certain price patterns will seem to jump out of the chart at you.

One of these patterns is the role reversal support pattern. We have found that this pattern can be seen on virtually every chart you look at. Day traders will see this pattern on intraday charts that measure increments of minutes while swing traders will find this pattern on daily charts over the course of the year. Even the long term investor will find this on weekly charts that include many years of data, so it doesn't really matter what time frame you are using, it will be there.

In our examples we will be using simple line charts that track the closing price of the stock each and every day. There are a couple of reasons why we use line charts. First, they're clean and simple, which makes it easier on the eye when going through your chart scans. Second, we put more weight in the closing price than any other price point. In order to understand the reasons why so many analysts favor the closing price over all of the other data points, we have to get into the mind of a professional trader. There is an old saying that the amateurs open the market each day, while the professionals close the market. At the end of each trading day, mutual fund companies go through the routine of settling their positions to calculate net asset value (NAV) for each fund they manage. This process includes teams of people who go through each and every company held in the fund to ensure that there are no price errors or mistakes made that would affect the NAV; otherwise, this could be costly to the fund company. There are times when news, either positive or negative, is released on one or more of the companies held in the fund, at which time the fund manager has to determine whether this news adds any risk to the fund and if, after consulting with the risk managers, the fund manager feels the risk outweighs the rewards of holding the position, the manager will liquidate some or all of the position to limit that risk. If you take our example of just one mutual fund company and multiply this by the many thousands of mutual funds that are traded each day, you will see why there are volume surges in the last hour of the trading day.

## Market Mechanics

Risk managers are doing what they do best which is minimizing downside exposure to the companies they work for. Along with the mutual fund companies, the market makers and hedge fund managers are adding to the closing volume of the market as they assess positions to determine whether they are comfortable with holding a particular long or short position overnight.

Before the Securities and Exchange Commission (SEC) began phasing in their special order handling rules in 1997, market makers had an easier time making money for the firms they worked for. The way it would work is if you, the investing public, entered an order to buy or sell a particular security, your order was entered through your broker and then routed to a market maker, who would then execute the transaction for you. The market makers had special privileges that allowed them to either take the opposite side of your order—meaning if you were a buyer of a stock, they could sell you that stock out of their inventory—or they could just show your order to the rest of the market makers, allowing them to take the other side of your buy order. The one thing you may not have known if you were an investor back in those days is that your market maker had the ability to buy stock for their account at prices below the price you were bidding. Understand that this is when stocks were trading in fractions of a dollar, so here is an example of what this might have looked like:

A particular market for a stock you may have been interested in might have shown a bid price of $24 and an offering price of $24½, at which time you may have entered an order to buy stock somewhere in the middle for 24¼. Your market maker was not obligated to show your buy order, and most of the time they wouldn't show your order to the open market. Instead, what they would do is post a bid for their own account through a system known as Instinet, which was a trading system reserved primarily for market makers and institutions. If the market maker posted a bid for $24⅛, there was a good chance they could buy stock an eighth of a dollar cheaper than your buy price. Therefore, if you were trying to buy 1,000 shares for 24¼, they would buy 1,000 shares for their own account at 24⅛ on Instinet, then quickly sell you your shares at 24¼ and pocket a quick profit of $125 with no risk at all to their own account. On top of this you were being charged a hefty commission for the transaction and in the end you probably thought you were getting a good deal from your broker.

For example:

1. Market for ABC stock is 24 bid offered at 24½.
2. You enter an order to buy 1,000 shares of ABC stock at 24¼.
3. Market maker buys 1,000 shares at 24⅛ on Instinet.
4. Market maker sells 1,000 shares to you at 24¼.
5. Realized profit for market maker is ⅛ × 1,000 = $125.

This would happen many thousands of times each day, but thanks to the SEC this abuse has, for the most part, been eliminated. What the SEC order handling rules have also done is force the market makers to take risk for their own accounts. This means that market makers now have to take open positions in the market in order to profit, and this opens them up to more risk.

What does this mean for you, the individual trader? It means that if you want to cut down on your own risk exposure, you don't want to be on the opposite side of these market makers. They see order flow better than you do, and they also have much deeper pockets than you do. In other words, although the SEC order-handling rules allow for full transparency for most small orders, not all orders are being shown. Larger orders, particularly those entered by the institutions, are not being displayed to the general public, and they like it this way. If you were an institutional trader looking to move a very large amount of money and you were thinking about buying a stock, do you think you would want to have everyone in the world knowing what your intentions were? Of course you wouldn't. If you entered a large buy order into the market that represented many millions of dollars in buying power, what do you think that would do to the price of the stock if everyone knew there was a big buyer coming in? First of all, it would scare away any of the smaller sellers. Second, it would cause any larger sellers to raise their sell limits to see how far the buyers would chase them. Finally, momentum traders would jump on the bandwagon and try to jump ahead of the big buy order to take a short ride with the intentions of making a quick profit on a price rally brought on buy this new demand in the stock. It would be the same on the sell side. If an institution decided to show a large sell order in the open market, the buyers would run for the hills and the price would drop like a rock.

Many times, the market makers are given discretion to complete the order over a series of days or even weeks. This allows them to fill the order little by little without drawing too much attention to themselves. They would just stay on the bid price if they had a big institutional buy order, or they would just stay on the offering price if they had a large sell order they were working. When market makers are not working any large institutional orders, they spend most of their day reading order flow. If they see that there is good news on a stock, chances are the majority of orders that come into their book that day will be buy orders. This is because the general pubic act like sheep and will react to this good news by buying the stock on the day the news is released. Market makers will favor the buy side in a situation like this because the good news adds to the price support as the news creates short-term demand for the shares. Also, should there be an unexpected price drop during the day, they can quickly get out by selling to the next buy order they have sitting in their *pending order file*. This allows them to efficiently manage loss to their own account. What they are doing here is using the public order flow as a stop loss feature. With the click of the mouse they can quickly sell out of their entire position if they feel the buy orders are starting to slow down. This is one of the great benefits of being a market maker, and it's a luxury you will have to live without as an individual trader.

Here is an example of how a market maker would use their order flow to profit in the market:

> The market for a particular stock is 24 bid offered at 24.02. The market maker sees that he has a large number of buyers in his order book who are stacked up on the bid side. There are a total of 10,000 shares in this pending order file, all bidding $24. So the market maker buys 10,000 shares at 24.02 for his own account. If the price of the stock goes up, the market maker will realize a profit. If the price of the stock does not go up, then the market maker will sell 10,000 shares from his account to those looking to buy stock at $24.

As you can see, this would cost the market maker only $200 if he is wrong. However, when he is right, he will make a lot more than $200 because as the price of the stock goes up, those buyers he had in his book will most likely chase the market. This is when people who were trying to buy the stock at $24 move their limits up because they did not get to buy the stock when it was lower. You may have done this yourself. Market makers count on the general public's chasing the market. There is even a term that's used to describe this action. It's called *stepping up*. Professional traders who trade for market making firms love it when you step up on your limit order. This allows them to capture profits pretty effortlessly.

Before you make a decision to day trade for a living, remember that your odds aren't even close to being as good as a market maker who earns a good living trading the markets. We want to reiterate the importance of having a fine-tuned discipline when managing risk in the market. Learning about how a market maker profits in the market will help you increase the odds in your favor when you are taking a position in the market for your own account.

From the examples we have given you so far with regard to how professional traders deal with risk in the market, you can see that a market maker will be siding with the order flow. If the order flow is on the buy side of the market, then chances are the market maker is going to be a buyer. If the order flow is on the sell side of the market, perhaps owing to bad news, then the market maker is going to be playing the short side of the market. If the market maker is aggressively attacking the long side of a trade, you can be certain that they have their eye on the downside risk and will be quick to take a loss if the buyers start to thin out in their pending book of orders. They are good at what they do, and they make money because they are reading the market with a trained eye and a strict set of rules for trading.

## Your Opinion Won't Move a Market

So why is it that so many traders who trade their own accounts from home lose money? The number one reason most people lose money trading their own accounts is that they have developed an opinion for the stock and this opinion draws them away from the obvious signals given through the price charts. Adding an opinion to a trading strategy will most likely doom the strategy from the very beginning.

From what we are seeing in our travels, there are still far too many people out there who are trying to buy stocks on yearly lows thinking that they have found the bottom. They do just enough research to justify the price as one of value, and at first glance this idea might seem sensible. But many times this bargain-hunting strategy quickly sours after this same stock drops to another 52-week low a short week later. The next thing they do is dig into the financial reports searching for a reason why they should hold on to this new losing position. Then they search the analyst reports, and after a while they commit to the good old strategy of "Just hold on; it will get better." From there, it develops into a "Hold on until I can get out at my breakeven point." There are price levels at which the general public reaches their goal in this amazing pursuit of breakeven, and we call it the role reversal point.

Our objective for this chapter is to bring you to a place where you have realized that the support line on the chart is also your financial lifeline. If you follow these easy steps in constructing a proper support line, you will find that this will allow you to absorb small losses when you are wrong, while allowing you to stay in the market by preserving your buying power. This will give you more opportunities to be right, which in turn means more profits down the road. We also encourage you to make sure you are buying your stocks as close as you can to a support level and not a resistance level. Should you do this, then you have once again increased the odds in your favor.

## Defining Role Reversal

In order to help you understand the ideas behind the role reversal point, we need to get into the minds of those who consistently lose money when trading the markets. One of the most popular misconceptions around is that in order to make money in the stock market you need to buy low and sell high. We have all heard it before, but what does this really mean? For most people this means that you should try to buy a stock at a lower price than where it is currently trading. Then the intention is to sell this position for a profit after the stock has gone up. If you dig deeper into this practice, you will find that in order for you to buy a stock at a lower price, the stock will have to fall to the price at which you are trying to buy it. Immediately, you are stacking the odds against you. Remember, the market makers are going to be happy to sell you the stock they own at this point because you are helping them limit their losses. Playing this scenario out, we will take this strategy to the next level, which is what the amateur traders do once they have realized that they were not lucky enough to pick the bottom. Once the buyer of this depressed stock suffers a downturn in the market, they justify the position by digging into the fundamentals of the company. After another round of analysis, they jump into the popular strategy called *cost averaging down.*

## Dollar Cost Averaging versus Cost Averaging Down

You may have heard of an investment strategy called *dollar cost averaging.* This is where investors deposit small amounts of money each month into an account that has been set up to automatically purchase shares in a mutual fund equal to the amount deposited. The goal is to accumulate shares in a retirement portfolio without having to suffer the pain of enduring extreme price swings brought on by market volatility. The most attractive thing about this strategy is that is allows us to accumulate more shares of the fund as the price drops, and over time we find that the shares we've accumulated at the lower price levels add to the performance of our portfolio when the price of the shares goes up to a new high. However, there is one catch: We need the mutual fund to go up in price for this to work. Otherwise, we have accumulated a lot of worthless shares in a retirement account designed to help us with a long-term plan for our golden years.

So with a dollar cost averaging strategy, it is wise to make sure your money is going into a fund that is in a steady, yet not too aggressive, upward trend. Notice in Figure 6.1 how a $250 per month

| Month | Share Price | Shares Purchased |
|---|---|---|
| 1 | $16.00 | 15.63 |
| 2 | $18.00 | 13.89 |
| 3 | $14.00 | 17.86 |
| 4 | $17.00 | 14.71 |
| 5 | $22.00 | 11.36 |
| 6 | $21.00 | 11.90 |
| 7 | $25.00 | 10.00 |
| 8 | $20.00 | 12.50 |
| 9 | $16.00 | 15.63 |
| 10 | $23.00 | 10.87 |
| 11 | $27.00 | 9.26 |
| 12 | $28.00 | 8.93 |
| Average | $20.58 | 12.71 |

**Figure 6.1    Dollar Cost Averaging with $250 per Month**

contribution smooths out the average price of the stock while giving us an average number of shares accumulated each and every month.

## A Good Plan Gone Bad

Dollar cost averaging is a very good plan for individuals who are putting money aside to supplement an existing pension plan or individual retirement account (IRA). However, as good as it is, you should not rely on this investment as a sole source of income for your retirement years unless you are contributing significant amounts of money each and every month to it (*significant* meaning percentages that exceed 15 percent of your gross annual income). Dollar cost averaging is considered an investment strategy, and although it is one that is recommended by most financial advisers, you should not try to combine this strategy with a short-term trading strategy.

Somewhere along the way this good plan went bad when someone decided to apply it to their trading account. What they wound up with is a common practice called *cost averaging down,* which is where amateur traders buy more of a stock that is going down in order to lower the cost basis of a stock that is hurting them. This is nothing more than an effort to trade out of a losing position. In the end, most people wind up with a very bad situation that ultimately loses very large sums of money. It's amazing to see just how many people have bought into this idea as being a good strategy.

The story usually starts off like this:

> Trader Bob decides to buy 1,000 shares of ABC stock at $30 per share. Immediately after purchasing these shares, the stock drops to $29 and Trader Bob gets a sick feeling in his stomach as he realizes that he made a bad decision. But does Trader Bob do anything to fix this problem? No! Instead, he makes a decision to hold on to this trade because he believes the stock will eventually rebound. The following day the stock drops to $26 per share, and instead of getting out and limiting his loss, Trader Bob makes a decision to buy another 1,000 shares at $26 in an effort to lower his cost basis $28 per share. Now Trader Bob is long twice as many shares, and the stock drops again, resulting in a doubling of the losses.

This story is told over and over again around the world, as many other traders do the same each and every day.

## Pursuit of the Breakeven Point

We work hard for our money, and it doesn't make sense to waste any of it gambling in the market. This market is too good for us to be pursuing the breakeven point. If you are planning to invest for your retirement, then do yourself and your family a favor and make sure you have a good, solid plan to follow. Dollar cost averaging is one of those good plans you can use if your plan is to invest a consistent amount of money in a retirement account each month. Just be sure that you are buying mutual funds, exchange-traded funds (ETFs), or

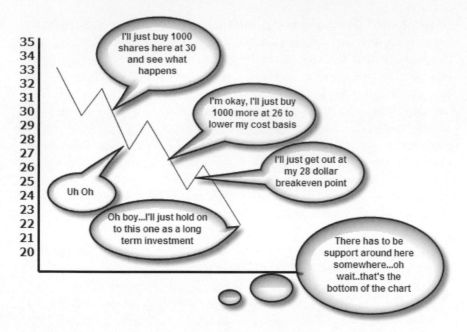

**Figure 6.2 The Thoughts of a Cost Averaging Down Trader**

index funds that are in upward-sloping trends. However, if your plan is to trade the markets for profit, then cost averaging down is a very bad way to go. Understand the differences and you will save yourself a lot of grief, stress, and money.

We have heard the same stories over and over again from people who think they are going to beat the market by buying more shares of the same stock that hurt them. Only gamblers put themselves into this sort of position, and we hope you will learn from the mistakes made by others who continue to throw their good money after bad trades. Figure 6.2 gives us a picture of what goes through the minds of those who use cost averaging down as a trading strategy.

## The Building Blocks of a Role Reversal Pattern

A role reversal occurs when a certain price level, once seen as a support on a price chart, is broken and then changes to an area of resistance. This occurs in a similar way with areas of resistance that change to support, but let's look at a typical role reversal pattern on the downside first.

In Figure 6.3 you see a candlestick chart with a role reversal identified. In this example you will see that at point A the stock was holding support around the $40 price range. Here, investors and traders alike thought that the price of the stock had reached a point of value. As a result, buyers came in and purchased shares, creating enough demand to overtake supply. As a result of this new money moving into the stock, the price moved up. This, as mentioned before, identifies an area of support. Keep in mind that the traders who were getting in at this point do so with a goal to take short-term profits on any price moves greater than $40. The stock rallied to $75 per share in just a few weeks. This works out to be an 87 percent price move. This return is good enough to force the swing traders to take their profits, which is what we see shortly after the $75 level is reached. This downturn is called *profit taking*, and it's something every trader should expect to see after a significant price rally.

After the profit-taking move, you can see that the stock traded back down to the $60 level. Another rally to over $90 was followed by a series of downturns that brought the stock right back down to the $40 support at point B. Moving on in time, you can see that after the stock had fallen below the support level of $40, it made one final attempt to rally before failing completely. After that, the stock continued to bump its head against the newly established resistance level.

**Figure 6.3   Role Reversal Support to Resistance**

## The Psychology behind the Move

If you were to study the reasons why this price pattern occurs so often, you would see that it is nothing more than large groups of people reacting in a similar way with regard to how they manage risk. Fundamentalist who debate the validity of technical analysis will argue that this is just self-fulfilling prophecy where herd mentality drives people to buy and sell at certain price points. The Market Guys have a good answer for that: "Who cares if it is self-fulfilling prophecy?" If we can make money because we have a good understanding of this herd mentality, great! We are simply following the money trail. If we notice that there are large groups of people getting out of a stock at a certain point and we know that there is a good chance this stock is going to hit resistance in the near future, then we just make sure we are not buyers at these newly established resistance points.

To fully understand why the role reversal is so predictable, you have to place yourself in the shoes of the person who has just bought the stock at $41 when it first bounced off of support but didn't take a profit when it traded up to $75. In fact, this may have happened to you at one point in time where you bought a stock and it went up right after you bought it. Imagine! A stock goes up right after you buy it and, to your surprise, it continues to go up. How sweet it is when this happens.

As we play out this scenario, we have to talk about a little driver called *greed*. This is the force behind why people don't take profits when they should. If you have played out this story in real time, then you know exactly what we are talking about here. Greed causes us to hold on even when our brains are screaming, "Take that profit! That's an 87 percent profit in weeks! Take it!" However, there is another side of your brain that is saying, "Let's go for double or nothing!" Then the stock drops, and you are right back to the place you first bought it. Almost everyone we know has gone through this pain when the stock proceeds to drop below the place you first bought it. What goes through your mind then? Of course, you start telling yourself that it's okay. It will go up again.

From there, you can probably finish the rest of the story line. What happens is that the stock doesn't go up right away, but instead it tortures all of those people who are hanging on to their hope strategy. This is the strategy where people hope that the stock will go back up to the place where they first bought it. All thoughts of profiting have vanished at this point, and people suddenly find religion. This is when traders all over the world start praying to the Market God: "Oh God, please get me out of this trade at breakeven and I promise I will never again listen to my brother-in-law, who got me into this stock in the first place. Amen."

We hope you are saving your prayers for better things in life than just to get out at breakeven, but the fact is that this is the story behind why stocks find resistance at the former support levels. People all over are trying to get out at breakeven. The opposite occurs when the resistance level is broken and then turns to support. In order to explain this, you need to know what is going through the mind of a short trader.

## The Role Reversal from the Short Side

As a trader, shorting the market should be as comfortable for you as taking a long position in the market. *Short selling* is a strategy that is used when you think a stock is going to drop in price. You borrow shares from your broker and sell them in the open market. Once you have sold these borrowed shares, you receive a cash credit to your account, which will be used later to buy back the shares at a lower price. If things work out as planned, and the stock moves lower, you then buy back the shares and return the shares to the original owner—in this case, your broker. What you are left with in the end is a profit equal to the difference between the sell price and the buy price.

Following is an example of short selling:

1. Trader borrows 1,000 shares of XYZ stock from his broker.
2. Trader then sells 1,000 shares at $24 and receives a credit of $24,000.
3. The stock drops to $22 per share, at which time the trader buys back 1,000 shares. This transaction costs the trader $22,000.
4. The result is a profit of $2,000, less the commission charged on both sides of the trade, along with a small amount charged for margin interest for the loan of the shares.

This is an exciting and profitable strategy because many times you will see stocks drop twice as fast as they go up. Of course, if the stock moved up in price after you had sold the shares, you would still have to repay the loan to your broker, which means you would have to purchase those shares at a higher price. This would result in a loss, so it's important that the short seller watch out for any upside risk.

The act of buying back shares that have been sold short is called *short covering*. In order for short sellers to realize their profits, they need to liquidate their positions by buying back the shares that were sold. Short selling usually occurs when traders believe a stock has reached an area of resistance and they think the stock will drop. If the stock breaks above resistance instead of going lower, short sellers are squeezed by day traders who generally buy into stocks that are breaking out to the upside.

The combination of both the momentum buyers and short covering results in an explosive rally we call a *short squeeze*. After the short squeeze has taken place, we usually see a drop in price. This is when the short-term buyers, who originally put the squeeze on the short sellers, begin to take their own profits. This new selling pressure adds to the supply, and we see the price drop to the original breakout point, hence the role reversal.

Figure 6.4 shows the points that mark the formation of the role reversal pattern to the upside. This is the sequence of events that drives the role reversal pattern, and we challenge you to look for it in every other chart you look at from now on. It's amazing how stocks have a tendency to reverse at the newly established support level, and many times the price will reverse within pennies of the original breakout point.

**Figure 6.4    Role Reversal Resistance to Support**

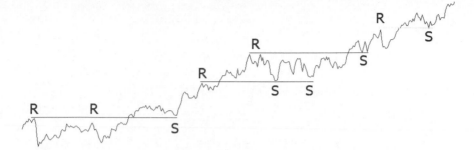

**Figure 6.5   Using a Line Chart to Identify Role Reversals**

In our last two examples we used a candle chart to show you the day-to-day price moves, but you can also use a line chart to find the reversal points. Many traders prefer the simplicity of the line chart, and if this is your choice, then make sure you are using a line chart that is tracking the closing price and not the opening price. Remember, we put more weight in the closing price for reasons previously mentioned.

Figure 6.5 is an example of how we would use the line chart to identify role reversal points. You will be able to find many stocks that are in steady upward trends, so this price pattern is one that you can use to find entry and exit points for your long-term investments as well. The short-term swing trader might use a daily chart going back 6 to 12 months, while longer-term investors would use a weekly chart going back 2 to 5 years. Once you familiarize yourself with this price pattern, you will find that, over time, your eye will be able to quickly pull it out of a chart with little effort.

In the chapters that follow, we will show you how to position yourself correctly using this price pattern and, more importantly, how to properly use the support line to minimize your risk in a trade.

## More Traders Drawing the Lines

As time goes on, you will see more and more people talking about role reversal patterns and their relevance to maximizing profits in the market. Thanks to organizations like the Market Technicians Association (MTA) and the International Federation of Technical Analysts (IFTA), who are both devoting their efforts to using and expanding the field to technical analysis, people all over the world are learning skills that help them better manage risk.

More people are talking about the charts today than ever before. As a result of this, more institutions and brokers are teaching their clients how to use the charts to minimize loss. There is a wave forming that is only going to get bigger. People will continue to resist using charts as a viable tool for selecting good investments, but eventually the overwhelming majority of people will be at least looking at price history to make a buy or sell decision. As the signals continue to be taught, then those very same signals will become more reliable.

The Market Guys started talking about technical analysis with some of the most popular brokers in the industry years ago. At first, we were met with heavy resistance, but when they eventually woke up and smelled the coffee, they realized that this form of analysis was helping their clients stay around longer. For the brokers, it became more profitable because their clients were trading longer and not losing as much money. For the traders, this newfound knowledge was exciting and profitable, and it gave a big boost to their confidence level. We expect the same to happen to you. Just give it time, relax with it, and you will see results soon enough.

CHAPTER 7

# Seventh-Inning Stretch

## MANAGING MARKET STRESS

The alarm sounded at 6:45 AM with a staccato note that roused Alex the Trader from his sleep (although, after a restless night of tossing and turning, it may not have been so much "sleep" as a fitful rest). There wasn't anything in particular that was bothering Alex lately; he just wasn't able to sleep through the night without waking and thinking. Usually, his mind wandered to the previous day's trades or some news that was coming out in the markets the following week. After churning the thoughts in his head, he would drift back into a hazy slumber, only to be jolted by the alarm mere minutes later—or so it seemed.

Alex roused himself and, in usual fashion, tried to shake off the sluggishness as he went through his morning routine. His reflection in the mirror was another reminder that stress and weight gain were taking its toll on his health. Shower, brush, dress, and walk to the office in the terrace room to fire up the computers and scan the day's news. Alex prided himself on his trading setup; no detail was overlooked in giving himself every advantage in the markets. If Alex were to miss a trade, it would not be for want of technology and information.

The screens flashed to life as he loaded his trading software and news feeds. The approaching market opening increased the rate of flow of information by the minute. The colors, headlines, charts, and indicators started painting a picture that would require Alex's experience and clear thinking to filter into the trades that he would execute today. This pretrading ritual consumed Alex's attention right up to the first trade, when the first pang of hunger caught his attention through the noise of the day. It was too late now for a proper breakfast, and besides, who has time for that? He knew that after the first hour settled down, he could break free for a quick snack before the lunch doldrums hit the market.

Two trades and 90 minutes later, Alex saw that the market was cooling, and he decided to not ignore his protesting stomach any longer—especially since his second trade was such a bust. How in the world could he have forgotten that the company was coming out with an earnings announcement that morning? Alex reluctantly acknowledged that he was becoming more forgetful with important information. He made a quick dash to the pantry and grabbed the last cherry cheese pastry. The microwaved cup of instant coffee with two tablespoons of sugar completed his mid-morning snack. Though Alex felt that familiar heaviness in his stomach, he did notice that his hunger was satisfied, and yet he felt impatient as the markets refused to break out of the late-morning trading range. He knew he was looking for trades that probably weren't there, but at least he felt alert—perhaps even jumpy. He blamed it on the coffee and the docile market. He decided not to sit and watch any longer, and he went long the oil market. When in doubt, he reasoned that oils will rise eventually with the uptrend that they've been riding.

Speaking of oil, Alex was disappointed that there wasn't any left over deep-fried fish and chips from yesterday's dinner. It was clearly the lunch slowdown now, so Alex decided to run out for a quick bite. As he waited in line at the café, he scrolled through the news headlines on his mobile phone. Even away from his office, Alex made sure that he kept the advantage on the markets. The one that caught his attention was the OPEC announcement; rising oil prices had prompted an increase in daily production to help stabilize the markets. Alex instantly knew what that news meant for his open position. He also knew that his leisurely lunch had just become a fast grab. Moving to the counter, he ordered the sausage roll (it was premade) and added a bag of crackers and a 24-ounce cola to the order.

Alex quickly returned to his office, eating his lunch along the way. As he looked at his position, he was surprised that it had dropped by only a marginal amount, although it was still trending downward. Experiencing an energy spike from his lunch break, he decided to pull his stop and actively manage this position. If it hadn't collapsed after the initial news, it would most likely rally later in the day.

By 1:30 in the afternoon Alex became increasingly drowsy, wondering what happened to his post-lunch energy surge. "Snap out of it," he said aloud as he prepared for some healthy trades. Running back to the pantry, Alex grabbed a bag of pretzels, two cookies, and a can of cola to increase his energy and mental focus. Unfortunately, Alex received only a momentary burst of energy accompanied by an anxious feeling. Slowly, Alex felt the drowsiness start to wash over him again. "It's not fun getting old!" Alex groaned.

Several hours of staring at the screen as the market close approached showed Alex that the downtrend in oil wasn't going to reverse today. It was slow, but it was steady. The only problem was that he was now so far out of the money that he couldn't close his position. He chose to hold it overnight and wait for the morning pop—or so he hoped. As he closed his trading office for the day, he knew he would be in a foul mood for the evening.

For dinner, Alex strolled out to his favorite Italian café. He wasn't sure if he wanted the double cheese with sausage pizza or the pasta; however, he was sure that he probably had another restless night ahead. Later that evening, Alex tried to relax in front of the television as he snacked on his favorite junk foods, potato chips and one more can of cola.

## Analyzing Alex

Let's revisit Alex's unfortunate trading day and look for some underlying health and diet issues that are sabotaging his ability to trade more effectively.

Let's start at the beginning with Alex's restless night. The brain needs sleep! Lack of sleep results in reduced productivity and increased errors throughout the day. Also, Alex is constantly being reminded by his reflection in the mirror of his stress and weight gain. What Alex is not aware of is the stress hormone called cortisol that is released in the brain during stressful situations (fight-or-flight response). This was an important chemical reaction in the brain when early humans were attacked by wild animals or in times of war, and the only choice was to fight for your life or run for your life. However, we were never created to be in a constant state of cortisol release. Cortisol is a powerful hormone that shuts down the immune system, making us more susceptible to illness. An abundance of cortisol also slows the metabolism, inhibits the absorption of protein, and promotes fat gain. But this is just the beginning of what's happening inside of Alex.

By skipping breakfast, Alex's metabolism slows down even more as it tries to adapt to long periods without food. By consuming all that sugar in the cherry cheese pastry and the coffee, Alex's insulin level quickly skyrockets and remains high, driving the sugar into the fat storage areas of his body. Within 20 minutes, Alex experiences an energy surge followed by lethargy. This unhealthy cycle of not eating for long periods of time and then consuming high-calorie, high-sugar foods promotes Alex's weight gain and prevents his ability to think clearly and remember important details about key companies or strategic trades.

Alex's premade sausage roll and cola lunch was high in saturated fat and sugar, giving him a temporary energy surge followed by a slump and more drowsiness. Alex tried to bring himself out of his mental fog by eating a bag of pretzels, cookies, and more cola. The afternoon snack gave another boost in energy, but lethargy set in, creating another food coma.

Alex's double cheese and meat pizza dinner was over 1,600 calories of saturated fat and simple carbohydrates, creating an environment of fat gain, clouded thinking, sleeplessness, and, eventually, even depression. Alex concluded his evening with chips and another can of cola, which packed on more empty calories and fat gain. This cycle assures no energy and promotes high blood pressure, high cholesterol, heart disease, cancer, obesity, fatigue, and premature aging.

### Alex's Action Plan

What should Alex do to reverse this destructive direction? Here are five highly effective action tips to get back on the road to high performance:

1. *Clean out the kitchen.* Remove all the junk such as empty-calorie snacks, cream-based sauces, processed or packaged foods, and sugary drinks. Protect your home as a healthy oasis in a toxic food environment. If you make it inconvenient to eat junk food, you'll have only one option—nutritious foods.
2. *Limit or eliminate visits to fast-food restaurants.* Pack a cooler with bottled water, fruit, vegetables, tuna on whole-wheat bread,

low-carbohydrate protein bars, and other high-quality food items that are high in protein and nutrients. Also, take a multivitamin with minerals every day.

3. *Drink plenty of water.* Our brain is 85 percent water, so it is imperative to stay well hydrated. The most efficient way to determine the *minimum* amount of water your body needs is to drink approximately one ounce of water per kilogram of body weight. If a person weighs 80 kilograms, or approximately 176 pounds, he should drink approximately 80 ounces of water, or almost two and a half liters. Some benefits of drinking water include:
   • Regulates body temperature.
   • Removes toxins and waste products.
   • Transports nutrients.
   • Maintains blood volume.
   • Protects against fatigue.
   • Curbs hunger pangs.
   • Every major system in our bodies begins to break down when water is low.
   • Concentration and reaction time drop substantially with a lack of water.
   • Soft drinks contribute zero nutrients or vitamins—only calories and chemicals.
   • Water has zero calories, yet fills you up.

4. *Exercise with free weights.* A daily workout releases brain chemicals, such as epinephrine and norepinephrine, which boost alertness. Regular exercise also raises levels of serotonin, a nerve chemical that boosts mood. Daily exercise naturally destresses the body by lowering blood levels of stress hormones, including cortisol.

   The rise in body temperature that results from a vigorous workout has a tranquilizing effect on the body, much like a soaking in a hot bath. Exercise is one of the best remedies for depression, many times better than medications or counseling. Physical exercise:
   • Arouses the body.
   • Sharpens the senses.
   • Increases blood flow to the muscles and brain.
   • Increases the transportation of oxygen and nutrients to the tissues.

- Speeds the removal of toxins and cellular debris.
- Reduces overall stress of the body.

Research indicates that active people think more clearly, concentrate better, remember more, and react more quickly than sedentary people. Furthermore, research also shows that individuals increase their memory and ability to multitask by up to 20 percent after participating in an exercise program.

5. *Eat brain foods and do mental gymnastics.* Research shows that memory and cognitive skills are greatly enhanced with a diet rich in antioxidants (vitamins B, C, and E and beta-carotene). Also, consuming omega-3 fatty acids found in fish will enhance the brain's ability to function. If you have an important morning meeting, eat a high-protein breakfast to help raise your serotonin levels, which produce hormones that make you feel more alert. An example of a "brain-empowering breakfast" would be five egg whites, salmon, berries, and at least 16 ounces of water.

Challenging your brain by learning new information stimulates blood flow and strengthens the connections, or synapses, between nerve cells in the brain. Memorizing data also encourages the brain to work more effectively and may reduce age-related memory loss.

## Sweet Nothings—Literally!

If you were to take time to read most of the labels found on some of the foods you were eating, you would be amazed to see just how much sugar you are consuming each and every day. For instance, a typical cola drink packaged in a 20-ounce container has in it 28 grams of sugars, which converts to seven full teaspoons! So-called "healthy" grain cereals might also surprise you when you check the ingredients on the side of the box. One very popular cereal brand identified by a Special Big Red letter in the alphabet (hint: the 11th letter) showed 11 grams of sugar for a serving size of ¾ cup. What is interesting is that most cereal boxes will state that a typical serving size is about 1 cup or 28 grams. Now when was the last time you sat down and consumed ¾ cup of anything? Just for the heck of it, pour what you would estimate to be an average bowl of cereal that you would normally eat then take the contents out of the bowl and measure it. Now you will see exactly how many servings you are really eating each morning. Chances are by the time you get finished filling your cereal bowl, it will measure out at least one and a half cups. This means the Special "health" cereal you are eating delivers a whopping 22 grams, or 5 teaspoons, of sugar into your bloodstream each morning.

Take time out to document your daily intake of sugar in the foods you eat, then think about how many "Alex" moments you run through during your trading day. Table 7.1 shows some of the things most people eat along with the sugar content for each serving.

In this chapter we have focused on diet and exercise for several reasons. Not only will this help you relieve stress, but these ideas will also help you live a more healthy and fruitful life. Think about it: What good would it do you if, for your whole life, you worked hard and traded the markets for profit only to see those profits eaten up with your having to fight an illness later on in life? Especially when that illness could have been avoided early on by following some simple ideas about diet and exercise?

Many believe that there will one day be a cure for cancer, and that day can not come soon enough, but until then many medical experts feel that preventative medicine is the best way to head off this disease. In fact, a report put out by the Wellness Directory of Minnesota, entitled "Cancer Loves Sugar," states that cancer metabolizes through the process of fermentation. Now, if you have ever tried to make your own wine, you will know that in order for fermentation to take place, you need to have sugar in the mix. In fact,

**Table 7.1    Sugar Content of Common Foods**

| Food | Serving Size | Grams of Sugar |
|------|-------------|----------------|
| Cola | 12 oz. | 40 |
| Fruit drink | 12 oz. | 25 |
| Chocolate bar | 1 oz. | 15 |
| Sherbet | ½ cup | 25 |
| Fruit sorbet | ½ cup | 28 |
| Donut | 1 | 24 |
| White bread | 1 slice | 12 |
| Honey | 1 tablespoon | 12 |
| Raisins | ½ cup | 16 |

Dr. Otto Warburg discovered years ago that cancerous cells can live and develop, even in the absence of oxygen:

> Cancer has only one prime cause. It is the replacement of normal oxygen respiration of the body's cells by an anaerobic [i.e., oxygen-deficient] cell respiration. (Dr. Otto Warburg, Nobel Prize winner in physiology/medicine, 1931)

So what else does Warburg's discovery tell us? It tells us that cancer metabolizes much differently than normal cells. Normal cells need oxygen; cancer cells despise oxygen. In fact, oxygen therapy is a favorite among many clinics around the world. So how can you improve on your health, relieve stress, and cut down on your risks of getting cancer? The answer is: Force oxygen into your bloodstream through aerobic exercise.

Now, we're not suddenly professing an extraordinary expertise in diet and nutrition. But in the same way that we read the markets and look for patterns and signals for our trading, we are also observers of behavior as it relates to diet, nutrition, and exercise. And our observations, coupled with some basic research available to anyone interested, tell us that there's more to success in the markets than just finding the right entry point for your stock. Hopefully, that great trade is just one part of an overall successful lifestyle.

## Trading Fingers of Steel

We would be leaving out half the formula if we concentrated on diet alone. We need exercise to stay healthy, and our brains need an invigorating blood flow to stay alert.

Oxygen-enriched blood flowing through your veins is good for you. Your body is a lot more efficient than you may imagine, and it continues to become more efficient as you change your diet and exercise routines. For example, let's say that you were thinking about going on a starvation diet, which is nothing more than stopping your caloric intake for long periods of time in order to lose weight. Under this stress, your body would react in a way that protects you from starvation. In other words, your body senses that food in not being digested, so what it does is slow down your metabolic rate (the rate at which your body expends energy). On top of that, your body will also become more efficient at storing fat. Why is that? Well, it's because your body doesn't want to die, and if you continued on with a starvation diet long enough, you would die. Your body needs food to survive, so while you may feel good about losing those unwanted pounds, you have in a sense trained your body to get better at storing fat. You will find that the next time you eat a meal, you will store even more fat than you did before you went on your diet. You may have met people who have gone through this experience where you'll see them take off amazing amounts of fat in a short period of time only to see them a year later heavier then they've ever been before. Chances are those people have only been dieting and not changing their lifestyles with regard to exercise.

If you are someone who is sitting in front of a computer all day trading the markets and eating like Alex the trader, chances are you are on the road to disaster. Instead, try little things that can help jump-start your exercise program. Make small changes that would not interfere with your trading or the way you conduct your business. For instance, try standing up the next time you pick up the phone instead of sitting down at your desk. Even if you were in a crowded office, this would not draw any unwanted attention to you. How about this: If you are in an office by yourself or at home, you can talk on the phone while doing calf-ups. This is when you stand flat on both feet with your weight evenly distributed and rock back and forth from your heels to your toes. Stand as tall as you can on your toes while you lift your heels off the ground. Try doing this a hundred times in a row, and you will definitely feel the soreness in your muscles the next day. I'm sure you have heard the old saying, "No pain, no gain." There is truth in that saying.

When you work your muscles, you are causing tiny tears in the muscle tissue. Your body then heals itself of these small tears and rebuilds the muscle, and this is why you feel achy after you have worked out. This is also known as "delayed-onset muscle soreness" or DOMS. As you repeat this process, the body becomes more efficient over time as you build muscle on top of muscle. As a result, your body burns more calories while you are at rest, and you will have increased your metabolism. Studies have shown that the majority of all calories burned (about 70 to 80 percent) are burned at the resting level. So imagine what a couple of hundred calf-ups can do for you each day. No extra time needed—just start your activities the next time the phone rings. If you are too embarrassed to do them in your office, then exercise while you are brushing your teeth.

**Table 7.2    Activity and Calorie Burn Chart**

| Activity | Calories per Hour |
|---|---|
| Washing car | 346 |
| Walking upstairs | 622 |
| Playing with kids | 306 |
| Playing guitar | 244 |
| Table tennis | 306 |
| Canoeing | 346 |
| Raking the lawn | 326 |
| Gardening | 418 |
| Stretching | 300 |

You can whip out a hundred calf-ups in no time, and your dentist will love you for it.

Now let's face it, we are all human, and every now and then we are going to give in to a freshly baked Krispy Kreme donut that's loaded with sugar and calories. Some of you may even be consuming these savory bits of sweetness to support your long stock position that you are still holding at $50 per share (ticker symbol: KKD).

So, in order to give you an edge in the battle of the bulge, we have come up with a list of activities that will fit nicely into your everyday life. Review Table 7.2, which shows the number of calories burned in a one-hour period for a person who weighs 170 pounds (77 kg). Notice how many of these activities keep us in shape without having to even step one foot in the gym.

## Small Steps, Big Changes

Most people wish they could do better when it comes to diet, nutrition, and exercise. If you find yourself in that majority, don't lose hope. We want to encourage you to make the changes necessary to enjoy the fruits of your labors and share them with your friends and family for many years. You don't have to make radical changes to enjoy radical benefits. Think about applying your own variation of the 1% Rule (discussed in Chapter 12) to your lifestyle. Reduce your sugar intake by 1 percent each month. Increase your exercise time by 1 percent each week. Add 1 percent more to your water intake each week. You see how the small changes will add up over time?

## Chatter Box—Rick

Many key points and information contained within this chapter were provided by a good friend of The Market Guys, Dean Rosson. Dean is a professional consultant who specializes in the areas of diet, nutrition, and fitness.

Dean tells the true story of a friend of his in Atlanta. This friend was at the top of his game; he was tremendously successful in business and seemed to possess the Midas touch. In fact, he was just completing an 11,000-square-foot addition to his home when he called Dean to mention that he was having trouble catching his breath. Dean encouraged him to visit his doctor as soon as possible. Dean's friend took a stress test on the following Monday. The doctor called him later that afternoon and told him that he was to check into the hospital at the first opportunity the next morning. It turned out that Dean's friend had between 70 and 90 percent blockages in all arteries and could literally drop dead at any moment. The man was only 40 years old.

Consider the situation. Here was a man with every success financially, but his lifestyle had him on a road to physical ruin. He was on the verge of creating wealth that he would never enjoy. Dean's friend was given the opportunity to make changes in his diet and exercise because of a warning shot fired by his own body. Had he ignored that warning, his family would be enjoying the fruits of his success without him. We're happy to say that this gentleman is still an active part of his family and on the road to recovery.

Managing risk and performing at your highest level are not based solely on how well you read the charts. Processing information and taking action—the essence of trading—is highly dependent on how well you take care of yourself. Don't neglect the trader while attending to the trading. You just might find that your life improves along with your profits!

# CHAPTER 8

# E Pluribus Unum

## OUT OF MANY STOCKS, ONE

*"The world I am trying to understand is one in which men think they want one thing and then upon getting it, find out to their dismay that they don't want it nearly as much as they thought or don't want it at all and that something else, of which they were hardly aware, is what they really want."*

Albert Hirschman,
*Shifting Involvements: Private Interest and Public Action,*
Princeton University Press, 1982

The above quote from Albert Hirschman captures the battle that every person feels when he's given too many options. We've all been in this situation at one time or another. You sit down at a restaurant with a pretty good idea of the steak you plan to order and how you wanted it prepared. But you open the menu to see 10 pages of everything, from salads to sandwiches to steaks to pastas. After a few minutes, you're considering the shrimp scampi or the bleu cheese–encrusted filet. By the time the server comes for your order, you're in a turmoil trying to figure out which meal to order that won't leave you regretting your choice. Inevitably, the meal that arrives for the person seated next to you looks even better than your own selection, and your dining experience has dropped a couple of notches. There's some age-old wisdom in Henry Ford's reputed comment regarding the Model T when he said, "The customer can have any color he wants so long as it's black." Ford's approach may have been self-serving, as he was establishing the efficiency of assembly-line production. However, with only one color from which to choose, thousands of hours in the showroom agonizing over various hues were doubtless avoided.

"The presumption is, self-determination is a good thing and choice is essential to self-determination," writes Barry Schwartz, author of *The Paradox of Choice: Why More Is Less* (New York: Harper Perennial, 2005). "But there's a point where all of this choice starts to be not only unproductive, but counterproductive—a source of pain, regret, worry about missed opportunities and unrealistically high expectations."

### Chatter Box—Rick

I've been known to frequent coffee shops on occasion to work on my laptop while enjoying a fresh cup of brew. AJ believes that I actually have a dark roast dependency. He supports this hypothesis by taking long call positions in Starbucks (ticker symbol: SBUX) when I have a lot of computer work ahead of me. In any event, I never cease to be amazed at the level of choices that one faces at the coffee shop counter. It reminds me of Tom Hanks's line from *You've Got Mail:* "The whole purpose of places like Starbucks is for people with no decision-making ability whatsoever to make six decisions just to buy one cup of coffee."

Starbucks acknowledges their myriad menu choices on their own web site with an interactive tutorial on how to order a cup of coffee! First, you can customize your drink with an add shot. Before you think you're facing a simple binary decision, consider that the shots are single, double, triple, quad, decaf, half decaf, or ristretto. According to the tutorial, the last option is a short pull of espresso, capturing only the sweetest part—as if to imply that the gallon of bitterness residing in a shot glass is only the result of the last few drops from the press. Next, you select your syrup additive. Here, you pick from two sugar-free varieties and nine straight blasts of flavored high-fructose corn syrup. The third step requires that you make your milk selection. There are six options in the milk category, including one that has been through the entire production process without ever even having seen a cow. Finally, you walk through a menu known as "Custom Options" where you can specify everything from the temperature to "wet" or "dry." I suppose the baristas receive some type of training on how to resuscitate a first-time customer who is reduced to a catatonic stare when she's faced with such a complex decision as the queue builds behind her.

Social psychologists Sheena Iyengar, PhD, a management professor at Columbia University Business School, and Mark Lepper, PhD, a psychology professor at Stanford University, were the first to empirically demonstrate the downside of too many choices. In a paper in the *Journal of Personality and Social Psychology* (Vol. 79, No. 6, 2000), the team showed that when shoppers are given the option of choosing among smaller and larger assortments of jam, they show more interest in the larger assortment. But when it comes time to pick just one, they're 10 times more likely to make a purchase if they choose among 6 rather than among 24 flavors of jam. The shoppers ostensibly wanted the larger assortment but responded more often to the smaller assortment. The fact that there were more choices in the latter situation actually proved to be demotivating when it came time to take action.

It goes against our intuition to think we could have more difficulty making a selection when there are four times as many options from which to pick. This very issue is addressed in *The Functions of the Executive* (Cambridge, MA: Harvard University Press), one of the few true and enduring management classics. Written by Chester I. Barnard in 1938, the book holds this observation: "Free will is limited also, it appears, because the power of choice is paralyzed in human beings if the number of equal opportunities is large. This is an induction from experience. For example, a man set adrift in a boat, awaking in a fog in the open sea, free to go in any direction, would be unable at once to choose a direction. Limitation of possibilities is necessary to choice."

The markets are sometimes the worst offenders when it comes to complicating our choices. At one time, we simply had to choose from many thousands of stocks. Now we have derivatives to add to the mix. As the world opens up, we can also choose from market exchanges from around the world. We need a process to sort through the choices and find the trade that works for us.

## It May Be a Small World but It's a Big Market

The New York Stock Exchange (NYSE) has around 3,000 listed securities. The Nasdaq has approximately the same. Within North America we can also add the American Stock Exchange (around 1,000) and the Toronto Stock Exchange (around 1,800). On the international scene there are numerous major exchanges, including the London Stock Exchange, the Frankfurt Stock Exchange, and the Hong Kong Exchange.

Each exchange has a major index that tracks the representative performance of that exchange. In the United States, traders will readily recognize the Dow Jones Industrial Average, or the Dow 30. This is represented by the tradable exchange-traded fund (ETF) called the Diamonds, named after the ticker symbol "DIA." Table 8.1 shows a small list of some other major indices and the exchanges that they represent.

Up to this time, we've talked only about equity issues. The next level beyond the equity is the option. The option has three additional parameters that must be considered before you decide what you want to trade: the strike price, the expiration, and which contract (call or put). Just to give you an idea of how the multiplying factor comes into play, let's look at the Nasdaq 100 tracking stock, the QQQQ. If we decide to trade the ETF directly, we can buy or sell the QQQQ. However, if we choose to trade the QQQQ option, we must first decide between a call and a put. Next, we choose the expiration month. At the time of this writing, the QQQQ has seven different expiration months, including the long-term equity anticipation security (LEAPS). As far as the strike price goes, we have

**Table 8.1 Major Exchanges and Indices**

| Location | Exchange | Index |
| --- | --- | --- |
| United States | New York | Dow Jones Industrial Average (DIA) |
| United States | Nasdaq | Nasdaq 100 (QQQQ) |
| United Kingdom | London | Financial Times 100 (FTSE) |
| Germany | Frankfurt | DAX 30 |
| Hong Kong | Hong Kong | Hang Seng 33 |
| Singapore | Singapore | Straits Times 55 |
| France | Paris | CAC 40 |
| South Korea | South Korea | KOSPI 200 |
| Japan | Tokyo | Nikkei 225 |

seven different price levels to pick from, in one-dollar increments above and below the current trade price. Taken altogether, we have a total of 98 ($2 \times 7 \times 7$) separate options from which to choose based on a single equity issue. When you look at all of the stocks that trade options (not all stocks have options traded), you can see that the pool of trading possibilities increases exponentially.

By the way, we haven't even started talking about futures, which may be traded on single stocks, indices, commodities, and more. Add to that the various ETFs, mutual funds, currencies, CFDs (contracts for difference), and multileg option spreads, and the task of deciding what to trade starts looking like too many jars of jam.

## Viva Simplicity!

### Chatter Box—AJ

I will admit that my strategy for going long Starbucks calls, just before joining Rick at his favorite coffee shop for a cup of hot java, has been profitable. However, there is nothing that beats the simplicity of ordering a double espresso (no sugar) and a bottle of San Pellegrino while sitting in the lounge of the Steigenberger Belvedere Hotel in Davos, Switzerland. The added bonus is that even at the top of one of the most beautiful mountain ranges in the world, I'm still able to place a trade through my computer via a wireless connection. Viva la Internet! Viva simplicity!

Our objective in screening stocks is to reduce the total population down to a reasonable pool from which we can select one or more trade setups. Simplicity is the name of the game here. The screening process, like the technical analysis process, will let you run down to the most arcane detail without so much as a whimper of a protest. You can create screens that, when applied to the total market, may yield only two or three candidates that match your criteria. The fact that you've narrowed the pool down to a handful of survivors does not in any fashion ensure that you've identified the perfect stock to trade. It simply means you're too picky.

In the same way that we advocate using the more robust and simple tools for technical analysis, we also suggest that the simple approach be applied to your screening methods. By nature, we tend to lend credibility to a decision in the same proportion as the degree of difficulty by which that decision was reached. When we don't fully understand something and we're having it explained to us by someone who, by all outward appearances, does understand it, we abrogate our judgment for theirs. Similarly, many traders will stroll through the carnival-like halls of a trading show and absorb the various technical screens, analysis packages, and cycle analyzers. Even though they may not fully understand what they're using, by virtue of the fact that many other traders seemingly profit from these tools, they put them to work in their own trading room.

We'll take a walk through the four most common screens and, hopefully, give you some ideas you've not considered. The following paragraphs are not meant to be the complete and final word, though. We're not sure it's possible to create a complete screening list. For that matter, we're not sure why anyone would attempt such a task. We're looking to separate the wheat from the chaff; we're not in search of the perfect grain of wheat.

## Back to the Basics

The first set of screening criteria that we'll examine is the basics. These are simple measures of the stock or the company that don't really fall into a technical or fundamental category, although some might choose to categorize them a bit differently. Here's where it's nice to be able to say, "It doesn't really make any difference." The categories that we're using are for the purpose of organizing the criteria and don't impact the final outcome.

- Price
- Exchange
- Sector or industry
- Market capitalization
- Options traded
- Recent initial public offering (IPO) versus established
- Included in a major index

We'll walk through them in short detail so as to explain our reason for including them in the list. As we provide the explanation, our goal is to stimulate your thinking about what other criteria you might use and, more importantly, why you would use it.

### *Price*

The first in the list is price. There's a reason that our lead-off batter is price; it's the only criterion whose change will directly and immediately impact your profits. With price, most traders will establish a minimum price and sometimes a maximum as well. For example, the price screen may specify that the stock price be at least $10 or $20 per share. The idea here is to eliminate the very low priced stocks. The so-called penny stocks tend to attract speculators who may be moving many thousands of shares. This often drives volatility, and hard swings may occur out of the blue for no apparent reason. Also, most institutions will avoid the very low priced stocks. Many of these stocks are trading at very low levels after having fallen from much higher prices, often due to news such as poor earnings.

It's easy to look at a very low priced stock and start dreaming about the day that your $1 stock is trading at $50. We can almost picture the profits that we'll rake in when the grand rally is staged. However, don't ever forget that the market tends to price a stock according to all of the information that is floating around. If a stock was trading at $40 last summer and is now at $1, it's most likely because the fundamentals have deteriorated so badly that the stock should be that low. Unfortunately, we've all met someone who claims to have purchased the stock that multiplied by a factor of 5, 10, 20, or more. You may have even experienced that situation. We're not saying that it can't happen. We're just pointing out that this is a flimsy foundation upon which to build your trading strategy. If you want to carve out a few dollars for a speculative play, that's fine. But please don't try to convince us that you have the regular insight into the stocks that will serve as your surrogate lottery ticket.

Screening for the higher-priced stocks is usually done because of a limitation in buying power rather than any indication of perceived value. If a trader has $50,000 buying power, she can choose between 1,000 shares of a $50 stock or 400 shares of a $125 stock. Since most traders think in terms of absolute dollar moves rather than percentage moves, a $1 advance in both stocks yields a 2 percent increase for the former but only a 0.8 percent increase for the latter. Looking at it another way, a $1 move for the 1,000 shares of a $50 stock will generate a $1,000 profit. But since the $50,000 buys only 400 shares of the $125 stock, the profit drops to $400. Of course, it would be expected that the absolute swings would be greater in the higher-priced stock.

Nevertheless, this is the reasoning behind an upper limit on the stock price.

### Exchange

The next criterion in our sample list for basic screens is the exchange. Here, we're talking about choosing a stock based on where it is traded. Older traders have a tendency to want to trade stocks that are listed on the NYSE. We suspect that this is due to the fact that the NYSE has an actual trading floor. It is possible to hop a flight to New York, take a taxi to Wall Street, and walk into the NYSE building. With a pass, you could actually look down onto the trading floor. The Nasdaq, on the other hand, exists only in the realm of computer servers. There is no physical Nasdaq trading floor; the exchange is strictly electronic. The NYSE is referred to as an auction market where two traders will execute transactions between themselves after matching one trader's bid to another trader's offer. The Nasdaq is a dealer market where trades must run through a dealer, known as a market maker. The specialists trading on the floor of the NYSE and the Nasdaq market maker are both charged with maintaining a smooth and orderly market, although their specific functions differ.

Speed of execution and spreads are two more considerations when screening for a specific exchange. In the early days of electronic trading, most traders expected to get faster fills through the fully electronic trading systems that the Nasdaq offered. The need to run NYSE trades through the specialist created a latent delay that day traders found unacceptable. At the time of this writing in 2007, the Nasdaq still posted its order execution speed as approximately twice as fast as the NYSE. The Nasdaq also posts the average effective spread as a third lower than the NYSE. The effective spread measures the difference in price between what investors and traders actually pay or receive for a stock versus the average buy or sell price. The lower the effective spread, the better for the trader.

Also, there are differences in the listing requirements between the two exchanges. Historically, the Nasdaq has been considered more of a technology and growth market. Part of the reason for this is the lower listing fees and listing requirements. Companies with limited capital have been able to obtain and maintain a listing more readily on the Nasdaq than on the NYSE. A company's ability to maintain an exchange listing is dependent upon such factors as minimum bid price, market capitalization, and liquidity. The liquidity is based on the float—the number of shares that are available for trading by the public as opposed to officers, directors, or controlling-interest investors. The NYSE has more stringent requirements and has been considered the home for the more mature, blue-chip firms and industrials. These are the companies that were around before most of today's traders were born. As such, there is a perception of safety that comes from trading companies with such a well-established pedigree.

### Sector or Industry

Screening for a specific market sector or industry is a common practice for many traders. Very few traders actually raised their hand as a child in primary school and proclaimed to the class that they were going to grow up to trade the equity and option markets. Wide-eyed blinks by fellow classmates and a mandatory trip down the hall to the guidance counselor would surely follow such a pronouncement. The reality is that most of us enter the world of trading after a stint in one or more nontrading fields. These past career fields provide an arena within which we're quite comfortable. As we mentioned in Chapter 5, many of our friends in Canada tend to gravitate toward the mining and energy sector. Those are strong industries in Canada, and many traders have spent years working with the mining and energy companies. As long as you don't fall prey to Mistake 1 (Marrying Your Stock and Finding Trades that Aren't There), covered in Chapter 5, there's nothing wrong with screening stocks for sectors and industries with which you are familiar.

Besides personal familiarity with a sector or industry, the fact is that sectors and industries often move as a group. For example, when crude oil prices are rising along with consumer and industrial demand, it should follow that the companies within the energy sector should benefit. Rising prices and rising demand can be expected to translate into rising earnings. It's natural to expect that the stock prices should rise to follow suit. A very profitable strategy in this scenario is to screen for stocks within the energy sector and open long positions in one or more. Alternatively, you could buy the energy ETF and capture the move of the sector or industry as a whole with a single trade. We can see two examples of key sector stocks moving

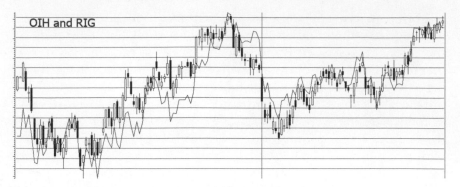

**Figure 8.1    Comparison of OIH Against RIG**

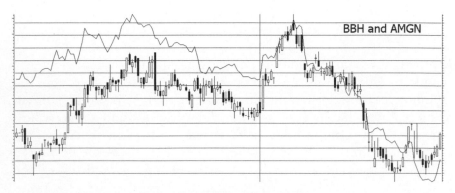

**Figure 8.2    Comparison of BBH Against AMGN**

in tandem with their respective sector ETF. The first, in Figure 8.1, is a comparison of the Oil HOLDR (ticker symbol: OIH) with one of the leading oil services stocks, Transocean Inc. (ticker symbol: RIG). In Figure 8.2, we see an overlay comparison of the Biotech HOLDR (ticker symbol: BBH) with a key biotech stock, Amgen (ticker symbol: AMGN). In each case, the leading stocks move quite closely with the overall sector. It becomes apparent why we want to screen for the sector or industry when we're trading a stock within that sector.

### Market Capitalization

Next up on our basic list is the market capitalization, also referred to simply as the *market cap*. Market cap is determined by multiplying the total outstanding shares by the share price. It's easy to think that the higher the share price, the larger the company. However, market cap is actually the better measure by which company size is determined. To illustrate this, consider two companies. Company A has 50 million shares outstanding with a per-share price of $25. Company B has 30 million shares outstanding with a per-share price of $40. It's tempting to look at Company B and conclude that it is the stronger company, based on stock price. However, Company A has a market cap of $1.25 billion, while Company B has a market cap of $1.2 billion. Comparing market caps, Company A is the stronger company, even though the Company B stock is 60 percent higher than the Company A stock.

Companies are generally grouped in size by market cap. Mega-cap or giant-cap companies have market caps over $200 billion. These are typically the bellwether companies or conglomerates that lead their industry. Below that are the large-cap companies with market caps from $10 billion to $200 billion. Many of the well-known blue-chip companies fall into this category. Next in the list are the mid-caps with market caps ranging from $2 billion to $10 billion. The mid-caps are typically growth stocks that may not be industry leaders yet, but may very well reach that stage as they grow. Below the mid-caps are the small-caps with market caps between $300 million and $2 billion. The small-caps are often young or emerging companies. They contain many companies with strong growth and appreciation potential but also carry a higher risk due to their lack of a corporate track record. Reaching even lower in valuation chain are the micro-caps with market caps from $50 million to $300 million. Micro-caps represent the balance between risk and reward; the downside is often as likely as the upside. What about the companies with market caps below $50 million? They're too small to trade on an exchange, so their prices are posted on a daily publication called the pink sheets. If you want to trade the pink sheet stocks then just remember: caveat emptor.

### Options Traded

Screening stocks based on whether the stock has options is another approach. The primary reason that a trader would want to eliminate stocks that don't have an associated option chain is that there is less flexibility in managing risk. The first risk management step that most traders learn to take is to place a sell stop order after buying a stock. However, managing risk by purchasing a protective put is becoming much more popular among traders. The reason is quite simple: A sell stop order is subject to gaps or fast moves during periods of high volatility. You can place a sell stop order at $48 for a stock that you bought for $50 and find that you sold it at $20 when the stock collapsed overnight on bad news. However, if you were the proud owner of a shiny new $45 put on that same stock, you could sell the stock for $45 even if it dropped to a penny. For that reason, many traders will screen for stocks that will allow them to manage risk through the use of options.

Besides managing risk, finding stocks that trade options will provide the opportunity to use a stock replacement strategy. A stock replacement strategy using options entails identifying a stock-trading candidate first. Let's assume you find a stock that is in a strong uptrend. Everything you see tells you that this is a stock you want to own. Of course, you could buy the stock. The alternative is to purchase the call option and effectively own the stock for a short time but with a smaller cash outlay. This is referred to as a stock replacement strategy and could multiply your returns since you pay less for the option than you would for the underlying stock.

### Recent IPO versus Established

Have you ever been to an amusement park and ridden the giant roller coaster? Once you've settled into your seat, the safety bar comes across your lap and then you're launched up the long, grinding climb. As you crest the top of the tracks, you hold up your hands and yell as the bottom drops out of the car and you speed into the curve. One minute you're going up, the next you're dropping.

With that mental picture in mind, trading an IPO can be the market's equivalent to the coaster ride. IPOs are stocks that have no market history and, therefore, no price chart to analyze. They can represent great opportunity and great risk at the same time. From a technical standpoint, you can't really use the Market Guys' Five Points for Trading Success because there is no uptrend, support level, or stop level that can be identified. Does that mean you should not trade IPOs? Not necessarily, but you need to understand the nature of an IPO. While not all IPOs behave like a four-year-old who just downed a bag of Skittles, more than a few have the kind of volatility that tests a trader's resolve. Take a look at the chart in Figure 8.3. Xtent Inc. (ticker symbol: XTNT) started trading on February 1, 2007. Within two weeks, it went from a high of $17.24 to a low of $13.75. As noted on the chart, one day's trading saw a range of $1.93.

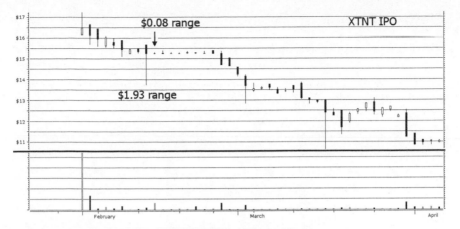

**Figure 8.3   Xtent Inc. Initial Public Offering Chart**

Suddenly, the stock fizzled as the trading range dropped to a mere $0.08 on triple the volume! Imagine—trading activity increased by three times, yet the stock flatlined. I don't know about you, but if I were in that trade and saw heavy volume and no movement, I would be jumping at every tick, waiting for the breakout.

### Included in a Major Index

Finally, the last screen that we include on the basic list is whether the stock is included on one of the major indices, such as the list shown in Table 8.1 (on page 152). If a stock is included in a major index such as the Dow Jones Industrial Average, then every fund and ETF that tracks the market based on that index must own the stock. Almost every mutual fund family includes an index fund for the major indices. If the stock price falls, you have the assurance that the large institutional holders of that stock aren't going to start selling out of their position. As long as the stock remains a component of the index, these holders will continue to own the stock.

Another consideration for trading stocks that are included in a major index is the fact that the index is intended to be representative of the overall market or economy. As such, you wouldn't expect to find fundamentally weak companies whose future is in doubt. That provides some measure of comfort for traders and investors who are buying that stock. However, if the stock should be dropped from the index, we'll refer you back to the mental picture of the coaster ride we created a few paragraphs ago.

## Getting Technical

The technical criteria for screening stocks may include any of the technical indicators that are used in technical analysis. The following list will give you some ideas of how and why you might use technical screens to pare down the stock pool:

- Volume changes
- High/low price
- Moving average trends
- Most active
- Gainers and losers
- Bollinger Bands
- Stochastics

### Volume Changes

Let's start the technical screening list with volume. Along with price, we consider volume to be the other member of the dynamic duo. If the trading police were to step up and tell us that we could have only two items with which to trade, we would have to go with price and volume. Take away either of the two of those and we'd be writing a book about catering wedding parties. We just couldn't trade without considering these two first.

For traders, volume looks like little green and red bars spread across the bottom of our charts. But consider the word in another context. Surely, most of our readers have attended a favorite sporting event such as the Olympics, a football game, or a college basketball playoff. You have two opponents meeting on the field of play, the home team (we'll call them the Bulls) and the visitors (let's call them the Bears). When the Bulls are sluggish and their play is sloppy, what happens to the crowd? Initially, perhaps, they'll voice their collective displeasure at the Bulls' performance. After a time, though, the crowd will generally settle into a lull. Substandard play by the Bulls will yield substandard support from the crowd. The result is that the volume in the arena is reduced to a low hum. At some point in the game, a couple of the players follow Rick to the concession stand for a quad-shot espresso. Upon returning to the action, these newly juiced players start playing with a new spark. They're advancing the ball down the court with an energy that the fans haven't seen so far. Now the crowd becomes engaged and with each advance by the Bulls, their voices crescendo until the arena is echoing with the volume of their support.

Can you see how we pick up the analogy for trading? Those little volume bars at the bottom of the chart represent more than just another line to analyzed. They give us an indication of how much support there is out there for the price movement. If the traders start advancing the price but the volume is very low, we have to be careful because that tells us that others aren't joining in the action. When volume spikes on the start of a price move, however, we can assume that the crowd is jumping into the action. Liquidity, as measured by volume, is the trader's friend for two reasons. First, more traders means faster fills. Second, increases in liquidity usually result in lower spreads—the difference between the bid price and the ask price. Faster fills and lower spreads actually serve to lower risk.

From a screening standpoint, there are two primary ways to use volume as a screening tool. The first is to set a minimum threshold for the average daily volume. A common measure is the five-day average daily trading volume. We could set the screen in such a way that it filters out stocks whose five-day average trading volume is below 500,000 shares. The only results that show up from this screen will be stocks that have traded on average at least 500,000 shares over each of the last five trading days. One word of caution here: Be sure to glance at the volume bars on your chart before you enter a trade that has passed through this screen. It's possible to have a stock with this trading history:

| | |
|---|---|
| Day 1 | 20,000 shares |
| Day 2 | 10,000 shares |
| Day 3 | 2.6 million shares |
| Day 4 | 35,000 shares |
| Day 5 | 15,000 shares |

This stock has a five-day average trading volume of 536,000 shares. That's enough to allow it to pass the screen we just set up. However, you can see that the average was skewed by a one-day spike and the true average is closer to about 15,000 shares. A quick look at the volume histogram will reveal any anomalies that need to be accounted for before entering the trade.

The second way to employ a volume screen is to look for stocks with an increase in trading volume. For example, we could set up a screen that shows us all stocks that have a 10-day average trading volume at least 25 percent greater than the 90-day average trading volume. In this case, we're looking for stocks where the fans in the arena are getting louder than they've been recently. If we're walking past 10 different arenas, we're trying to find the one with the most energy so that we can join in on that game. This screen will show us stocks that are increasing in volume and, therefore, are attracting more participation from the market. Remember, for the trader, volume drives price movement and helps to lower risk through higher liquidity.

### High/Low Price

Next on our technical list is the high/low screener. This is a simple but powerful tool that streams a list of stocks making new highs and stocks making new lows. Figure 8.4 shows an example of a high/low screening tool. On the left is the list of stocks making new lows.

| New Lows | | | New Highs | | |
|---|---|---|---|---|---|
| STOCK | PRICE | TALLY | STOCK | PRICE | TALLY |
| SHW | 42.1 | 37 | AXA | 28.29 | 29 |
| MHX | 8.41 | 11 | AU | 39.27 | 104 |
| TMG | 6.14 | 18 | FHR | 36.82 | 56 |
| MHX | 8.42 | 10 | CLX | 54.22 | 35 |
| RIOp | 38.41 | 37 | SFI | 35.4 | 46 |
| THO | 31.86 | 7 | KSE | 34.25 | 61 |
| LQD | 106.74 | 17 | MHS | 50.4 | 29 |
| SAX | 9.39 | 9 | MDC | 67.53 | 34 |
| IJJ | 68.44 | 22 | ARG | 28.77 | 55 |
| MRO | 59.16 | 67 | MWD | 52.6 | 73 |
| ROP | 37.58 | 3 | PEG | 62.55 | 20 |
| PRX | 25.71 | 31 | RMD | 39.1 | 30 |
| PLD | 40.95 | 16 | IRM | 43.21 | 133 |
| IJS | 63.1 | 21 | PGN | 43.4 | 49 |
| MNT | 55.19 | 34 | IAG | 6.74 | 14 |
| SBL | 10.12 | 28 | TE | 17.46 | 17 |
| BR | 69.41 | 100 | PGN | 43.36 | 48 |
| IJJ | 68.45 | 21 | GTK | 31.45 | 30 |
| KFN | 22.37 | 9 | NCI | 20.85 | 14 |
| RDK | 19.66 | 14 | MTN | 34.5 | 29 |
| FDG | 35.2 | 42 | PEG | 62.54 | 19 |
| SKO | 28.67 | 15 | IT | 12.62 | 42 |
| DD | 42.59 | 57 | MAS | 29.01 | 35 |

**Figure 8.4   High/Low Screening Tool**

The first column is the stock ticker symbol. The second column shows the trade price that generated the new low, and the third column is a running count of how many times during the day the stock has posted a new low. You can see at the top of the list that Sherwin Williams (ticker symbol: SHW) posted a trade price of $42.10, which was the 37th new low for that trading day. On the right side of the screener is the list of stocks making new highs for the day. Notice the listing for Iron Mountain Inc. (ticker symbol: IRM) about halfway down the list. That stock has a highlight across the entire line, indicating that the trade price is not only a daily high but also a 52-week high. When it posted a trade price of $43.21, that was the 133rd new high for the day as well as the highest trade price in the last 52 weeks.

The reason for screening for stocks that are making new highs and new lows is that we want to put our money where the money is flowing. Stocks make new highs when traders and investors are buying them. We want to buy stocks that are going up, and a great way to find stocks that are going up is to look for the new highs. On the flip side, when traders and investors are selling stocks, the prices will make new lows. We also want to sell stocks when the money is flowing out of them, and a great way to find falling stocks is to look for new lows. It's no more complicated than that. Like we've said many times, trading isn't easy, but it isn't complicated either. It's an ordinary endeavor that requires extraordinary discipline.

### Moving Average Trends

We've included screening for moving average trends on the list because it is a clean and simple way to identify an uptrend. Our favorite way to apply this screen is threefold:

1. Price is above the 20-day simple moving average (SMA).
2. 20-day SMA is above the 50-day SMA.
3. 20-day SMA and 50-day SMA are both trending up.

Clearly, you can adjust the period on the moving averages and create a screen that has different sensitivities. Using the 20-day and 50-day SMAs compares the short-term trend to the intermediate-term trend. You could just as easily use the 50-day SMA and the 200-day SMA to compare the intermediate-term trend against the long-term trend. Alternatively, you could use the exponential moving average

**Figure 8.5 Price > 20-day SMA > 50-day SMA**

(EMA) rather than the SMA. These adjustments are more a matter of personal preference than a correct versus incorrect application. The idea here is that we want to use a simple technical screen to generate stock candidates that are in an uptrend. When the price is trading above the moving averages, the moving average will act as support. The short-term moving average will only run above the intermediate-term moving average when the stock is accelerating in the uptrend. The picture that we see in Figure 8.5 is exactly what we're looking for with this screen.

### Most Active

The next two on the technical list are included to give you an idea of how to find stocks that others are trading. These stocks are not necessarily the best candidates in terms of the technical or fundamental criteria. Rather, the idea here is to find the stocks that are attracting the most attention based on volume or price movement. The most active stocks can usually be found on just about any report that measures the performance of the market. Most actives are generally reported by exchange, so we'll see the NYSE Most Actives, the Nasdaq Most Actives, and so on. Be aware that a stock may hit the most active list for any variety of reasons, good or bad. Making it to the most active list does not always entail a significant news event. Many of the stocks on the most active list are the widely held large-caps that almost every investor and institution trades as part of a portfolio. Sometimes, though, a stock hits the most active list when an earnings surprise is announced or there is pending litigation. In these instances, you have to be very careful about the increased volatility that comes with the increased volume. There's nothing wrong with running the rapids—just watch out for the waterfalls.

### Gainers and Losers

Looking at the top gainers and losers, in terms of both absolute and percentage movement, is a good approach to generating trading candidates. When using this screen, it's important to know the exchange or index from which these stocks originate. Figures 8.6 and 8.7 both show a list of the top gaining stocks. However, Figure 8.6 is generated from the American Stock Exchange (Amex), while Figure 8.7 is drawn from the S&P 500. All but two of the Amex stocks trade below $10 per share, while only one of the S&P 500 stocks is below the $10 threshold. The cheaper the stock, the less price movement is required to create a large percentage change. When you screen from the S&P 500, you're drawing from a pool of larger established companies, whereas a screen from the entire Amex would include many lower-priced stocks.

### Bollinger Bands

Finally, rounding out the technical screening list are two representative technical indicators: the Bollinger Bands and stochastics. We really don't need to go into the details of these indicators beyond what was covered in Chapter 4. These indicators are included in this list to show how any technical indicator may be used as a filter for screening. We saw how the Bollinger Bands may sometimes be used as an indication of a reversal for stocks that are channeling within the bands. One application of the Bollinger Bands as a screening tool is to look for stocks that are within a certain distance of the bands. For example, we could specify that we want stocks that are currently trading within 10 percent of the lower Bollinger Band. This will generate a list of stocks that are close to the lower Bollinger Band, and we would then scan the charts to see if the price is above or below the band. We eliminate the stocks trading below the band and then search for stocks that appear to be channeling within the bands. The ideal setup in this example would be a stock that is approaching the lower Bollinger Band and appears to be ready for a rally back into the channel.

## Top Gaining Stocks - Amex

| | | | |
|---|---|---|---|
| BPI Energy Holdings... BPG | 1.05 | +0.16 | (+17.98%) |
| MPC Corp MPZ | 1.09 | +0.15 | (+15.96%) |
| Peace Arch Entertai... PAE | 1.54 | +0.20 | (+14.93%) |
| American Mortgage A... AMC | 9.20 | +1.19 | (+14.86%) |
| Amcon Distributing ... DIT | 27.00 | +3.49 | (+14.84%) |
| IGI Inc IG | 0.90 | +0.11 | (+13.92%) |
| US Dataworks Inc UDW | 0.61 | +0.07 | (+12.96%) |
| IA Global Inc IAO | 0.35 | +0.04 | (+12.90%) |
| Hyperdynamics Corp HDY | 2.07 | +0.23 | (+12.50%) |
| Oilsands Quest Inc BQI | 3.63 | +0.40 | (+12.38%) |
| Eagle Broadband Inc EAG | 0.20 | +0.019 | (+10.50%) |
| Anooraq Resources C... ANO | 1.87 | +0.17 | (+10.00%) |
| CVD Equipment Corp CVV | 6.75 | +0.61 | (+9.93%) |
| Metalico Inc MEA | 5.22 | +0.47 | (+9.89%) |
| Titan Pharmaceutica... TTP | 2.62 | +0.22 | (+9.17%) |
| Isolagen Inc ILE | 4.03 | +0.33 | (+8.92%) |
| Virexx Medical Corp REX | 0.75 | +0.06 | (+8.70%) |
| Simulations Plus In... SLP | 14.20 | +1.13 | (+8.65%) |
| Birch Mountain Reso... BMD | 3.79 | +0.30 | (+8.60%) |
| Conversion Services... CVN | 0.301 | +0.021 | (+7.50%) |

**Figure 8.6   American Stock Exchange Top Percentage Gainers**

### Stochastics

In the same fashion, we noted that one application of the stochastic oscillator is to identify overbought and oversold conditions. In general, when a stock has a stochastic value below around 20 percent, we would consider that stock to be oversold. If we look for the price to correct in the direction of the stochastic, then this would be a

# Top Gaining Stocks - S&P 500

| | | | |
|---|---|---|---|
| NVIDIA Corp NVDA | 30.90 | +2.32 | (+8.12%) |
| Celgene Corp CELG | 58.03 | +2.53 | (+4.56%) |
| Janus Capital Group... JNS | 22.54 | +0.82 | (+3.78%) |
| Constellation Brand... STZ | 21.49 | +0.67 | (+3.22%) |
| PMC-Sierra Inc PMCS | 7.23 | +0.22 | (+3.14%) |
| Amgen Inc AMGN | 58.33 | +1.65 | (+2.91%) |
| General Motors Corp GM | 31.90 | +0.87 | (+2.80%) |
| Kraft Foods Inc KFT | 31.58 | +0.86 | (+2.80%) |
| Medimmune Inc MEDI | 36.38 | +0.94 | (+2.65%) |
| RadioShack Corp RSH | 27.61 | +0.71 | (+2.64%) |
| QLogic Corp QLGC | 17.13 | +0.42 | (+2.51%) |
| Forest Laboratories... FRX | 54.30 | +1.33 | (+2.51%) |
| Thermo Fisher Scien... TMO | 48.63 | +1.18 | (+2.49%) |
| Peabody Energy Corp BTU | 43.74 | +0.95 | (+2.22%) |
| Analog Devices Inc ADI | 36.13 | +0.76 | (+2.15%) |
| International Game ... IGT | 40.61 | +0.84 | (+2.11%) |
| Time Warner Inc TWX | 21.04 | +0.43 | (+2.09%) |
| Mattel Inc MAT | 29.65 | +0.60 | (+2.07%) |
| Applied Biosystems ... ABI | 30.04 | +0.60 | (+2.04%) |
| Corning Inc GLW | 23.59 | +0.47 | (+2.03%) |

**Figure 8.7   S&P 500 Top Percentage Gainers**

long candidate. To set up a screen using the stochastic, we could filter for any stock with a fast stochastic (%K) value less than 20 percent. Again, these values may all be adjusted to increase or decrease the number of stocks that pass the filter. Obviously, the smaller the stochastic number, the fewer the number of stocks that will pass the screen.

## Putting the Fun in Fundamentals

We know plenty of traders who will pass by this section because they place all of their stock into the basic and technical criteria. They're naturally suspicious of anything that gets reported by the accountants and analysts. After the wild ride that many investors experienced with such names as Enron, Lucent, and WorldCom, it would be tough to blame them. There are probably just as many investors who will skip the basic and technical sections, dismissing them as attempting to read the market tea leaves. They'll jump right to the fundamental list as the holy grail of finding the stocks. We like to balance the two, use the fundamentals to identify what to buy or sell, then apply the basic and technical screens to identify when to buy or sell.

- Earnings
- Price-to-earnings ratio (P/E)
- Price-to-book
- Analysts' ratings
- Revenue
- Sales per employee
- Ranking with sector or industry

### Earnings

Our fundamental list starts with two criteria that go hand-in-hand. The first is earnings, and the second is the P/E. Earnings are simply the profit generated by the company's operations for a specific reporting period, usually a fiscal quarter. The earnings are probably the most watched and analyzed measure of a company's performance. Part of the reason lies in the simplicity of the concept. We may be dazzled by some more arcane accounting metrics, but most of us can appreciate the answer to this one question: Is the company making money or losing money? During the gold-rush days of the 1990s' technology boom, many fast-growth companies were plowing every available dollar into business expansion and capturing market share. These companies were often given a free pass regarding their absence of earnings. A new measure was brought in to replace earnings—eyeballs. This was an attempt to justify losing money so long as the company was expanding into the marketplace. The problem was that eyeballs don't make purchases. It was a strange twist to watch companies explain that while they may be losing money, they're making it up in volume. That is to say, they used to be a small company losing a little money, now they're a big company losing a lot of money.

### P/E and Price-to-Book

As a way to benchmark the earnings, it's common to divide the per-share price of the stock by the per-share earnings. This yields a price-to-earnings ratio, or P/E. Different industries have different standards by which P/Es are evaluated. Technology companies, for example, are expected to have higher P/Es than utility companies. The stock price reflects the expected growth of the company and the industry that it represents. We mentioned a moment ago those companies that don't have any earnings. How do we evaluate a company if they don't have any "E" to "P" on? Again, creative accountants and analysts will highlight alternative measures such as price-to-sales or price-to-book. The book value of a company is the theoretical value of the company if all company assets were liquidated. Presumably, even zero-profit, high-flying technology companies could hawk their silk ficus trees and cubical partitions on eBay.

Either of these measures may be used to screen for trade candidates. Screening for earnings may be as straightforward as specifying that earnings are greater than zero. That screen will filter out any company that isn't reporting a profit. With the P/E, it is more common to determine the average P/E for the industry you're interested in and then using that average as the benchmark. A quick way to determine an industry average P/E is by looking at the ETF for that industry. The ETF P/E will be the weighted average of the constituent stocks within that ETF.

### Analysts' Ratings

Moving down the list we have the analysts' ratings. We'll do our dead-level best not to appear too jaundiced in discussing this point, but we really have seen some egregious failures by analysts. Recently, an analyst for a major Wall Street firm wrote an upbeat report on a company that specializes in making mortgages to cash-poor home buyers. The company, New Century Financial, had lost half its market value in the previous month, trading around $15 per share. The very next day, the company announced that it would cease writing new loans and needed emergency funding to survive. The stock collapsed to $3 per share and has since filed for bankruptcy protection. It makes you wonder if the analyst had inadvertently written up the wrong company. You'd be wondering only until you dug a bit deeper and found that the Wall Street firm reportedly had a long-standing relationship financing New Century Financial. The best advice we can give when it comes to reviewing analyst recommendations is to see which analysts are completely independent and which are tied to a banking or underwriting division. A good example of the former is Standard & Poors, which provides investment research, ratings, and risk assessments. S&P assigns ratings to companies on a one-star to five-star scale, with a five-star rating as the highest. It's quite easy to screen stocks based on a minimum S&P star rating. How much value do we assign to the latter? Modifying a saying from Rick's dad, "An analyst's rating and $3.50 will get you a cup of coffee."

### Revenue, Sales per Employee, and Ranking

The last three on the list, revenues, sales per employee, and sector or industry ranking, are all used primarily as comparative measures. As we mentioned earlier, this list isn't all that you have to choose from. Company strength, performance, and rankings are evaluated in a variety of ways, and any of the evaluation criteria may be used for a screen. As with the basic and technical screens, we would caution against applying too many criteria together and then assuming that the final list is worthy of your investment or trading dollars. Your trading plan should detail the process by which you arrive at your trading decision. Screening for stocks is a part of that process, not the entire process in and of itself.

## Buy the Rumor, Sell the News?

The final screening list is included because of the ubiquity of the phrase, "Buy the rumor, sell the news." The fact is, stock prices are very susceptible to rumor and news. Sometimes they present traders with opportunities; other times, it's best for the trader to step out of the game until the news and speculation pass. Screening for news usually requires scanning for keywords. For example, if you want to screen for earnings news, you may use such keywords as *earnings, whisper number,* or *beat the street.* The following list of criteria highlights some of the more common news items that bear further consideration:

- Legal news
- Added to or removed from index
- Earnings hit or miss
- Split announcement
- Insider trading
- Partnerships and alliances
- New market expansion

### Legal News

Legal news is always a price driver. Having an awareness of what's going on with the company in question is crucial before you scan for legal news. For example, you may be watching a company that has been involved in a patent infringement battle. A useful screen would be to look for keywords such as *settlement* or *damages.* It pays to use your judgment and experience here to decide on which keywords are most likely to appear in a news report that would affect your position. Drug and biotech companies are especially vulnerable to legal news, especially when their product line is subject to approval from a group like the U.S. Food and Drug Administration. These companies can see their stock prices double or halve on an approval or rejection announcement.

### Added to or Removed from Index

When the news reaches traders that a stock will be added to a major index, the volume will invariably rise and the price will often become more volatile. When a stock is dropped from an index, volume will again rise for a short time. This occurs because all of the index funds that held that stock must now liquidate their position to maintain their tracking of the index. After all of the index positions are sold, the volume in a dropped stock will start to dry up as traders move away from the discarded stock.

### Earnings Hit or Miss

We've talked about earnings at various times throughout this chapter. Earnings are one of those news events that draws in more rumor and news traders than any other we've seen. Companies are expected to give guidance to investors as the earnings announcement date approaches. The reason for this is the age-old adage that Wall Street hates surprises. In truth, Wall Street loves surprises as long as they're not the ones getting surprised. Also, there is a whisper number that is not the official company earnings but rather a consensus among analysts or individual investors regarding the earnings. The stock will often trade in response to the whisper number and then adjust as the official earnings number is released. The funny thing about the whisper number is that the plethora of blogs and market-reporting sites makes for some creative whisper numbers. Add to that the fact that the very venues that generate the whisper numbers also promote their use and you have to wonder why it's still even called the "whisper" number. Who is left to whisper it to?

### Split Announcement

A split announcement is something to watch out for when a stock price reaches levels that the company deems is counterproductive for investors. Interestingly, this can be too high or too low. In most instances, a traditional stock split is announced when the per-share stock price is so high that it discourages trading and investing by smaller investors. A stock that is trading at $300 per share may go through a three-for-one stock split. An investor with 100 shares at $300 per share would end up with 300 shares at $100 per share after the split. The total value of positions held and the company's total market value remains the same. However, a stock split is taken by the market as a sign that the company believes in the ability of the stock to continue rising, so it draws in more buyers and often pushes the price higher. Again, though, if there is speculation around a stock split, it is not unusual to see the stock rally on the rumor, only to sell off after the split is announced. This is a classic case of buying the rumor and selling the news. On the flip side, a stock that has seen its price hammered to very low levels may go through a reverse stock split. For example, a company may announce a one-for-three reverse split for their stock if it's trading at $3 per share. If you have 300 shares at $3 before the split, you'll have 100 shares at $9 per share after the split. Companies will often announce a reverse stock split when they believe that their stock price is too low to attract investors and traders.

### Insider Trading

*Insider trading* is a term that most investors have heard and usually associate with illegal conduct. While the illegal activity gets all the press, the term actually includes both legal and illegal trading. The legal version is when corporate insiders—officers, directors, and employees—buy and sell stock in their own companies. When corporate insiders trade in their own securities, they must report their trades to the Securities and Exchange Commission. These trades are readily available to anyone through a simple corporate financial overview site. We tend to pay more attention to insider buying rather than selling. Insiders will often sell company stock in order to diversify their portfolio. Corporate officers and others often receive a large portion of their compensation in company stock. If they continue to accumulate the company stock, they could very quickly find themselves with a high concentration of company stock in their portfolio. Even though they may believe in the strength of their own company, prudence requires that they sell large blocks of their own company stock in order to spread their investment risk. A stronger measure of insider activity for us is when the insiders are buying. This is especially true if the insiders are buying on the open market rather than exercising stock option grants. When insiders are willing to go to the same marketplace as you and I and purchase their stock, we look at that as a vote of confidence in the strength of the company.

### Partnerships and New Markets

Once again, we round out our list with a couple of miscellaneous screening ideas that may be used for news scans. Events that could move a stock price may include new partnerships or alliances, new product announcements, or entering new countries or markets. The key here is to have your finger on the pulse of the company and then use keywords in your news search that may give you some clues about upcoming events.

## "When You Come to a Fork in the Road, Take It"

We suppose not all decisions are as straightforward and obvious as the famous quote by Yogi Berra. But if you don't have a way to funnel the myriad stocks and other trading instruments down into a usable pool, you'll be as lost as the sailor in the fog, which opened this chapter. This is one area of trading that lets you test the waters. Try a screen and see what comes out. If you don't like the results, tweak it or discard it and start from scratch. Look at some of the predefined screens that are included in most trading web sites and software platforms. Use the canned screens as your base and build or adjust from there. You'll never make the trade if the choices leave you paralyzed.

And by the way, have fun while you're at it.

# POINT III

# WAIT FOR THE PIVOT POINT
## Strike with the Buyers

CHAPTER

# Going with the Flow

## DON'T JUMP IN TOO EARLY

Helio Gracie was the youngest son of Gastao and Cesalina Gracie. Helio was always a very physically frail child. He would run up a flight of stairs and have fainting spells. For two years, he would sit on the sidelines while his brother Carlos taught classes in a new martial arts style he was developing. One day when he was 16 years old, a student showed up for class and Carlos was not around. Helio, who had memorized all the moves and words of his older brother, offered to start the class. When the class was over, Carlos showed up very apologetic for his delay. The student didn't mind and, in fact, requested that further lessons be given by Helio. Carlos agreed, and Helio became an instructor.

He soon realized that some of the techniques he had memorized from watching Carlos teach were not very easy for him to execute. After all, he was only 140 pounds and not particularly strong. He then started to adapt those moves to his frail body's abilities, improving the leverage in the execution of some of those techniques. He drifted from the traditional jiu-jitsu his brothers had learned and continued to refine the skillful use of his opponent's momentum. From this beginning, Brazilian Gracie Jiu-Jitsu was born.

In 1951, Helio met Masahiko Kimura in a match watched by tens of thousands. Kimura was considered the greatest judo fighter of all time, and he also outweighed Helio by over 50 pounds. The match was so imbalanced that Kimura announced prior to the fight that if Helio could last three minutes in the ring, Helio should consider himself the victor. Helio fought with masterful skill, using his opponent's weight and momentum against him. The techniques he perfected in Brazil served him well in that title bout. Helio lasted 13 minutes before the fight was called when Kimura placed Helio in an arm lock. Helio later admitted in a 1994 interview that he had in fact been choked unconscious during the match but had revived and continued fighting. This was the ultimate testimony to the power of leverage and momentum over raw strength.

## Jiu-Jitsu Trading—Knowing When to Tap

Maneuvering within the markets is not at all unlike the match we described above. When we approach the market, we're the 140-pound small guy going up against the much larger opponent. For that reason, it's important that we move with the market and use it to our advantage rather than fight a losing battle. If you try to buy a falling stock, you may as well be pushing up against a 400-pound judo champion who is lying across your chest. During the match with Kimura, Helio felt his opponent begin to launch his trademark shoulder throw. Helio knew there was no way he could resist against such a large opponent, so he went limp and flowed with the throw, allowing him to continue the match. When the stock you're trading sets up for a strong move against you, it is fruitless—even reckless—to position yourself against the move. Rather, you should prepare to move with the action.

Sometimes, despite all of your training and maneuvering, you find yourself in a position from which you can't recover. The smart jiu-jitsu practitioner will tap out. Tapping out is just what it implies: The fighter taps his opponent several times to indicate that he's conceding the match. Tapping out stops the pain and injury and allows you to fight another day. If you stubbornly refuse to tap out, the pain and injury will continue and may cause enough damage to prevent you from fighting again.

If you ever get the chance to watch a jiu-jitsu match, one of the key differences between a novice fighter and an experienced practitioner is the patience displayed by the more experienced fighter. The novice will constantly squirm, scrap, and push as he tries to reach in for an attack. He's so focused on making something happen that he misses opportunities as they present themselves. The novice assumes that being in the ring means that you must always be moving. More often than not, his careless aggression leaves him exposed to the skillful counterattack of the veteran. You see, while the novice is a whirlwind of activity, the veteran will patiently defend against any attack until the right opportunity arises. You might even say that he's managing risk until he's ready to advance. It's almost boring at times to watch the veteran do nothing more than sit and position himself. Having saved his resources, though, he is ready to bring them to bear at any time against his opponent for the advantage. The veteran knows that while activity may be entertaining, his greatest profit comes from watching his opponent and moving at just the right time. Ultimately, he wins the match after having spent less energy and resources.

Do you see the picture we're drawing? You cannot defeat the market by scrapping and pushing against it. What you can do is move with the market and use momentum and leverage to your advantage. However, you will often find yourself in a situation from which you cannot recover. Your smartest move here is to tap out and protect your principal for future trades. Close the position, limit your losses, and look for the next opportunity to enter the ring.

## Identifying the Pivot Point

The concept of the pivot point is about how we move with the market. It is the early signal of what move the market is about to take, and we flow with that move as it progresses. Notice here that we're not anticipating the move before it occurs. That will often leave us struggling against the much larger opponent. Our goal is to recognize the move as early as possible and apply our trading action in the direction of the move. Simply put, when the stock begins to rally, we identify the uptrend and buy with the buyers.

The pivot point takes the form of a "V" in an uptrend or an inverse "V" in a downtrend. We use it in conjunction with the role reversal we discussed in Chapter 6. Figure 9.1 illustrates the pivot point from a role reversal in an uptrend. The first part of the setup occurs at the line marked by the "R." This is the price level at which the stock meets resistance. As is often the case, this level is tested more than once, indicating the strength with which the sellers are able to push the buyers back into a retreat. The curved line in the chart is the 200-day simple moving average (SMA). This line will usually act as a strong resistance level when the stock is trading below it. The stock rallies above the 200-day SMA at the point at which

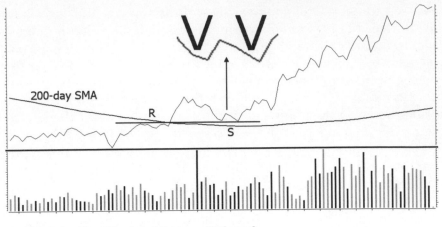

**Figure 9.1   The Pivot Point in an Uptrend**

it meets the role reversal line. In other words, the price level that acted as resistance at "R" is the same price level where the stock rallied through the 200-day SMA. This can be considered quite bullish when two strong resistance levels are breached. A short-term rally follows the break above resistance. Then the stock falls back and creates the role reversal line by showing support at the "S." It is here that we're watching for the pivot point to form. We've included an expanded view of the two distinct pivot points that formed above the role reversal line. Notice how both assume the "V" shape as the stock rises off the role reversal support level.

Even though we may anticipate the bounce off this support line, we don't enter the trade on the left leg of the "V." Entering this trade too early before the buyers complete the right leg of the "V" is akin to the fighter who presses for the advantage against the weight of a greater opponent. It is always possible that the move may yield a favorable outcome, but the smarter fighter displays patience until the opponent has begun to move in the desired direction. One point to note in Figure 9.1 is that the first pivot point failed to rally and led to the second pivot point. That's okay. You would protect yourself with a stop sell order placed below the role reversal support line. In this example, the role reversal support was not broken and you would have remained in the trade for the subsequent rally.

The same type of scenario occurs in a downtrend. Once again, in Figure 9.2, we start with identifying the role reversal line. In this example, we must first find a price level that acts as support.

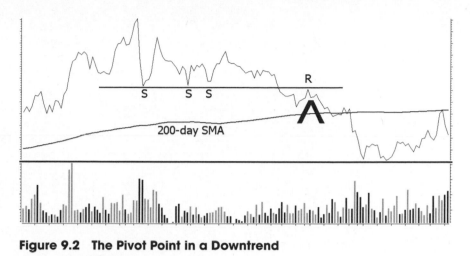

**Figure 9.2  The Pivot Point in a Downtrend**

This is highlighted by the three points marked with the letter "S." About three fourths of the way along the role reversal line, we see this support level broken as the stock falls. Shortly after breaking support, the stock rallies and is pushed back down from the same price level as the previous support. This established the role reversal line, and we now watch for the formation of a pivot point. We have clearly marked the inverted "V" shape of the pivot point in this example. Notice how the stock failed off the role reversal line and then dropped to the 200-day SMA. It spent several days testing the support of the 200-day SMA before finally dropping below. Once it dropped below, the fall accelerated before finding a short-term base. At the time of capturing this chart, it appears that another clear pivot point has formed below the 200-day SMA. We'll return to the writing of this chapter after we go enter our short trade.

Let's take a quick look at an example of what is more likely to happen if we jump the gun and enter a trade without a pivot point. Figure 9.3 shows a stock that is in a steady uptrend. We are able to strike a clean support line by connecting the lows in the uptrend. The stock has a history of dropping right down to the support line and obediently rising from there. If we look at a trend like this, it would be easy to convince ourselves that we can be lax about our requirement for waiting for the pivot point. After all, why leave money on the table when we can buy this stock right at the support line and grab the extra profit? The reason is given to us at the right side of the chart when the stock fails to form a pivot point after

**Figure 9.3    A Stock in an Uptrend without a Pivot Point**

reaching the support line. The long black candle shows us that the stock gapped down below support, briefly made an attempt to rise above the line, but then closed down heavily on high volume. We would not have been in this trade if we followed the rule of buying only on up days after the pivot point has been established. The last three candles before the big drop were all black candles, which tells us that the sellers are clearly in control. Money is flowing out of this stock, and until we see evidence that money has started moving back into the stock, we don't want to be buyers.

## The Pineapple Principle

It's often been said that the way to make money in the stock market is to buy low and sell high. The only problem with this approach is that we get the picture in our minds that we need to be able to identify the lowest point on a trend and somehow manage to also pick out the top of the trend. In all our years of working with traders around the world, we've yet to identify the first trader who can consistently pick the bottoms and tops. That said, we'd highly recommend against your attempt to be the first. A better slogan to adopt when trading trends is this: "Buy high and sell higher." Do you see how the picture changes in your mind? Now you're not conditioning yourself to buy against the downtrend in anticipation of finding the lowest point on the chart. You are executing the point of this chapter—namely, following the money trail.

When you wait for the pivot point in your trading, you are not going to be buying the low. The pivot point is formed when the low has been left behind. Very likely, you won't be selling at the highest point, either. That's fine to leave some money behind you and in front of you. Your goal is to find high-confidence trades and move in to take a bite out of the middle.

We want to encourage you to think about your trading like a pineapple, and we'll refer to this as the Pineapple Principle. (Our cursory literature search failed to uncover any widespread use of this term, so we'll be happy to take credit for introducing this to the financial world. Our guess is that this credit won't be accompanied by any significant monetary reward.) The idea is simple, yet useful. When you prepare a fresh pineapple, the first two steps are:

1. Choose a good pineapple.
2. Remove the top and bottom.

This is an appropriate analogy for the trader. The first objective is to choose a good trade, based on the criteria that we're outlining in this book. You want to identify the trend and follow the money trail. That's the good pineapple. Beyond that, though, is the idea of cutting off the top and bottom of the pineapple. Even though you've identified a good trend, you don't attempt to eat the whole thing. That is, don't waste your time looking for the top and bottom. The best trading in a trend is when you can jump into an established trend, ride it for a time for a profit, and then jump off. The trend may very well continue, but don't look back and lament the fact that you're out of the trade. Congratulate yourself for following your rules and making a profitable trade. According to the Pineapple Principle, trying to profit from the entire trend, however good the trend may be, is a bit like trying to eat the entire pineapple. The sweetest spot is in the middle.

## Pivot Point Patterns

As you can see, the concept of the pivot point is not a difficult one. Nor is it tough to recognize the pivot point when you see an example before you. The one aspect of trading with the pivot point that is subject to interpretation and causes the most questions for traders is exactly when the pivot point is considered complete. In other words, how much does the stock need to rally off the support level before you can consider the right leg of the "V" to be established well enough to say, "Here is the entry point?"

The Market Guys like to have simple rules that take the guesswork out of trading as much as possible. To that end, we'll spend the following pages reviewing some of our favorite candlestick chart patterns that we look for when we're waiting for a pivot point to form. The first section contains bullish pivot point patterns. These patterns occur in a long-term uptrend after the stock has had a brief pullback. The second section contains bearish pivot point patterns. On the flip side from the bullish patterns, these occur in an overall downtrend after the stock has experienced a short-term rally.

## Bullish Pivot Point Patterns

Multitudes of trading books and articles talk about various chart patterns. Some are fairly simple, while others require a special decoder ring to identify. The list that we have included is not comprehensive, but it does represent some of the more reliable patterns and signals for buyers.

- Bullish engulfing pattern
- Hammer
- Doji
- Piercing line

### Bullish Engulfing Pattern

The bullish engulfing pattern is one of our favorites because it creates such as strong indication of the return of the buyers after a short sell-off. This pattern does not require confirmation; it's okay to enter the trade on the day of the bullish engulfing candle without waiting for a follow-up day to show that the uptrend is continuing. Here are the key points of this pattern:

- The stock must be in a short-term downtrend within a longer uptrend. Remember, we don't want to be buying stocks with an overall bias toward the downside. This is just a pullback within a larger positive run.
- The first day of the pattern is a down day, as evidenced by a red or black candle. The black candle tells us that the short-term

downtrend is still controlled by the sellers, who are pushing the stock to lower levels.

- The second day's candle should be green or white, indicating that the buyers are in control for that day.
- Here's the key to the bullish engulfing pattern: The second day's body must completely engulf the first day's body. The open of the second day could be equal to the first day's close, although ideally the second day's open is lower than the first day's close. Likewise, while the second day's close may be equal to the first day's open, it's better if the second day closes above the previous open. Finally, while not required, it shows more strength if the second day's body completely engulfs the first day's body and shadows.

Figure 9.4 illustrates the formation of a pivot point with a bullish engulfing pattern. In this chart, we see that the prevailing trend is upward. As the stock moves higher, it takes a short breather, noted by the three black candles that drop to the role reversal support line. We've expanded the bullish engulfing pattern to reveal how the second day opened slightly below the first day's close. The stock then closed well above the high of the previous day. In fact, it closed higher than the two previous days' trading. When you see the stock forming this pattern, it's acceptable to enter the trade in the last 10 to 15 minutes of the trading day. Alternatively, you could wait until the next trading session to open your trade.

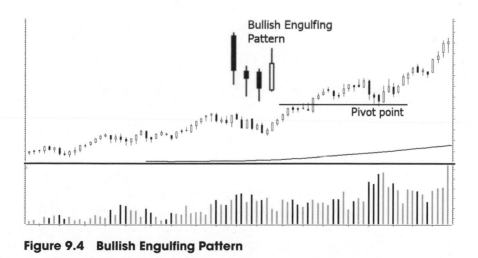

**Figure 9.4   Bullish Engulfing Pattern**

### *Hammer*

The hammer pattern develops at the bottom of a downtrend when the sellers continue their sell-off during the day but fail to hold it by the close. The long shadow below the candle body tells us how far the sellers took the price down before the buyers stepped in and forced them into a retreat. The hammer pattern does require confirmation. You need to wait until the day after the hammer pattern to verify that the buyers are going to continue pushing the stock back up. Also, the hammer pattern itself does not create a pivot point; it creates the apex of the "V." The pivot point is formed by the confirmation candle, which follows the hammer itself. Here are the key points of the hammer pattern:

- The stock is in a short-term downtrend, as shown by a series of lower highs and lower lows with black candle bodies.
- The hammer body is relatively small compared to previous day's candle bodies. The color of the body is not critical for the hammer.
- The lower shadow is at least 2 to 3 times as long as the body length. We tend to be a little cautious if the lower shadow is extremely long, however. For example, if the shadow is 10 times as long as the body, that tells us that the sellers were able to penetrate deeply into new low territory. We'd prefer to see a moderate testing but not a heavy sell-off, even though the buyers do push the price back up toward the end of the trading session.
- The top shadow should be no longer than the length of the candle body. It's also fine if there is no top shadow.

In Figure 9.5, we see an example of a hammer reversal during an uptrend. We've expanded the view on seven candles to highlight the setup and then the hammer with confirmation. The stock is clearly in an uptrend, with higher highs and higher lows. As the price crests one of the higher highs, we see the slight pullback in the expanded view. This is followed by the white hammer at point A in the large view. Remember that the hammer pattern does require confirmation, so we won't consider the reversal complete until we see the white day following the hammer. This tells us that the buyers are in control and we can enter a long trade after the following days' trading.

**Figure 9.5   Hammer Reversal Pattern**

### *Doji*

The doji is a single candle that represents indecision by the buyers and sellers. The interpretation of a doji is highly dependent on where it falls in relation to other types of candles. If a stock is printing a series of doji candles, that indicates that there is general indecision and it may not be resolved for quite some time. This is especially true if the volume is low. Indecision on low volume simply tells us that nobody is willing to commit to a direction and so the price just floats along. That type of stock does not offer good trading opportunities. However, if a stock is in a strong fall on heavy volume and then you see a doji immediately following a long black candle, that would be a strong sign that the sellers have lost the momentum. The doji always requires confirmation, since it signifies indecision rather than a change of direction. We want to see a confirmation of a new direction before we jump into the trade. The doji is very easy to identify:

- The open and close are the same price, or very nearly the same price. This creates a horizontal line in place of the body.
- The shadows create various styles of doji. A simple doji has a top and bottom shadow of approximately equal length. This creates the doji cross. The gravestone doji has no bottom shadow and a long top shadow. A dragonfly doji has no top shadow and a long bottom shadow. The four-price doji occurs

in the unique situation when the open, close, high, and low are all the same price. The four-price doji appears as simply a small dash.

Figure 9.6 is especially instructive because it gives us an example of a failed doji as well as a successful doji. Both of the doji candles appear within a short-term downtrend. Therefore, we would expect that a reversal signal would show us when the stock starts to rally. Doji 1 is noted on the chart as the first doji candle in the downtrend. Now, it would be tempting to look at doji 1 and reason that the stock should rally here because the three days prior to doji 1 all found support at about the same price. Notice how the low of each of the three previous days is approximately the same price as the low of doji 1. This is where our rules come into play.

The doji requires confirmation, so we wouldn't enter the long trade even though there are other factors that may tempt us. Our rules would have protected us from the long black candle that followed doji 1. Next, we see doji 2 appear after the long black candle. Follow the mind-set here: The stock had a support level that held for several days. This support was broken and the sellers pushed the price down and closed the stock very near the day's low. If the sellers still had control and momentum, we would expect to see more long black candles. Instead, we're given a doji, which tells us that

**Figure 9.6    Doji Reversal Pattern**

the fall was short-lived. Following our rules, we wait until the day after doji 2 before we enter the trade. The next day was a white day, indicating that the buyers had stepped back in, and it is there that we buy the stock. The second day after doji 2 might have rattled your nerves since it was a black candle, but don't lose sight of the fact that the stock still had a higher high and higher low. Doji 2 would have yielded a $2 move in four days if you waited for the proper confirmation. Jumping in too early on doji 1 would most likely have stopped you out at a loss.

### Piercing Line

Many of the reversal patterns that we look at have a counterpart for the opposite trend. The piercing line is a bullish reversal signal in a downtrend; the same type of pattern yields the dark cloud pattern at the top of an uptrend. The piercing line does not require confirmation like the doji and the hammer. Because the pattern itself is a strong show of buyer momentum, a long trade may be entered as soon as the pattern forms. The key points of the piercing line are as follows:

- The stock must be in an established short-term downtrend. A series of long red or black candles leading into the piercing line is especially strong. In any event, the day immediately preceding the piercing line must be a long black candle, indicating that the sellers are pushing the stock strongly downward.
- The piercing line is a green or white candle that opens below the low of the previous day. Ideally, the opening price of the piercing line candle will be below both the low and the close of the previous day. In order to create this scenario, the stock must gap down on the open of the piercing line day.
- The closing price of the piercing line candle must be between the previous day's open and body midpoint. This shows that the piercing line candle penetrates deeply into the previous day's trading range but doesn't fully engulf the previous candle. If the piercing line closed above the previous day's open, the pattern would be the bullish engulfing candle. It is best if the piercing line has little or no top shadow. We don't like to see a piercing line with a long top shadow because that tells us that the buyers were able to push the stock much higher but were repelled by the sellers.

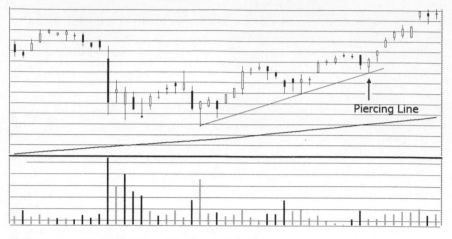

**Figure 9.7    Piercing Line Reversal Pattern**

Figure 9.7 shows an uptrend with the higher lows connected. Notice the long black candle as the stock pulls back to the trendline support just before the piercing line. On the piercing line day, the stock gapped down slightly, sold off to the trend line, and then rallied to close well within the previous day's body. There is a very small top shadow, which may very well have been some profit taking at the end of the day. A new long trade could be entered at the end of the piercing line day or during the next trading session.

## Bearish Pivot Point Patterns

As with buying patterns and signals, the selling patterns and signals are many and varied. Our goal is to find the signs that tell us that the sellers are once again in control of the trading. When we see the selling signals, we want to be sellers so as to put our money with the money flow. You will notice that some of the bearish pivot point patterns are simply the reverse of the bullish patterns.

- Bearish engulfing pattern
- Hanging man
- Shooting star
- Dark cloud

### Bearish Engulfing Pattern

Like its bullish counterpart, the bearish engulfing pattern is a strong, single-day indication of a reversal following a short-term uptrend.

The pattern is best used within a longer-term downtrend, when the stock is rallying toward resistance. The buyers push the stock higher for a few days but the momentum is halted by the bearish engulfing candle. We can recognize this pattern by following these points:

- The stock is in a short-term uptrend, characterized by green or white candles. The candle that immediately precedes the bearish engulfing candle must be a long white candle.
- The bearish engulfing candle must be a long black or red candle. This is our sign that the sellers have the upper hand.
- The bearish engulfing day must gap up at the open, so that the top of the bearish engulfing candle is above the previous day's close. Ideally, the gap will be higher than the previous day's high, so that the body engulfs the shadows as well as the previous body. While this is preferred, it is not required. Finally, the bearish engulfing candle must close below the previous day's open. Again, if the bearish engulfing day closes below the previous low, that's a bonus.

The first point to observe in Figure 9.8 is that both the trend line and the 200-day SMA (curved line) are trending down. Therefore, the overall trend is negative. The stock rallied from $29 to $32 just prior to the bearish engulfing day. This is the short-term uptrend that we want to see within the longer downtrend. As the stock reaches $32, it also bumps its head against the downtrend resistance

**Figure 9.8    Bearish Engulfing Reversal Pattern**

line. It is at this point that the bearish engulfing candle forms. The stock gaps up above the previous day's close, which also happens to be the high. The very small upper shadow tells us that the buyers pushed the stock marginally higher before the sellers came in and took control of the trading. While the bearish engulfing candle low is slightly higher than the previous low, the close is below the previous open. As we can see, the black body fully engulfs the prior white body. This pattern does not require confirmation, so you could enter a short trade at the close of the bearish engulfing day or during the following trading session.

### Hanging Man

We find it a bit funny that although many of the candle patterns have names that reflect their Japanese origin (doji, harami, marabozu, etc.), some of the patterns have less mystical origins. The hanging man falls into the latter category. With a small head and long body swinging from the top of an uptrend, the hanging man is a signal that the bears may be entering the arena once again. The hanging man definitely requires confirmation. Although the sellers pushed the stock lower during the trading day, the buyers stepped back in and brought the closing price closer to the open. For this reason, the hanging man signals indecision more than a reversal, so we need to see the sellers before we enter a short trade. The main points to look for with the hanging man are:

- The stock is in a short-term uptrend within a longer-term downtrend. Remember, we want the reversal to return to the prevailing trend.
- The body of the hanging man is relatively small compared to recent candle bodies. The color of the body isn't critical, although a red or black body does add strength to the sellers' movements.
- The top shadow should be smaller than the body length. It's also fine to have no top shadow at all. If there is no top shadow and the body is black, that means that the stock opened on the highest price of the day and only traded lower from there.
- The bottom shadow should be at least two to three times the length of the body. Once again, we're a little cautious if the bottom shadow is extremely long. There's not a hard

**Figure 9.9  Hanging Man Reversal Pattern**

definition for "extremely long" but, as U.S. Justice Potter Stewart said in 1964, "I know it when I see it." You, too, will develop the ability to know it when you see it.

The hanging man in Figure 9.9 occurs after a series of long white candles. Even though the overall trend is downward, as seen by the trend line connecting the lower highs, the stock is in a strong short-term rally. At the point noted in the chart, the black-body hanging man is formed. The hanging man appears right at the downtrend resistance line; this is a good reversal sign. The next day is a doji, so we don't actually get our confirmation until the second day following the hanging man. Here, we see a black candle dropping off the resistance line and that tells us that we can enter a short trade.

### Shooting Star

The shooting star has all of the characteristics of the hanging man, except that the long shadow occurs at the top instead of the bottom. We prefer the shooting star to the hanging man because it does a better job of showing the shift toward the sellers. With the shooting star, it is the buyers who make an attempt to continue the rally, but the sellers step in and push the close toward the low of the trading session. Most traders wait for confirmation with the shooting star; however, we don't mind entering a short trade on the shooting star if it forms against a key resistance level. The main points related to the shooting star are:

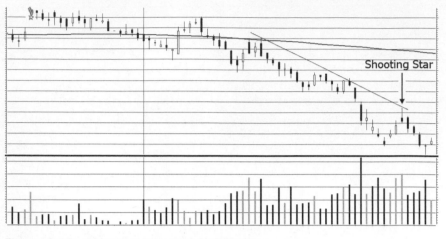

**Figure 9.10    Shooting Star Reversal Pattern**

- The stock must be in a short-term uptrend within a longer-term downtrend.
- The body must be small relative to recent candle bodies. If the body is black, that's an added bonus.
- The top shadow should be at least two to three times as long as the body. With the shooting star, we're not as concerned if the top shadow is relatively long. This tells us that the sellers pushed the stock down from much higher levels.
- The lower shadow should be nonexistent or at least less than the body length.

Figure 9.10 shows a classic shooting star pattern that formed against the downtrend line. Pay attention to how closely the top shadow ran up to the resistance line before the sellers started the retreat in price. We would be willing to enter the short trade at the open of the following day and use the resistance line to help us set our buy stop protection. If the price should rally back up through the downtrend resistance, it would be time to exit the trade.

### Dark Cloud

The dark cloud is the counterpart to the bullish piercing line pattern. Since the dark cloud penetrates deeply into the short-term uptrend, this pattern typically does not require confirmation.

## Chatter Box—Rick

The dark cloud is one of the first candlestick patterns that I learned to use and, as such, I overused it. In fact, I had programmed my trading software to identify the dark cloud pattern and back-tested the program to check its success. Sure enough, with the parameters I had set, this pattern formation yielded a high return with minimal drawdown. I was ready to battle the market. One of the first short positions I entered was on Dell Computer (ticker symbol: DELL) in the mid-1990s. Do I need to remind any of you what technology stocks were doing in the mid-1990s? My initial position quickly went out-of-the-money, so I shorted more. By the end of the day, I had an open short position with 6,000 shares, and the average cost basis was $8 out of the money. I went home that day with a $50,000 loss. The black dog visited me that night and I had almost no sleep. I tossed and turned and wondered how much my dog would fetch at auction.

I returned to the trading floor the next morning before the open and was met by grinning colleagues. It turned out that DELL was indicating a strong gap down at the open. I sat down at my trading terminal and watched the premarket activity. Just before the opening bell, my $50,000 loss position had turned into a $30,000 profit position. As soon as the market opened, I started selling at the market in 1,000-share blocks. The stock was so volatile that by the time I closed the entire position, I had made a net profit of less than $2,000. I thought surely there must be ways to make that kind of money without aging 10 years overnight.

The fatal flaws in my trading then were numerous, but I learned incredibly valuable lessons. First, I traded against the prevailing trend. A dark cloud in a raging bull market is nothing more than a breather—not an invitation to start short selling. Second, candlestick patterns are not infallible. You may have your favorite patterns, but sooner or later they will be completely wrong. That's when you need to tap out! Third, adding to a losing position just makes you a bigger loser. Don't do it!

Let's look at the factors that make up the dark cloud reversal pattern:

- The stock must be in a short-term uptrend within a longer-term downtrend.

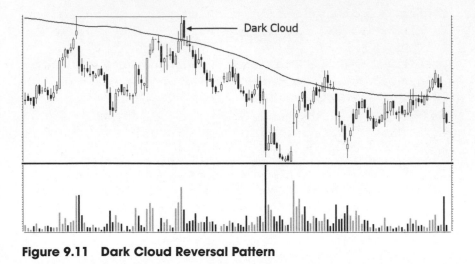

**Figure 9.11    Dark Cloud Reversal Pattern**

- The day before the dark cloud pattern must be a long white or green candle. This shows us that the buyers have strong momentum. It's even better if the several days prior to the dark cloud are long white candles.
- The dark cloud candle must gap up at the open. This gives us a candle body where the opening price of the dark cloud candle is higher than the previous day's close.
- The dark cloud's closing price must be above the previous day's open but below the previous day's midpoint. A small or nonexistent lower shadow just adds to the dark cloud's strength.

The dark cloud in Figure 9.11 is evident at the resistance line drawn on the chart. This is the same level from which the stock dropped in mid-October on the left side of the chart. Here, we see a short-term rally up to the resistance line. The stock gaps up on the dark cloud day and falls to form a long black candle. From the dark cloud to the subsequent low of the downtrend, the stock lost almost 50 percent of its value.

## Use the Market without Guilt

It's natural to try to find the secret that will allow you to buy when everyone else is selling. That crystal ball would be more than worth its weight in gold. Until you find it, the better suggestion for traders is to watch where the money is going and step in front of the flow as early as possible.

Your challenge is to learn to read the maneuvering of the market and then work that movement to your advantage. Like the jiu-jitsu fighter we described in the beginning of this chapter, you need to watch for the action that you can profit from. That's what the pivot point is designed to create for you. Have patience until the proper time, and you'll find success with less stress. In the end, isn't that what we're all after?

CHAPTER

# Essential Options, Part 1
## KNOWING YOUR OPTIONS

Even with all of the books and seminars that are available today, options remain one of the most misunderstood of all investment strategies in the financial world. Option trading can provide some of the best ways to leverage your money to make a profit without having to increase the risk to your portfolio. With that said, you would think everyone in the world would be an option trader. But the fact is that a large majority of investors have never even placed a single option trade. What is one of the reasons for this?

Fear.

Not only are options misunderstood, they are also the most feared. Human nature tells us to fear the unknown and for good reason. Imagine if we were to roam about the world without concern for our own safety. This would be foolish. Any traveler knows that you just don't enter into a foreign land without knowing where the danger areas are. Roaming about in such a manner would eventually get you into a dangerous situation. Therefore, it is a survival instinct, to be, at the very least, cautious of our surroundings.

One of the other reasons many people shy away from options is the misconception that they are extremely risky. As a result, those who have incorrectly traded options are left with an experience that was more like speculation or gambling. However, other investors feel that options are safe and are a great way to hedge a portfolio against risk similar to an insurance policy. This belief leads to a sense of security, making those who have traded them successfully feel that option strategies should be part of every investment portfolio. So how can the same asset cause people to have such opposite opinions? The reason is that options can be risky and speculative while at the same time be secure and prudent. This all depends on how you use them.

We see the same opinions in the credit markets. For those of you who have teenagers in the family, you know that a credit card can be a dangerous thing in the hands of a young adult who is unfamiliar with the dangers of going into debt. If you were to give the average college student a credit card in their own name, there is a good chance that student would run up the limit on that card within a 12-month period. This excessive spending could even wind up with that student's having to file bankruptcy to get out of this financial mess. On the other hand, you might have someone who just uses a credit card to take care of emergencies in the event they are traveling and run into a problem along the way. This person may also be inclined to pay off the balance of the credit card each month to ensure that the debt doesn't get out of hand.

When looking at this example, would you think credit cards are good or bad? Just like options, the answer depends on how you plan on using them. Back in the early 1970s, options were designed to reduce risk. Traders would use option contracts to hedge existing positions in a way that some people would use insurance policies. This, of course, would mean that for every person looking to use options to reduce risk there would be someone on the other side of the transaction willing to assume that risk. Using insurance as an example, you should already know that when you buy an insurance policy from an insurance company, the insurer is the party who is willing to assume the risk and you, the insured, in turn, pays that insurance company a premium to take risk from you. What's really interesting about options is that you may have one investor who may be using options to offset risk in a conservative way while at the same time you would have another investor who is speculating for profit by taking the other side of the trade. This relationship may be confusing if you are not familiar with options, and this confusion is another reason why many investors avoid trading options altogether.

It would be a mistake if you didn't make at least the smallest attempt to learn about options. Therefore, we have dedicated this chapter to the basic option concepts. In today's marketplace, options are the fastest-growing asset class in the world, and as our economies expand, you will see many more exchanges around the world offering options to their investors. As a result of this growth, you will also see many more trading opportunities open up, as new financial products come to the market. Options are by far the most important and powerful investment tool available to you, and they allow you to pick and choose the risks you decide to take or avoid. This is something that cannot be done with any other financial asset. Once you have finished this chapter, you might still decide not to trade options, but we must warn you that once you look beyond the basic ideas outlined in this chapter, and into the more intermediate to advanced ways of trading these little beauties, you may wind up wondering why you haven't been trading them already.

If this is the first time you have ever looked at an option, then understand you are in good hands. We are passionate about teaching option concepts, and you have come to the right place. Clear your mind, forget everything you have heard about them in the past, and let's start at the very beginning. Chances are, if you have heard about them through a friend or relative, you may have been misled in the way options work. It's amazing to see how even some of the skeptics have turned their way of thinking around after they have been to one of our option seminars. Sometimes you just need an idea or concept presented to you from a different angle for it to be clear in your mind. We will do our best to take this topic, as we usually do, in the famous Market Guy tradition of Keeping It Super Simple. So, with that, let's get started.

## What Is an Option?

There are two types of options: calls and puts. A *call option* gives the owner the right, not the obligation, to *buy* stock at a specific price over a given period of time. In other words, it gives you the right to "call" stock away from another person. A *put option*, conversely, gives the owner the right, not the obligation, to *sell* stock at a specific price through an expiration date. It gives you the right to "put" the stock back to the owner. Options only convey rights to buy or sell stock. If you own an option, you do not get any of the benefits that come with stock, such as dividends or voting privileges. Options are simply agreements between two people to buy and sell stock.

While options may sound like they would be used only by sophisticated investors, they are quite easy to understand and actually quite common in everyday life, although they are called by different names. In fact, we're sure that everyone reading this has used a call or put option at one time or another. If you still don't believe it, then just keep on reading. We're going to start with explaining calls first, and then we will move along to the puts.

## Call Options or Pizza Coupons

By now, you are thinking that there is no way you have ever used anything that would even resemble a call option, but think again:

A pizza coupon? Yes, this is actually just like a call option. Remember what we just said: A call gives the owner the right, not the obligation, to buy stock at a specified price. Well, isn't that what a pizza coupon does for you? In this case, the pizza coupon gives the holder the right to buy one large pizza. You wouldn't have an obligation to buy the pizza. If you weren't hungry, you would just hold on to the coupon for another day. When you finally do feel hungry, then, of course, you could walk into the restaurant and walk out with the pizza, as long as you were still holding on to your pizza coupon.

To help you get a better grasp on what a call is, just remember that the owner of a call has a right to call stock away from someone and take possession. If you run into difficulty later on when it's time for you to actually trade a call, be sure to remember the pizza coupon. Picture yourself making a "call" to your local pizza palace, then imagine yourself walking into the restaurant to take possession of the pizza. Finally, see yourself with a big smile on your face as the new owner of this wonderful, delicious pizza.

Now let's take a look at how a seller of an option contract would relate to the buyer of an option contract. Sellers of options don't have a right to do anything. In fact, they have an obligation to make a trade. The seller of call option has an obligation to deliver stock to you. One example that we could use is that the seller of a call option is like the pizza store owner who has an obligation to deliver a large pizza with two toppings should you present him with your pizza coupon. In other words, the pizza store owner is "short" the coupon and has an obligation to sell you the pizza should you ask him to.

Now, in the real world, the seller of the option receives money from the buyer of the option in exchange for accepting the obligation to deliver stock. This is not something that you would see with a pizza coupon because there is no real value attached to the coupon. Just remember that when you are selling an option, whether it is a call or a put, you have an obligation to make a trade.

### Chatter Box—AJ

Another real-life example of what a call might be is one that we would see in the real estate market. If you have ever gone to contract to buy a piece of property, you, the future owner, will pay the seller of the property a sum of money to lock in a sale price. This legal document that you sign is called a "contract," and it simply binds two parties to a sale that takes place at a specified time in the future at an agreed-upon price. In exchange for the money you have laid out for the contract, the seller of this contract obligates himself to deliver you the property on the closing date. This, too, is very similar to an option contract. I've had the opportunity to actually work out deals with real estate developers where I would buy an option on certain properties with the intent to close on the sale of these properties many months out in the future. These transactions have been some of my most profitable investments in real estate, and it was my experience in stock and commodity options that helped me to land those deals. So even if you decide not to trade stock options, this information can help you profit in other areas of investing.

Now let's get back to the pizza coupon in order to get a better understanding of the terminology we use as option traders.

In this coupon example, we would say the *underlying asset* is a pizza. Notice that we are limited to how many pizzas we can purchase; we are not able to purchase all the pizza we want. For stocks, the underlying asset for a call or a put represents 100 shares. There are times when the option contract would represent more than 100 shares for adjusted options, but for now let's just stick with 100 shares in our example. The value of an option, or the price we pay for the option, is derived from the underlying asset. This is the reason why options are considered to be one of many classes of *derivative* instruments. A derivative instrument is nothing more than a contract whose value is derived from another asset, whether it be a stock, commodity, bond, or currency.

If you take a look again at the coupon, you'll see that it includes a purchase price for the pizza. The benefit for you is that you have locked in a price of $7.99. Even if the price of pizzas around the world went up to $10, $15, $20, or more, you would still be able to buy your two-topping pizza for $7.99. If this were a call option, this stated price would be called the *strike price*. The strike price is the price at which the trade will be made should the option contract be exercised. The strike price is also known at the *exercise price*. The exercise price is determined at the time the option contract is formed. Also note that the coupon has on it an *expiration date*. You would be able to use this coupon, or exercise it, at any time up until the expiration date. After that, the coupon is worthless and no longer valid.

We hope this example simplifies the idea behind call options for you. Just like a call option, the coupon gives you the right to buy the pizza, not an obligation to buy a specific amount of the underlying asset for a fixed price over a given period of time, which is the exact definition of what a call option is. The main difference between a real call option and a pizza coupon is that you will have to pay money for a call option whereas you are given the coupon for free. The price you pay for the option, whether it is a call or a put, is called the *premium.*

All of this talk about pizza is making us hungry, but this coupon gives us the right to buy only one pizza. In the stock market, call options give the owner the right to buy a limited amount of stock. For most options, that amount is equal to 100 shares of the underlying stock. So, for instance, if you owned a call option on IBM, you would have the right to buy 100 shares of IBM stock. An important thing to remember is that option prices are quoted per share, so if you wanted to calculate what the total cost of that option is to you, you would take the option quote and multiply that by 100 shares, and that would give you the amount of money you would have to lay out for the trade. For instance, if you see that an option is priced at $2 (whether a call or a put), the total cost to you would be $2 × 100 shares = $200 plus commissions charged by your broker.

If you have ever looked at an option-trading screen, you have noticed that there are different strike prices listed for each stock that offers option contracts. This is the point at which most people start to feel the "pain in their brain" because now there are choices to make. Remember what we said at the beginning of this chapter about people fearing the things they don't understand. Well, if you are starting to feel your brain ache, don't worry, just relax and re-read what we have covered so far until you get it. It will absolutely be worth the time you spend learning this material because the time you spend trading options could be the most profitable. The reason options offer so many choices is that it allows the option trader a wider selection of premiums from which to pick. Calls and puts, combined with strike prices and premiums as well as expiration dates—oh, so many choices to pick from. Just take it one step at a time.

### Five Points to Remember

1. Options trade in units called contracts.
2. Each option contract controls 100 shares of stock.

3. To determine the total cost of an option, multiply the option quote by 100.
4. When you buy or sell an option, you are entering into a binding contract to buy or sell 100 shares of stock.
5. The strike price defines the agreed-upon trade price for the stock.

Options lock two parties to a particular trade, so what you are actually entering into is a binding contract. While this may sound like a tedious and time-consuming process, it's not. You can buy an option contract just as quickly as you can buy 100 shares of stock. Another point to remember about options is that they eventually *expire* because each option carries with it an *expiration date.* Just like in our pizza example, where you will see on the bottom of the coupon a date of expiration, the options also expire.

Another beautiful thing about options is that the option trader can choose from a variety of different expiration months, which allows you to buy and sell option contracts anytime, right up until the option expires. If, for example, you decide to buy a January option, whether a call or a put, the last day you will be able to trade this option will be on the third Friday of the expiration month that you are trading. In this case, it is the third Friday in the month of January. Technically, the option expires on the following Saturday, giving the Options Clearing Corporation (OCC) a chance to match up all of the buyers and the sellers, but you are most concerned about *Expiration Friday.* There is a misconception among traders who are new to the option markets in that they believe that once they have bought an option long or sold it short, they have to hold this position until the option expires. That is not correct; in fact, if you buy an option today, you can easily sell it on the same day.

This does not mean that we are encouraging you to day-trade options, even though you could. We are making sure you understand that the contract you get into is one that binds you to the other party who is making the trade with you, and at anytime you can cancel that contract by closing out of your option position.

### A Sample Option Quote

In Figure 10.1 you will see an example of an option quote screen that is also known as the *option chain.*

Stock: IBM        Last trade: $94.22        Expiration: January 2008

Calls                                        Puts

| Symbol | Tot. Volume | Last Price | Bid | Ask | Strike | Bid | Ask | Last Price | Tot. Volume | Symbol |
|--------|-------------|------------|-----|-----|--------|-----|-----|------------|-------------|--------|
| WIB AP | 4 | 17.30 | 17.10 | 17.30 | 80.00 | 0.95 | 1.05 | 1.05 | 2 | WIB MP |
| WIB AQ | 52 | 12.94 | 13.00 | 13.20 | 85.00 | 1.70 | 1.80 | 1.75 | 27 | WIB MQ |
| WIB AR | 127 | 9.40 | 9.30 | 9.50 | 90.00 | 2.90 | 3.00 | 2.85 | 4 | WIB MR |
| WIB AS | 30 | 6.40 | 6.20 | 6.40 | 95.00 | 4.70 | 4.90 | 4.50 | 25 | WIB MS |
| WIB AT | 274 | 3.90 | 3.90 | 4.00 | 100.00 | 7.50 | 7.70 | 7.60 | 21 | WIB MT |
| WIB AA | 86 | 2.15 | 2.20 | 2.30 | 105.00 | 11.20 | 11.40 | 11.00 | 0 | WIB MA |
| WIB AB | 11 | 1.20 | 1.20 | 1.25 | 110.00 | 15.80 | 16.00 | 15.50 | 1 | WIB MB |

**Figure 10.1    IBM Option Chain**

The call options are listed on the left, while the put options are listed on the right. The column in the middle of the calls and puts shows the strike price. This is the stated price per share in which IBM stock may be purchased (for a call) or sold (for a put) by the option holder upon exercise of the option contract. At the time these quotes were taken, IBM shares were trading $94.22, and the first strike price seen at the top of the list on the call side is the January 08 $80 calls. These are options that will expire on the third Friday in the month of January 2008.

This option chain reads very much like a Microsoft Excel spreadsheet. If you are reading this list from left to right, you will see that the first column shows the ticker symbol for each option in the chain, which is what's used to identify the option contract the way the ticker symbol would be used to identify the stock of a publicly traded company. The second column on the left displays the total volume traded in each option strike price for that particular day. The next column is the price of the last or most recent trade, followed by the *bid* and *ask* columns. Keep in mind that the bid column displays the price that is posted by buyers who are attempting to buy that particular option contract. So if you wanted to sell the January 80 calls *at the market*, then you would be selling to the buyer who is posting their *bid price* under the bid column, which in this case is 17.10. If you were looking to buy the January $80 calls at the market, you would have to buy those contracts at a price that's posted in the ask column. The *ask price* is the price where the sellers are willing to sell their option contracts.

If you are looking at options for the first time, it's important that you follow along in this section by referencing the option chain after each point is made to ensure that you are digesting this information at a comfortable pace. Otherwise, the information may seem overwhelming to you, and we don't want you to wind up in the group of people who are not trading options because it makes their brain ache.

---

### Chatter Box—AJ

I've found that one of the best ways to learn options is to try and teach it to someone who wants to learn how to trade them. Keep this chapter open on your lap and make an attempt to describe these ideas to your new student. Let your student know that you are just starting out and you'll need someone to work with. This method of "learning by teaching" will make you a better student because your student will ask questions, which forces you to find the answer if you can't come up with one right away. If you do not know the correct answer, go back to your book and look it up. This is a fun way to learn options. Having a partner helps start a dialogue that keeps you learning.

---

### Strike Prices

In our option chain you will see a column labeled "Strike." At the top of this column you will also see 80.00, which represents the agreed-upon price at which IBM will be traded should the option be exercised (Figure 10.2). It doesn't matter where IBM may be trading; the owner of this call option or "coupon" is locked into an $80 purchase price. Now this seems like a great deal since the stock is trading for $94.22, and it appears that if you bought the $80 call, you would be able to make an immediate profit of $14.22 (stock price of $94.22 minus the strike price of $80 = $14.22); however, what is the cost of

$80 is the price at which
IBM may be bought or sold ↘

| Symbol | Tot. Volume | Last Price | Bid | Ask | Strike | Bid | Ask | Last Price | Tot. Volume | Symbol |
|--------|-------------|------------|-------|-------|--------|-------|-------|------------|-------------|--------|
| WIB AP | 4 | 17.30 | 17.10 | 17.30 | 80.00 | 0.95 | 1.05 | 1.05 | 2 | WIB MP |
| WIB AQ | 52 | 12.94 | 13.00 | 13.20 | 85.00 | 1.70 | 1.80 | 1.75 | 27 | WIB MQ |
| WIB AR | 127 | 9.40 | 9.30 | 9.50 | 90.00 | 2.90 | 3.00 | 2.85 | 4 | WIB MR |
| WIB AS | 30 | 6.40 | 6.20 | 6.40 | 95.00 | 4.70 | 4.90 | 4.50 | 25 | WIB MS |
| WIB AT | 274 | 3.90 | 3.90 | 4.00 | 100.00 | 7.50 | 7.70 | 7.60 | 21 | WIB MT |
| WIB AA | 86 | 2.15 | 2.20 | 2.30 | 105.00 | 11.20 | 11.40 | 11.00 | 0 | WIB MA |
| WIB AB | 11 | 1.20 | 1.20 | 1.25 | 110.00 | 15.80 | 16.00 | 15.50 | 1 | WIB MB |

**Figure 10.2   Strike Prices for IBM—Note the $80 Strike**

the option? If you look at the ask column, you will see that the option would cost you $17.30. The big difference between option contracts and pizza coupons is that option contracts are not free.

Although you may be able to immediately make a profit of $14.22 as the owner of this call option, it will cost you $17.30 to buy it. The $14.22 profit built into the cost of this option is called *intrinsic value*. The amount over and above the intrinsic value is called *time premium* or *time value*. This is nothing more than the added premium you would pay for the life of the contract over and above the intrinsic value. The seller of this call option, who has an obligation to sell you IBM at $80, collects this time premium from you as soon as you buy the option contract from him. If we were looking at the pizza coupon again, you could say that the time premium is equivalent to any delivery charges that might be added to the cost of the pizza.

### Lower Strike Calls Are More Expensive

Take a look at the $85 strike price, which is displayed just below the $80 strike price, and you will see that the asking price for this option is $13.20, which is $4 less than the $80 call. Why? Well, there are many mathematical reasons why, but you now know enough about options to be able to figure this one out. Imagine that you walked into a pizza restaurant and found these two coupons lying on the counter (Figure 10.3). Which one would you choose? Both coupons offer the same pizza with the same expiration date at the bottom; the

**Figure 10.3  Comparing Two Coupons with Different Prices**

Lower strike price calls ———
cost more to purchase

| Symbol | Tot. Volume | Last Price | Bid | Ask | Strike | Bid | Ask | Last Price | Tot. Volume | Symbol |
|--------|-------------|-----------|------|------|--------|------|------|-----------|-------------|--------|
| WIB AP | 4 | 17.30 | 17.10 | 17.30 | 80.00 | 0.95 | 1.05 | 1.05 | 2 | WIB MP |
| WIB AQ | 52 | 12.94 | 13.00 | 13.20 | 85.00 | 1.70 | 1.80 | 1.75 | 27 | WIB MQ |
| WIB AR | 127 | 9.40 | 9.30 | 9.50 | 90.00 | 2.90 | 3.00 | 2.85 | 4 | WIB MR |
| WIB AS | 30 | 6.40 | 6.20 | 6.40 | 95.00 | 4.70 | 4.90 | 4.50 | 25 | WIB MS |
| WIB AT | 274 | 3.90 | 3.90 | 4.00 | 100.00 | 7.50 | 7.70 | 7.60 | 21 | WIB MT |
| WIB AA | 86 | 2.15 | 2.20 | 2.30 | 105.00 | 11.20 | 11.40 | 11.00 | 0 | WIB MA |
| WIB AB | 11 | 1.20 | 1.20 | 1.25 | 110.00 | 15.80 | 16.00 | 15.50 | 1 | WIB MB |

**Figure 10.4   Lower Strike Calls Cost More Than Higher Strike Price Calls**

only difference is that the coupon on the left allows you to buy the pizza for $3 less than the one on the right.

I'm sure you would select the coupon on the left because it has more intrinsic value, and the same thing occurs in the option markets. Traders see the value in paying less money for the same number of shares just like you saw value in picking up the coupon on the left, so as a result of this added value, traders will pay more money for this added value through an auction market. Look once again at the option chain and you will see that lower price strike prices on the call options are always priced higher than the higher strike prices (Figure 10.4).

By now, you are probably asking yourself why option traders would choose one call over another. Just remember that this chapter is just glancing over some basic option concepts, and to get into the core of option trading, we will have to write another book because there is that much information to cover. However, wait a few more pages and we will give you an outline of some of our favorite option strategies.

### Time Is Money

In Figure 10.5 you will see that the January 2009 calls are more expensive than the January 2008 calls seen in Figure 10.4. For example, the January 09 $85 calls are offered at $17.90, while the January 08 $85 calls are offered at $13.20. Why do the January 09 calls cost $4.70 more? Well, that's because the January 09 calls will expire a year later, giving the options more time to grow and increase in value. Since all of the other factors between these two options are the same, option traders are only bidding up the value of the additional time. However, why $4.70 more? One of the reasons has to do with interest rates. Remember, you are controlling 100 shares of a $94

Stock: IBM      Last trade: $94.22      Expiration: January 2009

Calls                                      Puts

| Symbol | Tot. Volume | Last Price | Bid | Ask | Strike | Bid | Ask | Last Price | Tot. Volume | Symbol |
|--------|-------------|-----------|-----|-----|--------|-----|-----|-----------|-------------|--------|
| VIB AP | 0 | 21.60 | 21.20 | 21.50 | 80.00 | 2.60 | 2.75 | 2.65 | 10 | VIB MP |
| VIB AQ | 0 | 17.90 | 17.60 | 17.90 | 85.00 | 3.60 | 3.90 | 3.60 | 29 | VIB MQ |
| VIB AR | 1 | 14.40 | 14.30 | 14.60 | 90.00 | 5.10 | 5.30 | 5.20 | 1 | VIB MR |
| VIB AS | 2 | 11.20 | 11.40 | 11.70 | 95.00 | 6.90 | 7.10 | 7.09 | 0 | VIB MS |
| VIB AT | 13 | 8.70 | 8.90 | 9.10 | 100.00 | 9.30 | 9.50 | 9.50 | 0 | VIB MT |
| VIB AA | 0 | 6.67 | 6.60 | 7.00 | 105.00 | 12.30 | 12.60 | 12.60 | 0 | VIB MA |
| VIB AB | 2 | 5.00 | 4.90 | 5.20 | 110.00 | 16.00 | 16.30 | 16.30 | 0 | VIB MB |

*This option series expires on the
3rd Friday in January 2009*

**Figure 10.5   More Time Means More Premium**

dollar stock for a fraction of the share price. So the cost to carry this position is much less than if you were to buy the shares outright.

For example: Owning 100 shares of a $94 stock will cost you $9,400 to carry this position for a year. Buying one call for $17.90 will cost you $1,790 ($17.09 × 100 shares per option contract = $1,790), which is a difference of $7,610. This money could be used to control more shares in another stock or could go to work in another option position. The point here is that there's value in your being able to control a stock such as IBM for a fraction of the cost. This, among other variables, is why we see the difference in price from one option month to the next.

### If You Buy a Call, You Are Not Required to Buy the Stock

It's important for you to understand that if you buy call options, you don't have to buy the stock or take delivery of the stock. You can buy and sell options in the open market just like you would buy and sell shares in the underlying stock. Even though owning the call allows you to buy stock at a certain price, most traders never exercise this right.

According to the Chicago Board Options Exchange (CBOE):

- *Approximately 10 percent of options are exercised,* which means the buyers of these options decided to go ahead and take a stock position by exercising their options (or using their coupon to collect their pizza).
- *Fifty to sixty percent of options positions are closed before expiration,* which is what we are referring to when we say you don't have

to buy the stock if you own calls. You can trade out of them before they expire.

- *The remaining (approximately 30 to 40 percent) are held to expiry.* This group includes those who are holding options that expire worthless.

### Exercise versus Assign

If you decide to use your "coupon," you must call up your broker and submit instructions to exercise your options. This is a simple process whereby you make a call to the institution that holds your trading account and tell the representative that you would like to use your call option to purchase stock. Throwing one more pizza analogy, it's like your calling up the restaurant telling them that you would like to have a pizza delivered and that you will be using your coupon. Instead, you would say "I would like to exercise my IBM January 80 call." Because the strike price is the price you pay if you exercise your option, it is also referred to as the exercise price. So if you hear the words *strike price* or *exercise price* they mean exactly the same thing. Once you've submitted your exercise instructions, you will receive 100 shares of stock in your account three business days later. This means that 100 shares of stock will be delivered for every call option held in your account. When the stock is delivered, a buy transaction will be entered, showing that you bought X number of shares at the strike price. In other words, if you are exercising one January $80 call, you will see a debit of $8,000 in your account. This represents 1 contract times 100 shares times $80 (strike price), which equals $8,000; at the same time, you will see 100 shares of IBM deposited to your account.

Now that you know how the person who owns the call option gets his shares of stock, you should know what happens to the person who has sold the call option contract. Remember that the person who has sold the option has the obligation to make the trade. In the case of the call option, the seller, also known as the *writer,* is now obligated to deliver the stock to your account. Once you have submitted your exercise instructions to your broker, an assignment notice goes out to the seller of the option. The short position holder or writer is said to be *assigned* on the call. Just to repeat what has already been said, the person who is long, or who owns the call, has a right to buy stock by exercising the option. On the other side of that, the person who is short the call has not rights but an obligation to deliver the shares to the owner of the option contract.

### Intrinsic Value Plus Time Value Equals Total Premium

We discussed earlier in our IBM example about the immediate benefit of the January $80 call when the stock was trading $94.22. If you were to exercise this call, you would have been able to immediately take a profit of $14.22. This profit is known as *intrinsic value.* Another way to describe an option contract that carries intrinsic value is to say that this option is *in-the-money.* In-the-money calls are options that have strike prices below the price at which the stock is trading. In Figure 10.6 you will see how the in-the-money options are listed on our option chain.

If you look at any of the in-the-money options highlighted in Figure 10.6, you will see that the ask price for each of these options are greater than the intrinsic value of each option. The January $80 call has intrinsic value of $14.22 yet is it offered at $17.30, the January $85 call has intrinsic value of $9.22 while offered at $13.22, and, finally, the January $90 call being in-the-money by $4.22 is offered at $9.50. This is because each option carries with it a time component. If today were options expiration day, the time value in each option would be zero and the options would be trading very close to intrinsic value. Because there is time left until expiration day, the options in our option chain will reflect this time value in the price of the option. If there is no intrinsic value in the option and there is still time left before the option expires, then the only value posted on the option screen will be reflecting time value alone. Options that have no intrinsic value are defined as being *out-of-the-money.* In Figure 10.7 you will see examples of calls that are showing premiums which only reflect time value.

Stock: IBM      Last trade: $94.22      Expiration: January 2008

Calls                                    Puts

| Symbol | Tot. Volume | Last Price | Bid | Ask | Strike | Bid | Ask | Last Price | Tot. Volume | Symbol |
|---|---|---|---|---|---|---|---|---|---|---|
| WIB AP | 4 | 17.30 | 17.10 | 17.30 | 80.00 | 0.95 | 1.05 | 1.05 | 2 | WIB MP |
| WIB AQ | 52 | 12.94 | 13.00 | 13.20 | 85.00 | 1.70 | 1.80 | 1.75 | 27 | WIB MQ |
| WIB AR | 127 | 9.40 | 9.30 | 9.50 | 90.00 | 2.90 | 3.00 | 2.85 | 4 | WIB MR |
| | | | | | 95.00 | 4.70 | 4.90 | 4.50 | 25 | WIB MS |
| | | | | | 100.00 | 7.50 | 7.70 | 7.60 | 21 | WIB MT |
| | | | | | 105.00 | 11.20 | 11.40 | 11.00 | 0 | WIB MA |
| | | | | | 110.00 | 15.80 | 16.00 | 15.50 | 1 | WIB MB |

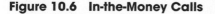

In-the-money calls have strike prices below the trading price

**Figure 10.6   In-the-Money Calls**

Stock: IBM       Last trade: $94.22        Expiration: January 2008

Calls                                              Puts

| Symbol | Tot. Volume | Last Price | Bid | Ask | Strike | Bid | Ask | Last Price | Tot. Volume | Symbol |
|--------|-------------|------------|-----|-----|--------|-----|-----|------------|-------------|--------|
|        |             |            |     |     | 80.00  | 0.95 | 1.05 | 1.05 | 2 | WIB MP |
|        |             |            |     |     | 85.00  | 1.70 | 1.80 | 1.75 | 27 | WIB MQ |
|        |             |            |     |     | 90.00  | 2.90 | 3.00 | 2.85 | 4 | WIB MR |
| WIB AS | 30 | 6.40 | 6.20 | 6.40 | 95.00 | | | | | |
| WIB AT | 274 | 3.90 | 3.90 | 4.00 | 100.00 | | | | | |
| WIB AA | 86 | 2.15 | 2.20 | 2.30 | 105.00 | | | | | |
| WIB AB | 11 | 1.20 | 1.20 | 1.25 | 110.00 | | | | | |

Out-of-the-money options have only time value in the premium

**Figure 10.7   Out-of-the-Money Options Include Only Time Value in the Premium**

### Time Premium Decays over Time

It is extremely important to know that this time value will decay on every option contract each and every day as we approach expiration day. There are some people who refuse to use options because of the fact that an option's price deteriorates over time. If you are one of those people, you are missing out on a very big piece of the equation. Your car loses value over time, doesn't it? The computer you use to trade with loses value. The fruits and vegetables that you eat deteriorate over time, too, yet these things still add value to your everyday life. Once you understand how to use options properly with regard to time decay, you will then see a whole new world of opportunity open up for you. So it really doesn't make sense to say that it's not worthwhile to invest in a decaying asset. You just have to make sure you are careful when you use them.

One of the biggest mistakes people make when first trading options is that they tend to buy the cheapest premiums on the board, thinking these are the best value options. Well, if this is something that you are considering, understand that these are the options that have no intrinsic value and the price you pay for these options is pure time value. Therefore, when you decide to buy such cheap options, you should know that you can't hold on to these for very long; otherwise, they will decay on you as quickly as a bunch of bananas sitting in a fruit bowl. Put them to use or you will wind up throwing them in the garbage. If you think about it, most assets that you buy depreciate over time. If you have ever owned a business where you had to buy equipment to run that business, you know that you have to get a return on that investment that is greater than the rate of depreciation. This is the same for options.

## Put Options

Now that we have covered some basic ideas of call options, we will now be able to move on the other option contracts we call puts. A *put* is a contract that gives the owner the right, but not an obligation, to sell a specified amount of stock at a set price (strike price) within a specified time. The general public usually finds it more difficult to understand the ideas behind put options, but, fortunately for you, most of the principles you've learned about the calls also hold true for puts. Things like strike price, expiration dates, and time decay are all the same, with one exception—puts work in the opposite direction. Maybe this is why the public is challenged in this area. They have to force themselves to think backwards. So in order to make this easier, let just say that put contracts are the insurance policies for the stock market.

Puts work very much like automobile insurance. With an auto policy, you pay a premium to the insurance company to cover your car for a fixed amount over a certain period of time. Most people buy car insurance from one calendar year to the next, and what you are doing is transferring risk from you to the insurance company. If you are a safe driver and you don't wreck your car, all you will have lost is the premium you paid for the policy. However, if you do wind up getting in an accident, your insurance company pays you an amount equal to what the value of the policy is. So, in a sense, you are a buyer of an automobile put, and the underlying asset that's covered is your car. Also, like an owner of a put you have to right to collect on your policy should you have a need to. You don't have an obligation to call up the insurance company but I'm sure you will anyway should you wreck your car. In the world of stock options you can look at it this way; should you own stock, and then buy a put on that stock, you are protected in the event you get into a "stock wreck" as a result of "market crash" (yes, pun intended).

Here is an example: You own IBM at $94 and you decide to buy a put with a strike price of $90; this guarantees that you will be able to sell your stock at $90 for as long as your put is in force, even if IBM goes to zero. If IBM goes to zero, you are still going to lose money, but it is not going to be a catastrophic loss. You own IBM at $94 and you will get to sell it at $90, therefore losing $4; plus, you will lose what you paid for the option. Well, isn't that just like automobile insurance? You might be driving around in a nice Mercedes that cost

Higher strike price puts
cost more to purchase

| Symbol | Tot. Volume | Last Price | Bid | Ask | Strike | Bid | Ask | Last Price | Tot. Volume | Symbol |
|---|---|---|---|---|---|---|---|---|---|---|
| WIB AP | 4 | 17.30 | 17.10 | 17.30 | 80.00 | 0.95 | 1.05 | 1.05 | 2 | WIB MP |
| WIB AQ | 52 | 12.94 | 13.00 | 13.20 | 85.00 | 1.70 | 1.80 | 1.75 | 27 | WIB MQ |
| WIB AR | 127 | 9.40 | 9.30 | 9.50 | 90.00 | 2.90 | 3.00 | 2.85 | 4 | WIB MR |
| WIB AS | 30 | 6.40 | 6.20 | 6.40 | 95.00 | 4.70 | 4.90 | 4.50 | 25 | WIB MS |
| WIB AT | 274 | 3.90 | 3.90 | 4.00 | 100.00 | 7.50 | 7.70 | 7.60 | 21 | WIB MT |
| WIB AA | 86 | 2.15 | 2.20 | 2.30 | 105.00 | 11.20 | 11.40 | 11.00 | 0 | WIB MA |
| WIB AB | 11 | 1.20 | 1.20 | 1.25 | 110.00 | 15.80 | 16.00 | 15.50 | 1 | WIB MB |

**Figure 10.8    Put Premium Increases with Strike Price**

you $94,000 but your insurance policy might pay out only $90,000 for the car, and on top of that you have to include what you paid for the insurance policy to begin with. Yes, you will have lost $4,000, but at least it wasn't a catastrophic loss. You can always buy more coverage next time so you don't lose on any other wrecks you might get into, but what would be the trade-off for a larger insurance policy? Yes, you would have to pay a higher premium to the insurance company. The same thing applies to put options. If you owned IBM at $94 per share and wanted to be guaranteed that you could sell those shares for $100 per share, you could do that. You would just have to pay a higher premium for the extra intrinsic value. The more coverage you want, the more money you have to lay out.

Take a look at Figure 10.8 and you will see the puts listed in the option chain. The strike price represents the locked-in sale price for the owner of the puts. See how the premium in the ask column goes up as the strike prices go up.

The cost of a put, like the call, has basically two parts to the premium. First is the intrinsic value, and second is the time value. The intrinsic value is what you would make as a profit should you exercise your option and collect on your policy. Anything left over from that is the time value, which, as discussed before, decays over time. This is the part that we like because, as you will see in the next chapter, this time premium actually works in our favor in a time premium collection strategy. Knowing how to buy an option is just one small piece of a much larger picture because if you understand how insurance policies work, you will know that the insurance companies make more money off of the policies they issue than the policyholders do when collecting on their claims.

### Obligations versus Rights for Puts

Selling puts places you in an obligation agreement that binds you to buy stock whenever the put owner wants to sell to you. In other words, you become the insurance company for the policyholder. This is an important point because if the stock drops in price, you will still have to buy the stock even if the stock goes to zero. Therefore, there is risk to you, the put seller. On the other hand, should the stock go up in price and not close below the strike price on expiration day, you still get to keep the premium that you collected when you first sold the put. We will be discussing some of the risks in selling options in the next chapter, so stay tuned for that.

### The Next Step

As we said earlier in this chapter, it's going to take time for you to fully understand the power of options and what they can do for you as a trader. There is a glossary of terms that you will find at the back of this book. Be sure to review these terms in order to become more familiar with the ideas behind these fantastic tools. Once you have memorized the definitions, it will be easier for you to pick up more educational material that will help you fine-tune your trading skills. With a little time and effort, your world will change as a result of your learning how to trade the option markets.

We will continue our introduction to options in the next chapter, where we start looking at how we can use them. Once we understand the basic definitions and concepts, we can start exploring which strategies to apply. Will we become hedgers or speculators? Should we collect premium or buy it? Do we use the coupon or the insurance? The world of trading really starts to open up when you realize that there is much more available to you than "Buy low and sell high."

CHAPTER

# Essential Options, Part 2

## KNOWING YOUR STRATEGIES

We have often said that learning option strategy is like learning a language. If you have ever attempted to speak a foreign language, you will know it starts off with one word at a time, a sentence at a time, then eventually you will learn how to speak in paragraphs. Before you know it, you will be able to have conversations with others who speak the language. With the exception of a few gifted individuals who have a knack for learning languages, most people will be able to become fluent in a few years, that is, of course, if the student submerges himself in the culture in which the language is spoken. Chapter 10 took you through some terms and concepts that will help you get started in the language option traders use most. This chapter will take you through some strategies that will help you maximize your profits. As with other trading strategies, it is always important to understand not only how the strategies work but also how to defend yourself in the event the market moves against you and the strategies do not work out as planned.

Before we get to the heart of our discussion regarding strategies, we will need to cover a few more terms that will help you get a better understanding of this new language. You will often hear option traders refer to option contracts as being in-the-money, at-the-money, and/or out-of-the-money. These are terms that are used to describe an option's "moneyness." An in-the-money option is one that has intrinsic value or, as discussed in Chapter 10, a call option is in-the-money when the option's strike price is below the price of the underlying security. Seasoned option traders will be able to quickly determine whether an option is in, at, or out of the money but for the beginner it will take some focus and practice before one is completely fluent. Figure 11.1 will help keep things easy for you. Just remember that an option will either have intrinsic value or not. So when expiration day comes along the option will be worth the intrinsic value or it will be worthless. Call options that have intrinsic value will be ones with strike prices below the price of the underlying stock. Options that have strike prices greater than or equal to the price of the underlying stock will have no intrinsic value attached. Below are some simple formulas that will help you with these definitions. You can copy this chart and put in a place near your computer so you can refer to it when needed.

Intrinsic value is just one of the parts that influence the price you might pay for an option. With intrinsic value options also carry with them premium known as *time value*. In general, in-the-money options will have a small time premium attach to them along with out-of-the money options. *At-the-money* options have the greatest amount of time premium associated with their strikes and over time, as you become more familiar with how time value works, you will see how time value can work either for or against you depending on what kind of option strategy you are using. Knowing how to quickly calculate the time value of an option will give you an advantage in being able to select the right option strategy for your portfolio.

One of the most important things you should know about time value is that time value decays from the premium of the option as you get closer to the expiration day for that particular option contract. If you are buying an option contract, whether it is a call or a put,

---

### For Call Options
**Stock Price > Strike Price = In-the-Money**
**Stock Price = Strike Price = At-the-Money**
**Stock Price < Strike Price = Out-of-the Money**

**Figure 11.1  Call Options Intrinsic Value Chart**

you need the stock to move in the direction that favors your option position otherwise you will lose money if the stock sits in a sideways trading range. One of the biggest mistakes novice option traders make when trading options is they have a tendency to reach for the cheapest options on the board thinking that these are the best valued options. In the world of options you should remember that you get what you pay for. If you are thinking about buying cheap options, then chances are you will wind up getting cheap performance. So if you are buying the front-month options, that are out-of-the-money, understand that the only thing left in the price of these options is time value.

This is why the front-month options cost so much less than the long-term options we call *LEAPS*. LEAPS is an acronym for long-term equity anticipation security. With more time until expiration, LEAPS have more life in them as compared to the front-month options. In turn, this gives the owner of the LEAPS more time in the market, which, in turn, gives them a greater chance to profit. The trade of for this luxury of time is simple: The more time you want to play in the market, the more premium you will have to pay. To help you with this idea, just think of an insurance policy—the longer the term, the higher the premium.

## On Expiration Day, the Option Must Be Worth at *Least* Intrinsic Value

Many people hear that all options expire worthless at expiration so let's put an end to this idea by saying this is definitely not true. It is only the time value of and option that becomes worthless. If there is any intrinsic value in the option it stays with that option.

For example, assume you own an option and today is expiration day for that option. In your position you hold a call with a strike price of $40 and the stock closes on expiration Friday at $45 per share.

You own one $40 call which gives you the right to buy 100 shares of the stock at $40 per share. If the stock closes that day at $45 per share that option is worth at least $500 at the close of the market on options expiration Friday. So the option is said to have $5 of intrinsic value.

You can also refer to the pizza coupon in Chapter 10 and see that if you had a pizza coupon that allowed you to buy a pizza for

$7.99 while the cost of pizzas around the world have now gone up to $12.99 your intrinsic value for this pizza coupon is now $5.

## Closing Your Option Position at Expiration

We said in the previous chapter that you are not required to ever buy the shares of stock if you own a call option, but you do have the right to do so. Most traders just take their profits by selling the contracts in the open market without ever buying the shares. Now that you know how to exercise your option contract and also understand how to calculate intrinsic values, we will now show you that there really isn't any difference between the two choices of either exercising your option or closing it in the open market at expiration.

Assume that that you buy a $40 call for $5 and, at expiration, the stock is trading for $50. You could call up your broker and tell them you want to exercise your call, which would require your having to pay $4,000 toward the purchase of the stock (remember each option contract represents 100 shares of stock). Then you could immediately sell 100 shares of stock at $50 per share and collect $5,000 on the transaction. This, of course, would leave you will a net profit of $500 because you originally paid $5 for the option (100 × $5 = $500) but collected a profit of $1,000, which was the difference between your sale price of $50 per-share times 100 shares less your buy price of $40 per share times 100 shares. Now, how would you do if you just sold your option without exercising it? With the stock trading $50 a share your $40 call would have an intrinsic value of $10 so if you sold it you would collect $1,000 (100 × $10 = $1,000), less the $500 you paid for the option, leaves you with a profit of $500. So you would have a gain whether you exercised your option and sold the stock in the open market or just sold the calls in the open market.

The big difference that you have to consider is what might happen after you have closed out your position. If the stock goes higher on the Monday after expiration Friday you may wish that you just exercised the option and held on to the long stock position. Then again, there is always the chance that the stock could drop after you exercise your call option. This is a matter of how much risk you want to take in the overall position. Just make sure the decision you make is in favor of the trend that exists in that stock at that particular point in time.

## Closing Your Option Prior to Expiration Friday

Okay, so there is no difference to us whether we close out of an option at expiration when compared to exercising it and selling the stock in the open market. What about if we wish to close out of the option position prior to expiration? Well, now, this does make a difference and sometimes it makes a big difference. Assume you that you buy a longer-term call option that has two months left before expiration and you purchased a $40 call for $7 when the stock was trading $45 per share. Let's also say that the stock is now trading for $47 a share.

If you decide to go ahead and exercise your $40 call you will again have to call up your broker and put in a request to exercise your option. Once you do this you will have to pay out $4,000 to buy 100 shares of the stock at $40 per share. You would then sell your stock at $47 per share and collect $4,700. The credit received for this transaction would be the difference between your sell price and the exercise price which is $4,700 minus $4,000 or a profit of $700. But don't forget you paid $7 for the option, which works out to be a cost of $700 (100 shares × $7 = $700). When you subtract the cost of the option from the profit on the trade you are left with a net profit of ZERO. When you exercise an option early, you forfeit the time premium and prematurely give it away to the person who sold you the option in the first place. Therefore, the majority of the time, you would not want to exercise your option when there is time value left in the premium.

Looking at the other scenario, we have the same position:

Long one $40 call with two months left until expiration. Your purchase price for the option was $7 when the stock was trading $45 per share. Now that the stock is trading $47 per share, the premium on that option has also gone up to $8.50. Should you close the position by selling the call in the open market you will be able to collect a credit of $850 (100 × $8.50 = $850). This credit of $850 less the $700 you paid for the option allows you to collect a net profit of $150. So you need to be careful before you decide to exercise your options. Carefully consider how much time value you would be giving up before you call up your broker to go through with you exercise instructions. The reason there is no difference between exercising a call at expiration when compared to selling it in the open market is because there is no time value left in the option. There is no time remaining on Expiration Friday, and the time value is therefore nothing. Prior to expiration, time value does count and there can be significant differences between the two choices.

As you become more familiar with options, you'll hear caveats to the "don't exercise early" rule such as only exercise early to capture a dividend. Exercising early may make sense, but it really only offsets some small losses. Most dividends are small and usually not our concern as traders of call options (unless it is a large, surprise dividend). But, for now, just understand that in the vast majority of cases, it is never to your advantage to exercise a call option early. If you wish to take profits, simply sell the call option in the open market. Now you see why the majority of contracts are just closed in the open market. Most traders never intend to buy the shares and just buy and sell the contracts by themselves.

## Let's Talk Volatility

Okay, we have talked about the basics of call options, and we've said that they are not that much different from pizza coupons other than the fact that options have value. So why do you suppose that pizza coupons have no value whereas call options do? Many are inclined to say that it's due to the prices and that stocks are far more expensive than options. That's partially true, but the bigger reason is because of the uncertainty of prices. You can be almost certain that the $7.99 pizza price will stay just about the same and as competitive the pizza market is, there is a good chance that the price of pizza may even fall. Because we are fairly certain about the prices we will pay for pizza next week, next month or even next year for pizza, there's no reason we would want to "lock in" the price of pizza. As a consequence, pizza coupons have no real value other than a slight discount off of the normal price of a pie.

Options, however, do carry value since stock prices can change so unpredictably. One day, the stock will be up and the next day it could be down 10 percent or more. We just never know what is going to happen to the price from one day to the next. Because of this uncertainty, traders and investors are very willing to pay for the right to lock in a price for the stock. Their goal is to avoid holding the stock and having to lay out large sums of money in the process. Stock prices that exhibit dramatic price ranges are considered to be more volatile than one that does not. While there are many ways to measure the *volatility* of a stock, just understand that the more volatile the stock's price, the more money people are willing to pay for an option. Therefore, a one-month, at-the-money option on a more volatile stock will be much more expensive than a one-month, at-the-money option on a less volatile stock. In the next section, we will talk about some easy-to-learn strategies that will help you profit from both sides of the market—the upside and downside—while at the same time considering how volatility comes into play.

## Long Calls

Let's start with one of the most basic option strategies: the long call position. We've shown that call options get more valuable as the stock price rises. For any given strike or "coupon" price you hold, the higher the price, the more someone will be willing to buy your coupon for and as a result they will bid a higher price in order to hold it.

Let's compare two traders, Trader A and Trader B, who are both looking to trade 1,000 shares of Wal-Mart (ticker symbol: WMT). Trader A will be using stock, while Trader B uses options. In Figure 11.2 you can see that Trader A has laid out $48,000 to buy 1,000 shares of Wal-Mart. Having this much money in this position means that it's possible to lose a significant amount should Wal-Mart shares crash.

Trader B can accomplish the same thing with less risk by buying 10 of the call options. Buying 10 option contracts for $3.50 will cost

Trader A:

Buys 1000 shares of Walmart at $48
for a $48,000 cash outlay

Trader B:
Buys 10 June 45 Calls for $3.50
and has a $3500 cash debit

(10 contracts x 100 shares/contract x $3.50 = $3500)

Commissions not included

**Figure 11.2   Long Stock vs. Long Calls**

a total of $3,500 plus commissions and no matter what happens to the price of Wal-Mart between now and June expiration, Trader B has a defined maximum loss potential of $3,500. Notice that Trader A does not have a defined loss potential even if he uses a stop loss order. Stop loss orders do not define maximum loss potential should the stock move against you. Trader A is now long 1,000 shares of WMT while Trader B owns 10 $45 calls. If Wal-Mart falls more than $3.50 per share or lower by expiration, Trader A is going to wish he had bought the calls instead. Trader A will continue to suffer losses for all prices below $44.50, whereas Trader B will no longer have to suffer a loss below the $3.50 paid for the option. You can only lose what you pay for an option and no more.

Now let's take a look at the stock to see what would happen if the stock were to rise. Let's assume that Wal-Mart rises and is now trading $55 per share (see Figure 11.3). Trader A paid $48 per share and sold it at $55 per share for a profit of $7,000 less commissions.

This $7-per-share gain works out to be a profit of 14.6 percent. However, with a $7 rise in the stock the June $45 calls now have intrinsic value of $10. Trader B paid $3.50 for the calls and can now sell them for at least $10 in the open market for a $6.50 gain, which works out to be a profit of 186 percent.

This is just one simple example of how a trader can get leverage in the market without having to lay out large sums of money to trade, and this example shows what can happen if the stock makes a big percentage move in price. The other thing to consider is that

---

Walmart is now trading at $55 per share

Trader A:

Owns 1000 shares with $48 cost basis
Profit is $7000 or 14.6%

Trader B:

Owns 10 June 45 Calls with $3.50 cost basis
Intrinsic value is $10
for a profit of $6500 or 186%

($10-$3.50 x 10 contracts x 100 shares/contract = $6500)

Commissions not included

**Figure 11.3  Stock vs. Option Profit when Wal-Mart Is $55**

when you buy options, you need the stock to move. We need speed for the option to be most effective and if the stock drops just below the strike price and closes there, the owner of the option will lose that amount paid for the option because at that point there will be no intrinsic value in the option and the calls will expire worthless. This is the trade-off when compared to trading a stock position. Shares of stock do not have expiration dates, so you will be able to hold on to the stock position long after the options have expired, and should the stock rally afterward, you could eventually get a return on your investment. So the lesson you need to learn here is to make sure you are buying calls that help you position yourself in the direction of the trend, and should the stock continue in an upward trend, the returns can be far better than if you had just purchased the shares alone.

## Long Puts

Let's now assume that you are bearish on Wal-Mart and you wish to short shares of the stock. For many people, the concept of shorting is still very unfamiliar. *Short selling* is simply a way for you to sell stock that you do not own in order to profit from a downturn in the stock. To do this, you would borrow stock from your broker with a promise to return those shares to them at a later date. Once you have borrowed the stock, you would then sell those shares in the open market with the intention of buying them back at a lower price. So the idea is to sell high and buy low, then keep the difference. However, should you sell the shares that you borrowed from your broker and the price of that stock goes up after you have taken the short position, you subject yourself to unlimited loss potential because there is no limit to how high a stock can go. Eventually, you will have to buy back the stock in order to repay your loan, and this unlimited loss potential is one of the reasons most people shy away from the short-selling strategy.

Buying puts allows you to take advantage of a downturn in the market without subjecting yourself to the unlimited loss potential. In Chapter 10, we discussed how puts act as insurance policies for the person who owns stock. But you don't have to own stock to buy puts; you can own an asset that acts like a short stock position. The terms we used for calls, with regard to the "moneyness" of the option, also apply for puts with one exception: Put premiums go up when the stock price goes down. Figure 11.4 will help you understand the difference between in-, at-, or out-of-the-money strike prices for puts.

The best thing about owning a put versus shorting the stock is that the most you can lose is the amount you paid for the put.

Let's revisit Traders A and B to see how they compare when trading the "short side" strategies. Trader A has decided to borrow 1,000 shares of Wal-Mart from his broker and sell them in the open market for $48 per share (Figure 11.5). Trader B has chosen to buy 10 June $50 puts for $2.50, which costs a total of $2,500 for the total option position plus the cost of commissions.

Both traders want the stock to drop to maximize their profit potential, but let's first look at the risk to the upside in both positions. Remember that Trader A has a loan to pay back, which is to deliver the shares he has borrowed from his broker, so should the stock go up by $10 per share, Trader A would have to buy back the stock at a

---

**For Put Options**

Stock Price < Strike Price = In-the-Money
Stock Price = Strike Price = At-the-Money
Stock Price > Strike Price = Out-of-the Money

**Figure 11.4   Put Options Intrinsic Value Chart**

---

Trader A:

Sells short 1000 shares of Walmart at $48
and receives a $48,000 credit

Trader B:

Buys 10 June 50 Puts for $2.50
and has a $2500 cash debit

(10 contracts x 100 shares/contract x $2.50 = $2500)

*Commissions not included*

**Figure 11.5   Short Stock versus Long Puts**

higher price than where he sold it in the first place. Trader A has to make a decision to either buy back the shares at $58 or not buy back the shares and continue to stay exposed to an unlimited risk position. For now, let's just say Trader A decides to get out of this position that's hurting him and takes the loss. Buying back 1,000 shares at $58 would create a loss of $10,000 ($58 − $48 × 1,000 shares = $10,000). After the shares are bought back, Trader A returns the shares back to his broker and is left with the loss in his account.

Trader B, however, has a different position to deal with. With a long put position that is totally paid for, Trader B is now long the 10 June $50 puts. With the stock trading at $58, these puts have no intrinsic value; however, if there is any time left before Expiration Friday, the June $50 puts may still have some time value left in them. The great thing about owning the put versus selling the stock short is that Trader A is completely out of his position with no chance to recover a profit, while Trader B still has a chance to make a profit even though the puts are worth less than the price he paid to open the position.

On the positive side, puts work very well to leverage buying power in that stocks have a tendency to drop faster than they rally. This has a lot to do with the emotional charge of the market. As mentioned in previous chapters, fear has a way of charging the market with volatility, and volatility is an option trader's best friend. If the stock were to drop to $40, this would allow Trader B to lock in $10 or intrinsic value. Owning the $50 puts gives Trader B the right to sell stock at $50, so once the trader buys the stock at $40, he can immediately sell those shares for $50. This $10 profit less the cost of the puts ($2.50) winds up giving Trader B a $7.50 profit which is close to a 300 percent return after commissions are paid out. It's not uncommon to see these types of returns in the option markets. Of course, you should not expect to profit on every single trade you make but the important thing to remember is that your downside risk is precalculated so you are more likely to stay consistent in your performance if you have mastered the stock selection process we have outlined for you.

## Cash-Secured Put Selling

The long put gives us the right to sell stock at a predetermined price, but one of our favorite strategies is to sell puts in stocks that show signs of good strong support or stocks that indicate upward trends with positive volume on the technical charts. Before you initiate a strategy such as this, it's important for you to understand that you would never consider selling puts in stocks that are breaking down below key support levels or in stocks that are in downward trends. Should you do this, you would be placing yourself in a high-risk position. You should approach a short put strategy in the same way an insurance company would approach a potential policy holder. Would an insurance company issue a life insurance policy on a person who was terminally ill? Or . . . would the insurance agent ever insure a driver who had a long history of drunk driving? Of course not—insurance companies hire actuaries, who make sure the companies they work for are not taking unnecessary risk. Unless the premiums were out of this world and over the top, insurance companies would go bankrupt if they made it a policy to insure only high-risk individuals, so why would you, the put seller, ever consider high-risk stocks?

The put-selling strategy we teach is one where you would sell puts only in stocks that you would consider owning. If you were willing to buy shares of Wal-Mart, you could obligate yourself to buy the stock at a given strike price and in return receive a premium for the risk you take. The strike price you sell is the agreed-upon price at which you would commit to purchase the shares. So the role you take in this example is that of the insurer. You would collect a premium for providing the put buyer with the peace of mind of knowing that if the stock drops, you will be there to limit their loss. However, you want the stock to stay flat or go up from that point. The last thing you want to happen is for the stock to crash. Similarly, the last thing the insurance company would want to have happen is for you to crash your car after they have insured you. Do people crash their cars from time to time? Yes, but the insurance company assumes this risk, betting that you will not crash your car. Therefore, they look to insure safe drivers who have a clean history of accident-free driving.

Stocks that show strong signs of support and ones that have good upward trends are the types of stocks you would want to insure. When you find stocks like this, you would put up enough cash in your account to secure the purchase of the shares; should you be "put" the stock—in other words, be asked to fulfill your obligation—the cash moves out of your money market fund and you buy the stock. As an insurer of stock price, it's also important for you to know where your breakeven point is for the stock. If the stock trades from

Shares of Walmart are trading at $48 per share
You sell the June 45 Puts and collect $1.50 premium

Your obligation is to buy the stock at $45
if it closes below $45 on expiration day.

If the stock is "Put" to you, your net
cost basis is $43.50

| | |
|---|---|
| Purchase price | ($45.00) |
| Less premium collected | $ 1.50 |
| Cost basis | ($43.50) |

*Commissions not included*

**Figure 11.6    Cash-Secured Put-Selling Example**

$48 per share down to $44 per share, you will still be able to make a profit because, although the stock is below the strike price, your cost basis is still below $44.

This is where your technical analysis skills will come into play. If you see that the stock has good, strong support around the $43 area, you might make a decision to hold on to this new long stock position because there is a chance that it could rally from this point. Your cost basis is $43.50 so even though the stock is trading at $44 you may still be able to squeak out a profit of $.50. However, if you see that the stock is not holding support, you would make a decision to close out of your position to minimize risk. Remember that you don't want to be buying stocks that are crashing. In this chapter we are just grazing over some of the basic strategies we use, and you will need to delve into more of the details surrounding these concepts to become more fluent in this put-selling strategy. The label we use to identify this strategy is *cash-secured put selling*. Figure 11.6 is an example of what this would look like in your trading account.

## The Covered Call

Most traders who are new to options will always hear about the covered call since it is considered to be a basic, safe strategy. Let's take a look at how it works.

Let's assume you own 300 shares of Wal-Mart at $45 (maybe you got assigned on a short put—hopefully, you're starting to see how you can combine option strategies to gain even more flexibility).

You're willing to hold the shares and are now waiting for it to rise. Rather than wait, you can sell a call against your shares. By selling a call, you have an obligation to sell shares if the long call holder decides to exercise his right to buy. You could sell three contracts of the July $50 calls at $2.75, which is a total credit of $300 \times \$2.75 = \$825$. Again, this cash is available for your immediate use to use however you wish.

You would just call your broker and say, "Sell to open, three contracts, of the Wal-Mart July $50 calls, at market." You would then be long 300 shares of stock and short three $50 calls.

If the stock rises above $50 at expiration, you would be required to sell for $50. If the stock stays still, you get to keep the $825, which is something that the long stock holder will never see. Notice that this credit provides a little downside protection, too. If the stock falls $2.75 below your cost basis, you're still at breakeven. The initial credit from the sale acts as a cushion against adverse stock price movements.

The reason this is called a "covered call" is that you already own shares of the underlying stock. In other words, the upside risk of a short call is already "covered" by the long shares of stock. You have no need to worry about being able to deliver the shares if the stock rises. Of course, you still have all of the downside risk that the long stock owner has, but you were willing to assume that anyway. What if you weren't willing to hold the shares but entered the covered call anyway? Now you're speculating with options, and it is then considered a risky position. The risk in options depends on how you are using them.

### Chatter Box—AJ

With over two and a half decades spent in the option markets, I have, for the most part, favored selling option premiums. I feel comfortable taking on the role of "the insurance company" for stock traders, but before you begin selling option premiums, please make it a point to understand all of your risk points. This includes your obligated buy or sell points, breakeven points, and strategies you would use to bail out of a risky situation should the stock price move against you.

While living in Florida, I've learned a great deal from insurance companies that insure homeowners during hurricane season. When the skies begin to darken and the seas start to swell, insurance companies will send out the alarm to all of their representatives to cease all activity with regard to accepting new insurance applications. Why do they do this? It's simple: There is a much greater chance that they will have to pay out claims as the storm heads for the coast. So they do this in an effort to eliminate additional risk should the storm hit.

A perfect example of this was when Hurricane Katrina came ripping through Florida. Rick and I were actually recording one of our radio shows when Katrina first hit the east coast of Florida. I was stuck in a hotel room in Palm Beach after finishing up a seminar, and we were talking about the possibility of this whopper of a storm regrouping in the Gulf of Mexico. While we had no idea this would be the deadliest storm in U.S. history, it just so happened that the topic of our discussion was risk management. We were using this storm as an analogy to describe what investors would do to limit risk in a financial storm. We have this show archived on the Internet where we mentioned that if Katrina strengthened in the Gulf, it would be a powerful one, and those who lived on the Gulf shores should run for cover. It's unfortunate that more people didn't listen to the warnings we put out, but our point is if you are insuring stock price, you had better heed the warnings when the financial storm front approaches. If you are ever in doubt about what to do when you're in a risky position, it is best to just close that position out and take the loss rather than to attempt to ride out the storm. I have seen too many people bury their heads in the sand when they get confused. This ostrich approach to trading is not a strategy at all and can wind up with only one outcome: big losses. Just be smart and use your common sense.

### Rick

It has been said that common sense is the least common sense of all. Unfortunately, many traders who are otherwise very smart and calculating individuals tend to ignore the warnings that the market gives them. Perhaps it really is the same mind-set that affects the beach dwellers in hurricane country. They figure that they've made it through the storms this far without taking a direct hit. They're lulled into a sense of invincibility that is broken only by the catastrophic loss. If AJ and I can get you to take away only one point in this discussion, it is this: Learn from those who have been through the storm and know its power. You can really profit from trading, but only when you give the market the respect it requires.

## Now You Have Options

The strategies we covered in this chapter are just a small fraction of what's available to you. You can even combine strategies to create risk/reward profiles that are better suited for your tastes—and that is something that cannot be done with stock alone.

Options were created as a way to buy and sell risk. If there is a risk you're willing to assume, you can now get paid to assume it. If there is a risk you don't want, you can pay someone to assume it for you. Once you understand that options are about reducing risk, you'll see that they are not meant to be risky at all. Of course, someone can speculate and bet lots of money just because they have a hunch that the stock will rise or fall. That person is a speculator. But you must realize that doesn't mean that the whole options market is comprised of speculators. These risk seekers may be buying or selling options to traders and investors who are using them to reduce the risk in their portfolios. The options market is the only forum that allows us to meet speculators and trade risk.

Not all option strategies are speculative; it all depends on how they are used. If you think you've found some interesting aspects to options trading, we encourage you to find out more. If not, there's no harm done and you can at least say you know more about them than when you started. Either way, you're a better investor or trader for taking the time to learn about this fascinating market!

# POINT IV

# THE 1% RULE
## Protect Your Position

# Managing Risk

## LEARNING TO LOSE MONEY THE RIGHT WAY

Is it reasonable to trade the markets and expect not to lose money? The answer is no, of course. So the challenge for any trader or investor is to know when to close a trade at a loss so that you can stay to trade another day. We refer to this as learning to lose the right way. The stunned looks on the faces of our audience still amuse us when we step before a new group at a financial conference and announce that our first goal is to teach the correct way to lose money. More than a few people reply that they already have that part of the game down pat, no more instruction needed. Joking aside, do you really know how to lose money in such a way that you can remain in the markets for the profits?

The Market Guys' approach to limiting losses is called the 1% Rule. In a nutshell, you shouldn't lose more than 1 percent of your trading account value on any given trade. Let's break the rule down a little before we move forward.

First, your trading account is not your net worth. We don't recommend actively trading with more than about 20 percent of your portfolio value. The rest of the 80 percent should be allocated according to your overall financial plan and may include such investments as cash, bonds, real estate, and dividend stocks or funds. To keep the numbers easy, let's assume that your entire portfolio is worth $500,000. In that case, your trading account should not be greater than $100,000.

Second, each and every trade is capped to a loss of 1 percent of the trading account. Your first trade in our example account should not lose more than 1 percent of $100,000, or $1,000. If you have two open positions, they each get $1,000 for a total possible loss of $2,000. Notice that we're not saying anything about the stock yet. The stock may fall 10 percent, but the corresponding loss in your account should not exceed $1,000. We'll explain how to tie these two concepts together later in the chapter.

Finally, there is nothing magical about 1 percent. It's a good number that we have found to work very well in practice. If you tend to be an active day trader, you might want to reduce the 1 percent to ½ percent. However, if you trade less often and tend to hold your trades for six months or longer, you would do well with a 2 percent limit. The point that we want to stress is that you shouldn't adjust it on the fly. If you're using the 1% Rule, then every trade should follow the rule.

## Is There Really Such Thing as a Safe Investment?

Certainly, some investments carry different types and degrees of risk, but you need to recognize that every financial venture includes risk. Even if you have insider information that would guarantee your returns, you assume the risk of getting a call from the attorney general about your trading patterns prior to the release of the news that propelled your stock.

In order to understand the bigger picture of risk in the markets, it's helpful to list the risks and see where we might encounter them. By reviewing the variety of ways that we may be impacted, you develop an appreciation of the inherent nature of financial risk and how to best manage these risks.

> *Market risk.* Market risk is the risk associated with falling stock prices when the market moves as a whole. This is the risk most familiar to traders because it captures the loss of value when the equity drops due to market forces. Market risk is generally associated with an entire market, asset class, or segment of the broad market. As the name implies, it is a risk to our position when the overall market forces conspire against us. The old saying about a rising tide lifting all boats is another way to describe market risk. In the same way, a falling tide tends to leave even the good boats stranded on the beach.

*Business risk.* The risk that is unique to the specific business that you're trading or investing in is known as the business risk. The overall market may be doing just fine, but you read in the press that your company just announced they're starting a new series of internal seminars entitled, "Keeping the Books the ENRON Way." This would likely create a business risk that would have a somewhat deleterious impact on the stock price.

*Credit risk.* The risk associated with bonds is commonly known as credit risk. This is the possibility of a default by the bond issuer where they are unable to pay interest or principle in a timely manner. Credit risk is higher with corporate bonds than with government bonds since corporate bonds are backed by the strength of the issuing company, whereas government bonds are backed by the taxing authority of the issuing municipality.

*Interest rate risk.* When a debt security such as a bond decreases in value as the interest rates rise, this is called interest rate risk. Bond values generally drop with a rise in interest rates, even though the bond will continue to pay its stated interest rate until maturity. For example, let's assume you buy a bond with a 6 percent coupon when the prevailing interest rate is 6 percent. You would most likely pay par, or the face value of the bond. However, if you wanted to buy a 6 percent coupon when the prevailing interest rate is 4 percent, you would pay a premium over par for the added value of a higher coupon. Likewise, if you bought this same bond at a premium and then interest rates rose to 10 percent, your coupon would be worth less and, therefore, you would have to discount your bond if you wanted to sell it. That is how interest rate risk affects a debt security investment.

*Currency risk.* Currency risk is the risk that comes from volatility in exchange rates between various currencies. Many companies that have extensive international business also have hedging programs to mitigate the impact of currency risk. This risk comes into play when you buy a company with substantial international exposure. However, it may also impact you directly when you trade on a foreign exchange and need to convert your currency for trading. This is also known as exchange rate risk. With the growth in forex trading, many individual traders are able to create their own currency hedges to protect against this type of risk.

*Country risk.* As we write this book, Venezuela's President Chavez is seeking to exert greater national control over the banks and industries within his country. He is quoted as telling one steelmaker, "I'll grab your company." As a result, the main index of the Caracas stock exchange fell almost 3 percent while Venezuela's currency, the bolivar, also fell about 3 percent. This type of country-specific volatility is known as country risk. It is usually political in nature, but the results are directly seen in investments that are exposed to the country's turmoil.

*Liquidity risk.* If you own an investment that is not readily turned into cash when you're ready to sell it, you are subject to liquidity risk. Hard assets such as real estate and vehicles are most susceptible to liquidity risk. However, stocks with very low volume or funds that aren't publicly traded also run into liquidity risk. If you buy 100,000 shares of a penny stock that trades only 5,000 shares per day on average, it will be very difficult for you to sell your position without driving down the stock price.

*Inflation risk.* Inflation risk is what you encounter when you have such a distrust of the markets that you invest only in your mattress fund. Every dollar you invest goes right into the sack under your mattress. Even in this case, your money isn't growing to keep up with inflation and, while your principal doesn't decrease, your buying power falls. It's easy to see how $50 that was stashed in a coffee can in 1950 isn't going to get you the same level of goods and services today as it did then.

*Regulatory risk.* Will Rogers is quoted as saying, "The only difference between death and taxes is that death doesn't get worse every time Congress meets." He was creatively describing what is known as regulatory risk. This is the unknown and unpredictable consequences of changing laws and regulations. Whether we're talking about long-term versus short-term capital gains, distribution requirements for retirement accounts, or corporate tax policy, the activities of our elected officials represent an undercurrent of risk in every financial venture.

## I'd Like to Buy a Vowel

Now that we've described the myriad ways in which your money can shrink beyond recognition, where does that leave us? Some readers at this point may be thinking that any trade or investment is simply a spin on their own personal Wheel of Fortune. "Since I can't control my financial destiny, I may as well spin for the new car!" they reason to themselves. Of course, there are many varied risks that we face, but it should rather leave us with the clear understanding that risk is ever present and that we shouldn't attempt to avoid risk. Risk is a factor that must be recognized and properly managed, not avoided entirely.

One of the problems with managing risk is our skewed perception of the risks that we face. In *Against the Gods: The Remarkable Story of Risk* (New York: John Wiley & Sons, 1996), Peter Bernstein relates this story:

> One winter night during one of the many German air raids on Moscow in World War II, a distinguished Soviet professor of statistics showed up in his local air-raid shelter. He had never appeared there before. "There are seven million people in Moscow," he used to say. "Why should I expect them to hit me?" His friends were astonished to see him and asked what had happened to change his mind. "Look," he explained, "there are seven million people in Moscow and one elephant. Last night they got the elephant."

We recently presented a seminar at the Chicago Board Options Exchange. Just prior to the start of the second day, one of the attendees was talking to his brother, who had purchased 200 out-of-the-money call contracts on Yahoo! (ticker symbol: YHOO). On this particular morning, rumors were rampant about a possible buyout of Yahoo! by Microsoft. The contracts that were purchased for mere pennies were now over $3 in-the-money. Absent a major news event such as this, it is quite likely that the contracts would have expired worthless. Now, our friend's brother was enjoying a profit of more than $60,000. The next time this trader picks up a load of cheap out-of-the-money options, how much confidence of making a profit do you think he'll display? Most likely, he will be thinking about this last trade and considering the possibility of doing it all over again, even though the likelihood is quite small.

On the other side of the trade, consider the trader who sold the contracts. Especially consider the scene if the trader sold them naked; that is, he didn't own shares of Yahoo! to deliver when the options were assigned to him. In effect, he is short the stock and has to come up with $60,000 cash to cover his exposed position. How likely do you think this same trader will be to sell uncovered calls again? Once again, the probability of losing money from selling the calls is very small. It is just as likely as our friend's brother making money by purchasing the same contracts. But his experience showed him that it can happen, and all future decisions will be clouded by that experience.

This is the contemporary market version of the *Port-Royal Logic,* published in 1662. Antoine Arnauld and Pierre Nicole noted that people overestimated the probability of being struck by lightning in a thunderstorm. Statistically, the odds of such an occurrence may be very low but the consequences are high and, therefore, add weight to the fears beyond the mere likelihood of occurrence. Furthermore, any experience with a lightning strike (having witnessed a strike, knowing an acquaintance that experienced a strike, etc.) only added to the fears. The underlying probability didn't change, but the *perception* is greatly influenced by these other factors. When we experience a "highly unlikely" market event, it's all but impossible not to take the event into account when we face future risk/reward decisions.

## Everyone Should Be Above Average

We've talked many times about the importance of having a trading plan that removes your emotion from the decision process and holds you accountable for your defined strategy. The biases we just discussed that we bring to our degree of confidence in trading and investing decisions are another reason for having a strict risk management plan. Some traders like to adjust their risk levels as their confidence in a trade rises or falls. As a rule, this will not serve your best interests. We offer this advice more from a practical standpoint than from an empirical study. We have watched traders take this approach, and it usually comes back to bite them.

As much as we'd all like to believe that we're different, there is also a fundamental misunderstanding of probability and statistics among the general population. There's a reason that college freshmen refer to this subject as "Probability and Sadistics." For most of us, we're not going to improve our lot by estimating probabilities in trading and investing decisions.

Perhaps the most famous evangelist on the subject of statistics-based decision making was W. Edwards Deming. Dr. Deming worked with Japan in the rebuilding of the post–World War II economy, teaching the principles of statistical quality improvement. In 1960, the emperor of Japan awarded him the Second Order Medal of the Sacred Treasure for his contributions. In 1982, he published his classic book, *Out of the Crisis* (Cambridge, MA: MIT Press), highlighting his approach to decision making through data analysis. Dr. Deming included the following two news articles that demonstrate how statistical misunderstanding can be our Achilles heel in making sound decisions. The first article, published in 1983, is from the *San Diego Union*. Author Bob Dvorchak writes:

> "In general, we have been blessed with above-average leadership," said Robert K. Murray, who is tabulating the responses of 970 historians questioned in the survey.

> "We've been remarkably lucky, considering the relatively haphazard way we select a president. Historians have determined that almost one out of every four has been great or near great, and over half are above average," said the professor of history at Pennsylvania State University.

It's important to note that "greatness" is defined as being in the top 25 percent. Should we not, therefore, expect that one in four would end up in the top 25 percent? What a travesty that one in four should be in the bottom 25 percent!

The next article was published in 1983 in the *Wisconsin State Journal* under the headline, "Half Still under Median":

> Despite the increase, union officials said, more than half the league's players earned less than the league-wide median of $75,000 a year.

Recognizing that the median, by definition, is the point that separates the top half from the bottom half, how do we resolve the problem stated above? Should we not be equally concerned about the fact that nobody makes more than the top-paid player? Nobody!

Let's take one more example to illustrate the disconnect between probability and expected outcome. The lottery is quite similar to the trader who speculates with very cheap options or penny stocks. In both cases, the cash outlay is very small and the likelihood of success is correspondingly small. Nevertheless, our judgment is clouded by visions of what we'll do when the 15-cent option is now trading with $5 of intrinsic value. One of the top lotteries in the United States is the Mega Millions game. This lottery requires the player to choose five numbers from 56 choices. On top of this, the player selects one Mega Millions number from a total of 46 choices. The jackpot is hit when all six numbers match the winning drawing. The Mega Millions site lists the odds of winning the jackpot at 1 in 175,711,536. Ask any player at the local convenience store what they think about their chances of winning and they'll always admit to an inflated possibility. "Someone has to win," they'll reason. However, their interests are not served by "someone" winning; their interests are served when they win. And the likelihood of someone's winning is much greater than the likelihood of their winning.

## Five Principles of Risk Management

There are myriad reasons to employ a solid risk management strategy. If you distill the reasons down to the simplest concept, it is the fact that risk management is the single most important key to success in the markets. Gamblers in Vegas make money from time to time. These runs are called streaks, and they occur in the markets, too. However, whether a streak is long or short, there will come a time when the markets zig at the very moment we think they will zag. When that moment arrives, our lifesaver will be our risk management plan. Here are five principles of The Market Guys' approach to managing risk:

1. Risk management moves you from emotion to discipline.
2. Risk management allows for more losses.
3. Risk management requires an understanding of technical analysis.
4. Risk management starts with stock selection.
5. Risk management is non-negotiable.

### 1. Risk Management Moves You from Emotion to Discipline

Have you received the message by now that our emotions don't treat us well when it comes to managing our money? Left to our own devices, we tend to do stupid things with our money. Granted, that's not the most technical presentation of the facts, but it is the truth. For that reason, when we develop a plan to manage trading risk, it is imperative that the plan be designed in such a way as to minimize our interference in the execution of the plan. Simply, we need to create a foolproof plan and recognize that it is ourselves that we're protecting against.

To illustrate this, we can look at a popular experimental economics game referred to as the "Ultimatum Game." In the Ultimatum Game, two players are given the opportunity to divide a sum of money, and there is no reciprocation. That is, each player only has to make one decision and the game is over. To start, player A is told to divide an amount, say $10, between player A and player B. The split can be any ratio, with one exception: Player A cannot keep the entire amount. The worst case split for player B is that player A will choose to keep $9 and give $1 to player B. The next step is for player B to decide whether to accept or reject player A's offer. If player B accepts the offer, then both players get the amount of money set forth in the offer. If player B chooses to reject the offer, then both players walk away empty-handed. Here's the key question: When is it advantageous for player B to reject an offer? The answer, of course, is never! In the worst-case scenario, if player B accepts the offer, he will still receive $1 that he otherwise wouldn't have. However, experimental results show that offers of less than 20 percent ($2 in our example) are often rejected. Subsequent investigation reveals that there is an element of "fairness" that's considered by player B, and if the offer is perceived as "unfair," then the offer is rejected. Player B would choose the defense of perceived fairness rather than improve his financial condition if they appear to be mutually exclusive choices.

Before you think that you're the exceptional trader who can overcome this propensity through sheer determination, consider this: A research study scanned the brains of Ultimatum Game players as they responded to fair and unfair proposals. The results were published in a 2003 article in *Science* magazine entitled "The Neural Basis of Economic Decision-Making in the Ultimatum Game." It was shown that unfair offers elicited activity in brain areas related to emotion, which suggests an important role for emotions in decision making. The conclusion for the trader is that we have to recognize that our emotions are an integral part of our financial decision making and then take the necessary steps to ensure that we don't harm ourselves in the process. Of all professions, the trader must take care to address this point since financial decisions are made every trading day.

### 2. Risk Management Allows for More Losses

It doesn't make any difference how well you trade if you get kicked out of the game. You may trade for profits for years, and one moment of careless trading without proper risk management may wipe out your accumulated profits. Managing risk in a systematic and disciplined way will let you take more losses without a catastrophic loss. In the next section, we provide the steps for applying the 1% Rule to your trading. For now, consider the trader who loses only 1 percent of his trading account each time he has a losing trade. The sequence of losses and account balance would look like the one shown in Table 12.1.

**Table 12.1   Sequence of 1 Percent Losses**

| Trade | Loss | Account Balance |
|-------|------|-----------------|
|       |      | $100,000 |
| 1 | $1,000 | $ 99,000 |
| 2 | $ 990 | $ 98,010 |
| 3 | $ 980 | $ 97,030 |
| 4 | $ 970 | $ 96,060 |
| 5 | $ 961 | $ 95,099 |
| 6 | $ 951 | $ 94,148 |
| 7 | $ 941 | $ 93,207 |
| 8 | $ 932 | $ 92,274 |
| 9 | $ 923 | $ 91,352 |
| 10 | $ 914 | $ 90,438 |
| 11 | $ 904 | $ 89,534 |
| 12 | $ 895 | $ 88,638 |
| 13 | $ 886 | $ 87,752 |
| 14 | $ 878 | $ 86,875 |
| 15 | $ 869 | $ 86,006 |
| 16 | $ 860 | $ 85,146 |
| 17 | $ 851 | $ 84,294 |
| 18 | $ 843 | $ 83,451 |
| 19 | $ 835 | $ 82,617 |
| 20 | $ 826 | $ 81,791 |

Notice how this trader could start with a $100,000 account and then have 20 losses in a row. After the twentieth loss, he would still have almost $82,000 in his trading account. This highlights how a good risk management plan allows you to take more losses and still remain in the markets.

An analysis of how well we tend to accept losses was developed by Daniel Kahneman and Amos Tversky, in their landmark research into Prospect Theory. The short description of Prospect Theory is that people are much more willing to gamble with losses than with profits. This concept is actually quite familiar to traders because we are quick to lock in a profit while allowing losses to continue, in the hope that our patience will be rewarded by a rebound in the stock price. Gambling with a loss is known as *loss aversion:* the tendency for people to strongly prefer avoiding losses over acquiring gains. Conversely, when we quickly lock in our profits, we're exercising *risk aversion:* we shun any risk when we have a profit in hand. Some studies suggest that losses are as much as twice as psychologically powerful as gains. This phenomenon serves to dramatically increase the level of risk that a trader will accept with a losing position. We don't want to accept the negative emotions that come with a loss and will go to great lengths to avoid a loss. However, many times, the losses are not avoided but rather deferred. When we practice loss aversion and watch the unrealized losses continue to grow, we'll eventually reach a point where even the unrealized loss becomes untenable and the position is closed.

In the markets, the movement that occurs when masses of traders finally realize a loss that has become unbearable is known as capitulation selling. The rapid downward drop in price with a corresponding spike in volume is often the result of emotional decision making rather than a thoughtful, well-executed risk management plan.

### 3. Risk Management Requires an Understanding of Technical Analysis

If you buy a stock, you make money when the stock price goes up. That sounds like we're stating the obvious, but many traders will talk about the company management, sales forecasts, and market caps while ignoring the basic fact that their stock is falling. Technical analysis will tell you what's happening with the stock price, regardless of what may be transpiring within the company fundamentals. The market really does tend to price in the various news and information that circulates on a company. By focusing on the technical analysis, we see what people are doing rather than just what they're saying. We've all seen the stock that fell after the analyst upgrade. Only through the chart analysis will we see that the highs are falling on increasing volume in spite of the good news that the financial shows may be feeding us.

If you tend to resist the whole study of technical analysis, as many skeptical first-time traders and investors do, then think about it another way. You don't need to discard your fundamental research when you begin to use technical analysis. Think about fundamental analysis as showing you what to buy or sell and technical analysis as showing you when to buy or sell.

The alternative danger for the trader is in assigning too much confidence in the predictive power of technical indicators. This is often followed by a relaxing of the rules of risk management. The logic used is expressed in such phrases as "I can afford to keep this position open even though it is moving against me because the (fill in your favorite technical indicator) indicates that the stock will recover." Many very well-intentioned traders spend countless hours searching for the market equivalent of String Theory: the perfect algorithm that will allow them to predict future price movement. The well-known lesson of Long-Term Capital Management is that the best minds and tools must still employ a rigorous risk management discipline. The economist John Maynard Keynes is said to have warned investors that although markets do tend toward rational positions in the long run, "the market can stay irrational longer than you can stay solvent." The power of technical tools is most fully realized when you understand the inherent limitations of any technical analysis.

The rule of thumb for the trader is this: Use technical indicators in the same way that a drunk uses a lamppost—for support, not illumination.

### 4. Risk Management Starts with Stock Selection

Within this book we've devoted an entire chapter to the techniques of stock screening and selection. A key reason for spending so much time on the subject is that it is a large factor in mitigating risk. You may be familiar with the assertion that one could randomly pick stocks and still make money with a proper money management plan. While we agree that the position management is a crucial component, we also recognize that it certainly helps to stack the odds in your favor. It's a simple fact of the markets that momentum will tend to continue until forces create a reversal. This is a basic tenet of Dow Theory. With that being the case, wouldn't you rather buy a stock in an uptrend than a downtrend?

Think about this concept another way. There are probably more than a few of you who have looked at your trading history and thought, "If I'd only bought when I sold and sold when I bought, I'd be making loads of money by now!" We've observed that this is often the result of the never-ending pursuit of the reversal. You watch a stock drop and think that you'll pick the bottom and profit from the following bounce. Instead, the stock continues on its free-fall because it is in a downtrend and money is moving out of the stock. Stock selection is the discipline of choosing stocks based on their adherence to your trading strategy, rather than a roll-of-the-dice emotional guess.

### 5. Risk Management Is Non-negotiable

Do you have any non-negotiables in your life? We would certainly hope that you do. The non-negotiables are those issues, beliefs, and actions that are not subject to the whims of circumstance. You hold those items inviolable regardless of what may happen around you. Risk management should be one of the trader's non-negotiables. It's just too easy to come up with creative reasons why this particular trade is different from the many trades you've done before. Just about the time you negotiate with yourself and allow yourself a pass on strictly managing the losses, you find that you're in too deep. The relaxing of the rules that started innocently enough now threatens your ability to continue trading.

## Chatter Box—Rick

I remember when I was a rookie pilot and I flew my private plane to the west coast of Florida to pick up a friend who was visiting for the week. It was a sunny day, as is usually the case in central Florida, and the flying was terrific. Everything went smoothly as I passed south of Tampa and followed the coastline down to my destination. In no time,

*(Continued)*

I had reached the airport and was coming in on final approach. As I descended toward the airfield, I trimmed the plane for landing. This involves setting the control surfaces of the aileron so that the plane angles downward without as much effort on the controls. I landed the plane safely and taxied toward the office, where my friend was waiting.

After a brief stop in the office, we loaded his bags and taxied back out to the runway for take-off. I brought the plane around to the end of the runway, applied power, and started my take-off roll. The runway faced directly toward the Gulf of Mexico to take advantage of the headwinds, which assist in lifting the plane during take-off. Just as I reached the speed at which I needed to lift off, I pulled back on the controls and felt a heavy resistance. The plane was actually fighting me as I attempted to lift it into the air and we were racing toward the open water. In an instant, I realized that I still had the plane trimmed for landing. Still pulling back on the controls, I reached down and spun the trim back into the take-off position as we climbed out over the water and started our trip home.

With flying, the take-off and landing checklists are considered non-negotiables. Had I followed the procedures that I full well knew I should have followed, there would not have been any problem. Instead, I acted too quickly without making sure I was following my risk management plan and I left myself open to trouble. The same thing happens every day in the financial markets. Traders start to think they know the routine by heart, and they ignore the rules that brought them to where they are. Or a trader will think that somehow this particular trade is unique and should be treated with a little more flexibility. Folks, the bottom line is simple: Risk management is a non-negotiable part of your trading plan.

## Risk Management Action Steps

The best theory in the world is just theory until you can figure out how to apply it to real life. This is where the rubber meets the road in managing risk. Now that you've determined to limit your losses, what do you do tomorrow when the next trade shows up on your screen? This list of risk management action steps can be copied to a note card and taped to the side of your trading monitor. The next time you're ready to trade, check off the steps in this list:

1. Identify the market and sector trends.
2. Identify stocks within the trends.
3. Identify your entry price.
4. Identify your stop price.
5. Calculate your position size using the 1% Rule.
6. Execute your opening trade and stop order.

### 1. Identify the Market and Sector Trends

The first step in managing risk is to be aware of the environment in which you're trading. You have to know what's happening in the market and sector that you're using as your candidate pool. We just mentioned in the previous section that a key point of risk management is that it begins with stock selection. As part of the selection process, it's important to know what market or sector forces are at work.

If you're trading the U.S. markets, your first course of action should be to chart the Dow, the Nasdaq, and the S&P 500. These will not always move in tandem, although they do often display bullish and bearish sentiment together. The simplest way to get a feel for the broad markets is to plot the ETFs on a simple line chart. The Dow, Nasdaq, and S&P 500 exchange-traded funds (ETFs) are DIA, QQQQ, and SPY, respectively. Don't get too caught up in the detailed technical indicators at this stage. If you start at this step with a market chart covered with fast and slow stochastics, moving average convergence divergence (MACD) and Fibonacci retracements, then you're probably already overcomplicating the analysis. The danger when you do that is you lose a sense for the market direction and get lost in the market noise. Remember, we want to see where the forest is here, not count how many oak trees the forest contains.

After putting your finger on the pulse of the broad market, drill down to individual sectors that you're considering. If you don't have any specific sectors in mind, then you can screen for rising or falling sectors. For example, if you search for sector ETFs that have rising 20-day and 50-day moving averages, the result will include sectors that are in a short- to intermediate-term uptrend. Many basic web sites include a top 10–style list of ETF performance. These lists will often display the ETFs with the best returns for the year, for example. It stands to reason that the ETFs on this list would be trending upward.

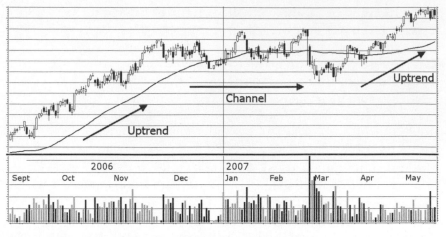

**Figure 12.1   Identifying the Broad Market Trends**

Figure 12.1 shows the Dow Jones Industrial Average ETF (ticker symbol: DIA) from September 2006 through May 2007. While the chart is a simple candlestick chart with one intermediate-term moving average along with volume, it does a very good job of pointing out the intermediate trends within this broad market. At a glance, we can identify the three trends; the initial uptrend that carried forward from early 2006, the channel from November through March and then the uptrend into May. We don't need some complicated analysis that includes the inverted Christmas tree oscillator to tell us the general direction of the market here. (Please don't spend too much time trying to find out about the inverted Christmas tree oscillator!)

### 2. Identify Stocks within the Trends

Once you have determined the current direction of the market and the sectors you wish to trade, now it is time to find specific stock candidates. Pay attention to the fact that we state, "determined the current direction." This is a much different analysis than "determined where the market is going." Remember that we don't need to predict the future or develop an opinion about where the market might be in six months. Our responsibility lies in determining what forces are at work in the market today.

At this point, you have several choices in finding trade candidates. You could begin by trading the broad market directly through the index ETF. You could also trade the sector ETF directly if you've found a sector that is trending according to your strategy. For example, if you charted the biotech sector (ticker symbol: BBH) and found that it was in a steady uptrend with good support levels then you may decide to trade BBH directly. Finally, you could select specific stocks within the sector. To find these stocks, you need only find a list of the stocks that make up the ETF in question. Some research sites list only the top holdings within the ETF; others will include the entire list of stocks within the ETF.

After obtaining a list of the stocks that comprise the ETF, the next step is to scan the stock charts in the same way we scanned the market charts in Step 1. The objective is to sort out the stocks that are not following the trend we're after. If the market is trending upward and the sector is trending upward, we naturally want to identify those stocks that are also trending upward. There will almost certainly be individual underperformers within the list and the chart scan will reveal these to you.

### 3. Identify Your Entry Price

Now we're ready to take aim at our stock and decide on our point of entry. Figure 12.2 highlights three possible entry points in the DIA if we had decided to trade the Dow Jones Industrial Average directly. These points are not the only possible entry points; we've selected

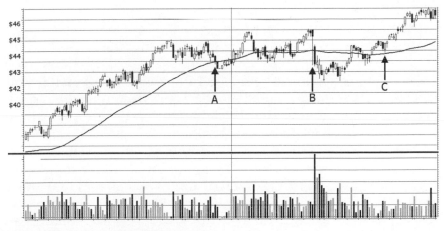

**Figure 12.2   Possible Entry Points**

them to illustrate some key considerations regarding position entry. At point A, the stock is in an uptrend and settling on support. However, the reason we wouldn't enter at point A is that the sellers are in control as evidenced by the black candle. The following day saw the stock move below the support line for the first time in the chart window. That should give us pause since it tells us that the buyers are not holding the support with the same strength as previously.

Point B is our next choice for entry. At first blush, this appears to be showing strength since the sellers had pushed the stock below support only to be overcome by the buyers. At the end of the day, the stock had rallied back above support on strong volume. However, the sell-off occurred at a level that had been resistance just a few weeks before in early January. When we see the sellers show that kind of strength at a key resistance level, we should wait for confirmation before entering a new trade. Our caution would have paid off as the next day saw a continuation of the selling below the moving average support line.

Our third choice is point C, where we see a white candle resting on support. Notice that this occurs after the stock had rallied above support and then pulled back to test the moving average again. Furthermore, the stock closed very near its high for the day on fairly strong volume. It appears that point C has several positive factors that would let us buy this stock on the open of the following day. Based on the chart, our entry price would likely have been around $44.50.

### 4. Identify Your Stop Price

Now we need to answer the key question, "Where am I going to get out of this trade if I'm wrong?" If you don't answer this question right up front, you will find yourself in the middle of a mind game, coming up with creative excuses for continuing to hold a losing trade. The simple rule that you should follow is this: Failure of the reason you entered the trade should be the reason you exit the trade. In our example, we bought the stock at point C because it was showing strength above the support line. Therefore, we need to sell the stock when it shows weakness below the support line.

If we look at the moving average support in Figure 12.2, it looks like the line is near the $44 mark. But we don't want to place our stop on this line. Why not? By definition, support is the level at which the buyers overcome the sellers and the stock rises again. If we place the stop order on support, that doesn't indicate anything other than normal, expected movement in the stock. We really won't know that we're wrong unless the stock drops below the support line. At that point, we can see that the sellers are pushing the buyers down to new lows and that's when we need to exit.

A key question for many beginning traders is, "How far below support should the stop be placed?" While there really isn't a reliable way to quantify that distance, it's encouraging to know that your eye will do a pretty good job with estimating. When you look at how the stock responds to the support line in the recent chart history, pay attention to the list below:

- Does the stock drop right to support before bouncing?
- Does the stock penetrate the support during the day before closing above support?
- Does the stock have a tendency to swing sharply below support and rally above shortly afterward?
- Does volatility tend to increase (longer candle bodies) or decrease (smaller candle bodies) as it approaches support?
- Has the support held for a long time, or is it newly established?

The answers to these questions will allow you to develop a sense for the proper distance below support for your stop. More volatility in a stock means that you have to give it more room below support. Otherwise, you'll find yourself constantly getting stopped out just as the stock is ready to bounce.

The entry point C shows a candle that formed a lower shadow, which touches right on the moving average support. A week earlier, this support level was the resistance level, giving us a role reversal in addition to a moving average support. We see also that the moving average has started trending upward again, so we'll place our stop slightly below the moving average, assuming that the stock will follow this support line as it rises. In this case, let's use $43.50 as our stop level. This price is not too close to the moving average, yet it will show us that the stock has clearly broken the support.

### 5. Calculate Your Position Size Using the 1% Rule

Are you ready to bring this all together? In our opening example, we assumed that we have a $100,000 trading account. Based on the

1% Rule, we cannot lose more than $1,000 on this trade. This maximum loss number was determined before we ever set eyes on our chart.

Next, we need to determine our risk per share in this trade. The risk per share is simply the entry price minus the stop price. How's that for easy math? Written as an equation, it looks like this:

$$\text{Risk per share} = \$44.50 - \$43.50 = \$1.00$$

Notice that if the stock drops by $1, that represents a 2.2 percent drop in the stock. Many people mistakenly think that the stock can drop only 1 percent according to this rule. That's not the case. The stock may drop by more or less than 1 percent, but the impact on our trading account is limited to 1 percent.

The last step here is to calculate your position size or how many shares you may trade. The following equation is used to determine position size:

$$\text{Position size} = \text{Risk amount}/\text{Risk per share}$$

In the example we're creating, the position size is found as follows:

$$\text{Position size} = \$1,000/\$1.00 = 1,000 \text{ shares}$$

What this tells us is that based on the chart setup that we've analyzed, we can buy 1,000 shares of DIA at $44.50. If it should drop to our stop level of $43.50, we would lose $1,000, which is our maximum loss set by the 1% Rule.

There are two factors that influence our position size. The first is the account value. As the account value increases, the value of 1 percent of the account increases and vice versa. Second, as the risk per share increases, the number of shares that we can purchase decreases. This is how we accommodate the higher risk trades. If we had to purchase this stock at $45.50, our risk per share would have increased to $2. Using the same $1,000 maximum loss, we could now buy only 500 shares in order to stay within our defined risk plan.

What happens if we had to buy this stock at $53.50? Now we have a risk per share of $10, and we could buy only 100 shares. Some traders would raise the stop in order to allow them to buy more shares.

This is absolutely the wrong approach because we'd be placing our stop above support and we should expect to get stopped out for a loss. Never tell the market what you need or want; it doesn't care. Your placement of the stop order should be based on the chart alone. If the trade doesn't meet your standard, then go find another trade.

### 6. Execute Your Opening Trade and Stop Order

It's as simple as that; you've found the trade, now take the risk. How soon after the opening trade should you place your stop order? Let's list the tasks that may not be done until the stop order is placed:

- Get coffee
- Use the restroom
- Answer the phone
- Sneeze
- Breathe

Are you getting the picture? Once your opening trade is filled, you should immediately enter your stop order. If you give it any more time, you're just inviting trouble. And, as we've said many times, the stop order must be physically entered with your broker. Don't keep the infamous mental stop because it has a nasty habit of failing to fire when the stop level is reached.

## Managing Risk in a Probabilistic World

The issue of managing risk for the trader essentially boils down to the fact that we are required to take specific action in a market that is probabilistic rather than deterministic. We can make our best-effort guess at what the future holds, but it can never be known with certainty. Dr. Lloyd S. Nelson, director of statistical methods for the Nashua Corporation, is quoted as saying, "The most important figures that one needs for management are unknown or unknowable, but successful management must nevertheless take account of them." Extending that concept to the trading community tells us that sometimes the most important considerations are not to be found in the relative strength index (RSI) percentage or whether the candlestick has a bottom shadow. These may serve as guidelines for our action, but the analysis is sometimes trumped by factors beyond our control: an unexpected economic report, litigation against the company, accounting irregularities, and so on. These are the trader's "unknown or unknowable," but successful trading must nevertheless take account of them.

Our probabilistic world may not be the most predictable or, at times, the most profitable. Nevertheless, the lure of the market continues to reside in the challenge of navigating through the uncertainty. Navigate with care and you'll be amply rewarded.

CHAPTER

# Trading Hall of Shame
## TRADERS YOU DON'T WANT TO IMITATE

Over the years that we have worked with traders, both new and experienced, we have seen some personalities emerge. Some traders exhibited more of these personality characteristics than others. Some traders captured various characteristics from several personality types.

We used to joke about the trader who always bought the high and sold the low. No matter what he tried, he was always on the wrong side of the trade. That led his fellow traders to consider him a reliable contrarian indicator. When the predictable loser would buy, his fellow traders would all quietly sell. As long as you took the other side of the trade, profits were almost guaranteed.

In the United States, Chapter 13 is the bankruptcy law that allows for reorganization. Filing a straight bankruptcy forces you into liquidation and does not allow for redeeming yourself. Chapter 13 gives you the breathing room to recognize the problem and implement corrective action. If you see yourself in the profiles that follow, then consider this Chapter 13 to be your path toward reorganization.

In that light, and with perhaps a bit of lightheartedness, we offer the trader personalities on the following pages. While these characters are fictional (for the most part), they really do exist in the market. Your goal is to make sure you are not one of them. We'll start by describing the characters, including their quirks and trading habits. Following each character development is the prescription for curing the bad habits. It doesn't do any good to point out a problem without providing a solution. Read both sections for your enjoyment and, if necessary, your improvement.

## Barry the Bottom Fisher: Always Buys the Low (Until It Makes a New Low)

Barry is the type of person who buys bulk toilet paper because it's his way of getting a bargain. The caption under his high school yearbook picture reads "Penny wise, pound foolish" and he still thinks that price is everything. The truth is he'll drive across town to save a penny per gallon on gas just as quickly as he'll change his broker to save on commissions. He is so resistant to paying up for an option contract that the tattoo on his arm reads "The further the strike the more I like."

He is, by far, the most popular guest at the dinner party because his friends consider him to be the ultimate contrarian indicator. He's even been known to break up a party or two by talking about his trading positions during the course of a meal. Hosts have since learned not to schedule any more parties during trading hours as people will tend to race home to place a trade once they've found out that they have the same stocks as Barry. He tries hard to convince others of the favorite trading strategies he's learned from long-time buddy Double-Down Dan, and often wonders why his positions never move from the average cost basis. It just so happens that Barry *is* the average cost basis, and you will find that he holds over a million shares of stock, but his account equity is still hovering about the $12,000 mark. Barry never has trouble identifying support for his stocks. He simply uses the bottom of the chart. His trend lines look like the flight path of a homesick groundhog in freefall.

His great grandfather Phil Orkillit just happened to be the author who introduced the buy and hold strategy in his 1928 best seller, *Buy Till You Die*. Feeling confident that time is on his side, Barry would never ever consider using a stop loss order because this would interfere with his plan to accumulate the position. He will spend many long hours studying the fundamentals of a company to help him make a buy decision, and once he is in, he is committed to that stock.

### Prescription

Barry the Bottom Fisher obviously has it in his head that buying a stock when it's on a 52-week low means the stock is selling for a bargain. There is nothing further from the truth. Of course, there will be times when you will get lucky and actually be the person who buys the 52-week low, but in all our years in the market, we have yet to meet the person who does this consistently.

If your strategy is to "bottom fish" in the market, then there is a good chance you have at one point or another, bought a stock, watched it go down, bought more, and had it go down again; then, after you ran out of buying power, you grabbed the analyst report to find reasons why you should hold on to this stock for the long term. Experienced traders do not trade this way. The great traders buy high to sell higher. If you find yourself trying to predict the bottom for a stock move, change your approach and make it a point to only buy a stock that has evidence of a support level and one that is already on its way up after it has bounced off of the support line.

Another thing you can try in order to change your strategy is to look for stocks that are in upward trends and try to buy the highs. This will feel a little uncomfortable for you in the beginning, but after you have had some success with this, you will feel much better about it later on.

With regard to shopping for a lower commission, please don't pinch pennies by changing brokers every time the competition lowers the cost of a trade. Building a relationship with your broker is a very important part of your business. If you are a long-time client who is active in the markets, your broker will be more willing to fight for you the next time you get a bad trade execution. If you ask for it, there will be times where your broker will give you a customer service adjustment just to keep you happy (this one piece of information could pay for the cost of this book). If you are trading 50 to 120 times per year, you are categorized as an active trader in the eyes of your broker. Even if you consider yourself to be a long-term investor, 50 to 100 trades per year make you a very valuable client who generates revenue for the company you have your account with. If you left your broker, it could cost them anywhere from \$2,000 to \$10,000 to replace you. You represent a very competitive segment of the market, and most brokers will fight for your business.

Take time and get to know the people you are speaking with on the phone and shop for good customer service and not a cheaper commission. Think about it—even if you trade as much as 200 times per year, is it worth leaving a good company just to save a dollar or two per trade? We are talking about a \$200 to \$400 difference.

Would you trade good service for $400? If your answer is yes, then you are focusing your attention in the wrong direction. A good broker who gives good service could save you many thousands of dollars over time.

We have a good time whenever we talk about Barry the Bottom Fisher because his character is based on a real person who actually lives in London. Barry has called in to our radio show a few times, and we are happy to say he has kept a good sense of humor when we discuss his losses in front of the world. Note to Barry: If you are reading this, we do hope you have learned your lessons.

## Breakeven Betty: Forget Profits, Breaking Even Is Her Goal

Fifty-two years old, slightly optimistic, and full of ideas, Betty doesn't embrace success—she absolutely fears it. She drives a hybrid to work because acceleration frightens her. The bumper sticker on her rear window reads "Born to be Mild."

Betty is the type of person who so badly wants to be a trader she can taste it, but somehow she's never been able to get in a groove. Her timing is always just a little off. The stocks she picked in the past always seemed like good ones at first, but when they turned on her, she'd always find a way to hold on. She loved all of her stocks equally and maybe that was her problem—she didn't quite know how to let go of them when the price moved against her. When Betty was younger, she always dreamed of having an only child because she didn't think she could handle sibling rivalries.

Once in a while her friends would come over to visit for some Reg-T and crumpets. Her trades took on personalities of their own, with Betty occasionally naming them. Betty's friends became her support group, and they would hold her accountable by asking the tough questions: "Why do you like this guy so much? If you hold on any longer, you are not only going to waste your precious time but also a lot of money carrying this loser." Sooner or later, her friends were right. She would hold on to these guys just long enough to get back the money she had invested in them, and then she would boot them out.

### Prescription

The number one thing we can learn from Betty is that that you should not marry your stocks. Dump them just as quickly as you would an abusive relationship. The longer you wait for things to get better, the worse it will get and the more money it will cost you.

You'll find that the only time Betty sells a stock is when it has come back up to her entry price. You see, she buys the stock, suffers all the pain of the crash, and then exits just as it breaks even. That is often the point when the buyers have regained control, and the pain is amplified by the fact that Betty watches the stock she just sold move into a profit. The fatal flaw is that Betty buys on the way down and sells on the way up. That is the exact opposite strategy from the Market Guys' Five Points for Trading Success.

Another rule that is good to follow is this: If you ever find yourself in a *margin call,* the first thing you should do is sell out of the losing position and move to cash. This is the safest thing to do; then, once you are in cash, you can always find another stock that will treat you better. Just because Betty has her broker's margin department on speed dial doesn't mean you have to. From our experience, we have seen that the majority of the time traders will receive a second and sometimes third margin call after they have deposited funds in their trading accounts to meet the minimum cash requirement set by the Federal Reserve Board. If you get a margin call from your broker, this means your stock is not working out the way you thought it would. Otherwise, you would be making money from your investment. If you are holding on to a stock that is collapsing and you give money to your broker to finance this losing position, chances are the stock will continue in the direction that is hurting you, much like a bad relationship.

## Seminar Sal: He's Everywhere, But Is He Making Money?

On day one of the Super Swingtrader Software Symposium, you will see him standing at the check-in door like a homesick puppy. Genuinely a nice guy, very outgoing, wide-eyed, and one who idolizes the seminar speakers, Sal actually reads the expo agenda in order to time his lunch breaks around the speaker schedule.

He doesn't bother to pick up the exhibitor schwag bag because he has his own monogrammed leather schwag bag custom-made to accommodate the inventory of pens he picks up along the way. In fact, he's made more money selling exhibitor-branded stress balls on eBay then he has the whole time he's been trading. Even in the warmest weather he comes with four jackets so he can save seats at his favorite seminars. You'll know who he is because he's the one in the crowd who laughs uproariously before each punch line simply because he's heard all the jokes before.

Like Indiana Jones in search of the Holy Grail, he arrives at each expo with the eager anticipation that this is the event where he will find the elusive black box for trading. In fact, it's been rumored that he really does carry a whip at the bottom of that schwag bag. He has never visited a city that doesn't have a trading expo because seminars are his only reason to travel. He is hoping that Kalamazoo will one day host a trading expo because that's where his mom lives.

### Prescription

We meet Seminar Sal at every money show and trader expo. When are you going to learn that there is no Holy Grail for trading? A good friend of ours, Martin Pring, has told us that you have bought every book he has written and he has told you the same, yet you are still searching for the golden secret. Sal, it's time for you to Keep It Super Simple.

It's important for us to tell you that there are a lot of good things you can get from a seminar. The markets will continue to evolve and you will be able to learn how to trade an exchange-traded fund (ETF) or you may learn how to correctly invest in a hedge fund, but at the same time it's important for you to know that there are snake oil salesmen out there who will try to sell you the useless software package that will cost you many thousands of dollars. Here are some pointers that will help you get the most out of a trade show:

- Avoid the impulse buy and don't get caught up in the emotion of the moment. The vendor at the trade show will have little time to capture your attention; therefore, their approach will be enthusiastic and one that plays on your emotions. Be aware of this; make sure you have all of the facts and take the information home with you so you can make your decision without the influence of the enthusiastic salesperson.
- Watch out for false claims. Check the performance record of anyone who is making income claims. In other words, vet your source and see if your expert is willing to show you the losing trades along with the winners. This goes for money managers as well. Many times, we have seen people just highlighting the

best of show while they ignore the worst performers. Don't fall for the sales gimmicks.

- Make sure you know your financial objectives before you get to the show. This will help you get the most of the show, and you will be able to focus your attention on topics most important to you.
- Get a copy of the speaker schedule and cross off anyone who uses language that appeals to the person who is looking to get rich quick.
- Allocate your time and frequent the speakers who showcase risk management strategies.
- Visit the brokerage firms to see what they are doing to stay competitive with the other firms. Don't focus as much on commissions, but rather what they are doing to improve customer service and availability.

Once you have your trading platform in place, you should be ready to go. Stick with some basic strategies that will help you stay consistent in the market and try not to jump from one idea to the next because this will lead you off on tangents that could distract you from your most profitable trades.

## The Frozen Chosen: Holding Back Because of Fear

As one of the Frozen Chosen, Margarita knows it all, but she can't seem to get herself to make a trade. We met with her the other day in an effort to help her with her trading problem and found that there is more to her story than meets the eye. Here are just some of the notes we took away from our meeting:

- She is difficult to drive with because she tends to want to stop at green lights.
- She's an enthusiastic individual, but one who pays a monthly fee for a dummy account on her trading software.
- She doesn't really care what commissions cost her because she's never paid one.
- She will lose sleep at night over a bad paper trade.
- She has a collection of dice from the craps tables at Vegas because she could never bring herself to throw them.
- Fearful of making a commitment, things went terribly wrong at her wedding ceremony when she said, "I might."

- On her birthday she makes it a point to blow out all but one candle on her cake, for fear that her wish might come true.
- She has never won the pick-six lottery because she will only pick five numbers.
- She knows that the early bird catches the worm, but she's fearful that she may be the early worm. This may be something she learned from her father, whose favorite quote was, "Eagles may soar, but moles don't get sucked into jet engines."
- She attempted to place a trade one day, but it scared her half to death. Now she wonders, "What happens if you get scared half to death twice?"

### Prescription

The solution for Margarita is for her to overcome her fears, not just in trading but in every aspect of her life. This may sound like an easy thing to do, but if you have conditioned yourself to react to challenges in a fearful way, this can be a very tough step to take. We are talking about changing a mind-set, and the only way to reverse this way of thinking is for you to condition yourself to take action.

From a trading standpoint, the best way to overcome the fear of the trade is to start small. Buy 50 shares of the stock that you're considering. You may be thinking that it will be difficult to make a profit on 50 shares. Your goal is not to make a profit but rather to overcome your fear of the market. You will find that 50 shares are easy to manage. You can buy them quickly, sell them quickly, and you won't lose sleep if the stock moves in the wrong direction.

Once you are comfortable with trading 50 shares, move up to 100 shares. Continue building your confidence until you are ready to fully implement the Market Guys' Five Points for Trading Success Point IV (The 1% Rule). At that point, you will have the confidence to trade 500 or 1,000 shares.

We might also suggest some of the following activities that many of our friends around the world have found useful:

- Read a short motivational book once a month for a year. Consider starting with *The Generosity Factor* by Ken Blanchard and S. Truett Cathy (Grand Rapids, MI: Zondervan, 2002), or *Wins, Losses, and Lessons* by Lou Holz (New York: William Morrow, 2006).

- Join a local gym and hire a personal trainer who will push you to your limits. Exercise is a not only a stress reliever (scc Chapter 7), but you will find that it will help you sleep better at night. Keeping your mind and body strong and rested will help you make better business decisions.
- Take a self-defense class. You will be amazed to see how well this builds self-confidence. After you break your first board, you will feel invincible, and this feeling will eliminate any fears you have about the world around you.
- Make new friends. Go out there and try to find people who have qualities you admire. Those who are optimistic, confident, friendly, and helpful to those around them will most likely influence the way you evaluate risk. If you surround yourself with successful people, then your chances of success become much greater.
- Pray. We are not ashamed to talk about the power of prayer. It's positive, it's relaxing, it's exciting if you do it right, and, above all, you will truly be inspired to make good choices not just in your investments but in your personal life as well. Start by going to a comfortable, quiet corner in your home or lock yourself in your car if you have to and just close your eyes and be still. Be thankful for what you have and relax. Spend time with your creator and believe in miracles.
- Go out and help someone who really needs your help. Giving back to the community is a great way to build up your confidence and sense of self-worth. Not only is this rewarding, but you will be amazed to see just how many people will return those kind gestures. What goes around comes around.

## Larry the Lemming: Follows the Crowd, Not the Money

This is the guy who believes what he sees on television is true and will actually buy on an analyst upgrade. His favorite game as a kid was Simon Says, but he never aspired to be Simon.

Larry just loves driving down one-way streets because he doesn't have to make a decision, and he always seems to have a hard time when he gets to the forks in the road. When he eats out with friends, he always orders "what he's having." Larry books his travel with a group even if he doesn't know them. One of his favorite activities is to go to football games just to participate in the wave.

As a career employee of the consensus bureau, he loves his job but will often catch himself reminiscing of the days when he knocked on doors to ask people's opinions. When he was a child, his mother asked him, "If all of your friends jumped off a bridge, would you jump, too?" He meekly replied, "Yes."

These days, you will often find Larry putting long hard hours into his stock research. Although this is done through the late night chat rooms while on his computer, he does manage to find time for his closest friends, who happen to be avatars. He tried trading by himself for a while by going long Coca-Cola, but that position just fizzled out. Then he tried buying into the mining equipment sector, and that idea hit rock before he tried again to trade International Paper, and that position just stayed stationary for years. Then, on his final attempt, he tried trading pencils, but after he lost a few points he just decided to give up trying to make decisions for himself.

### Prescription

We know this is corny, but what we have just described to you in Larry characterizes many thousands of people who trade the market each year. If you find yourself always asking for a second opinion about a stock you are about to trade, then chances are you are not willing to take the risk on your own.

Do you take stock tips from your neighbor? Are you always checking the analyst reports to see if they are in line with your positions? If you wait for everyone else to get into a stock before you get into the stock, chances are you are on the wrong side of the trade because by the time you get in, the people who bought first are already thinking about getting out to take their profits. When they sell, who do you think they will be selling to? Yes, you.

Here is one way you can solve this problem. Instead of following the crowd, follow the money trail. Get good at reading simple line charts, and as soon as you see the pivot point that we described in Point III (Chapter 9), buy your stock and soon others will be following you instead of the other way around.

Larry is a close cousin to Frozen Margarita, because he trades with fear, too. That's why he always needs to find the consensus. The big difference between Larry and Margarita is that Larry is at least willing to place the trade. If you find that you are like Larry, we would suggest you follow the suggestions we gave Margarita. If you need to run with the crowd, at least make sure you are running with a group of success-minded individuals. Think like a winner, act like a winner, believe you are a winner, and then *be* a winner.

## Norman Is an Island: Trades in Seclusion, to His Theme Song, "All by Myself"

As an only child, Norman's favorite game was solitaire. You would often find him riding across town on his unicycle. A skeptic at heart, he's often wondered why psychics have to ask you for your name and doesn't allow anyone to influence his own opinion.

He lives in a one-room house at the end of a cul-de-sac, and when he eats out he makes sure to only use the drive-through window. Norman is an investor whom the brokerage firms would label "self-directed," and his biggest challenge is knowing when to get out of a stock.

Norman has never been strong on accountability. He assumes that any association with other traders would simply be a ticket to passage on a ship of fools. His trading software is direct access, but Level 1 suits him just fine. He has yet to return his broker's phone message asking him if she can help in any way.

### Prescription

One of the reasons we see so many people like Norman is the advancement in technology. It's easy to sit at home or in your office all by yourself at the computer to trade in and out of the markets. With the click of the mouse you can buy and sell stocks just like the professionals. But the big difference between your sitting there all by yourself and the professional is that the professional trader is not sitting there all by himself. He has many other traders around him, with a head trader who is keeping a very careful watch on the risk levels.

If you are like Norman, alone at your computer, who is there to help you manage the risk? Chances are, nobody is helping you manage risk. Norman avoids accountability. This is why we suggest you try to partner with either your spouse or a friend. Their role is not to give you a second opinion about the stocks you pick; they are there to help hold you accountable to the exit points. In other words, if you buy a stock at $25 and you have calculated your stop loss point to be $23, let your partner know that you are getting out at $23. Then ask them to help you track the progress of the stock over time. If the stock drops to $23 or lower, hopefully your friend will let you know about it. This will be a "backup" plan to the stop loss order you should already have in place.

Please reward your partner every time they help you get out of a bad position. This will reinforce this behavior pattern, and over time you may even have trained a good trading buddy, who may one day be the next great portfolio manager. What you need to do is find a place that brings you somewhere between Norman and our next character, who is quite the opposite.

## Urgent Carl: He's Trading, but He's Not Weaned

Carl is willing to make any trade but will not make the trade by himself. If there were a trader's 9-1-1 line, they would know Carl by name. Carl needs validation on every stock before he enters the position, and he has an endless list of questions. Furthermore, when he gets a trade idea in his mind, the best time to place the trade was an hour ago. Every minute that passes without the trade is surely sucking every last penny out of his potential profits. Carl lives for the next market emergency.

Some of the things we noticed about Urgent Carl are:

- He's only read part of *I'm OK, You're OK* because he is not really sure he is okay.
- He is so unsure of his own abilities that he refuses to give himself discretionary trading authority in his own account.
- He carries with him a hyperventilation bag for those times when he can't reach his trading coach.
- Armed with the latest and greatest technology, he is a wiz on the Bluetooth and can spit out a text message in a flash for instant, quick-response backup support.
- He is actually a very nice guy but is having a hard time fighting the stalking charges filed by his last trading coach.
- On his account application he listed his personal trading coach as a codependent.
- By himself he wouldn't trade a dollar for a five-dollar bill, but with the right validation would trade a complex forex spread.

*Prescription*

There is some overlap here with Carl's behavior and that of Larry the Lemming in that they are both validators, but Carl is at least able to make his own trade decisions. His only problem is that he is quite unsure of the decisions he is making. To accommodate his lack of confidence, he gathers one or more trading coaches around him. These coaches may be other traders, technical analysts, or financial advisers. Whoever they are, they become Carl's lifeline when his insecurities rise to a boiling point.

## Chatter Box—AJ

There was a time when I was handling a trader who lived in Annapolis, Maryland. A dentist who loved to trade IBM, he would call me during the trading day to see how the stock was looking on the technical charts. I would give a quote to him, he would ask if the stock was still holding support, and then he would hang up and go back to work. Five minutes later, my phone would ring again and I would once again pull up IBM to talk about price support and any news that would come up on the stock. If you've ever tracked IBM, you know that there are hundreds of press releases that go out on this company each and every week, and at times it can be pretty tedious going through all of those stories to analyze what affect this news will have on the stock. Well, I had to end our relationship after the day when the number of inbound calls topped 37 and that was all during the six-and-a-half-hour trading day. This worked out to be about one call every 11 minutes. After I ended that relationship, I found out his calls were coming in between each patient who came to visit him at his office. Needless to say, this individual was quite unsure of his own ability to manage risk and needed me to reinforce the risk management plan.

Here are some solutions that will help build confidence in your ability to trade the markets without your crutches:

- Start off by trading with a small amount of money in your trading account. Remember Margarita? This will relieve some of the stress and get you in a rhythm that will help build a profitable trading account. Then, once you are in the groove, you can increase the number of shares according to your comfort level and risk tolerance.

- Make sure you are using stop loss orders and accept the fact that you will be wrong once in a while (maybe even more than once in a while). Setting your expectations in this way will eliminate any surprises that will contribute to financial stress.
- Back up your stop loss orders with e-mail alert services that notify you when a stock drops below key support levels.
- Trade within your education and expertise level. Don't trade options if you don't know the difference between a call and a put.
- Turn off the television. Financial news programs play on the emotions of investors and will only result in your reacting in a "knee jerk" fashion.
- Don't stare at your trading platform every minute of every trading day. Go out and get a massage and relax. The market will be there when you get back. Looking at the markets too much will result in a condition we call "tickeritis," which is a compulsive disorder causing one to crave stock quotes every 11 minutes.
- Switch to decaf.

By now, you may have picked up on a common trend seen in several of our characters. Lack of confidence, low sense of self-worth, fearfulness, and uncertainty are all factors that will contribute to making poor financial decisions. Moving on to our last couple, you will see that this theme continues.

## Oz and Trish: The Couple that Vows to Ignore Any Losing Position

As head-in-the-sand traders, Oz and Trish still believe WorldCom will come back. They find it curious that most of the stock ticker symbols in their portfolio end with a "Q." They didn't actually prepare for Y2K—they just set their clocks back. Oz was once overheard telling Trish that stop orders are issued by police for speeding, and he believes the best way to handle a losing position is to turn off the computer and go on vacation.

Many people are motivated by various inspirational posters, books, and tapes. Oz and Trish have a placard hanging above their computer that reads, "It Isn't a Loss until You Sell It." They never made any trades on margin, so they have the luxury of riding their losing positions to the bitter end. Neither knew the meaning of the word *asymptotic* until a friend once used it to describe the line chart of their favorite stock.

Oz and Trish are living proof that misery loves company, yet they have come to a place where they are actually comfortable with their losing positions. They have always been traders, but somewhere along the way they morphed into long-term investors as their losing trades accumulated. A common practice of theirs is to sell other stocks that allow them to take a profit in order to finance the stocks that are losing money.

### Prescription

Oz and Trish live among us more frequently than you might guess. When we have the opportunity to explain to them what they are doing wrong, they understand everything we tell them. They are at the seminars taking copious notes; they hear what we say and know that it makes complete sense. But when we talk to them days after our advice was given, to check on what they did to get out of their downtrending stocks, we see no action taken. It's almost as if someone put a spell on them that causes them to ignore all losses whatsoever.

Whatever you do, don't become an Oz and Trish couple. This is not a strategy to manage risk, and it will never work as a strategy to profit in the markets. Imagine if money managers all over the world ignored risk management ideas. This would be the same as a captain sailing off toward the open seas knowing that there were holes in the bottom of his boat and not doing anything to plug the holes.

This type of a mind-set is a very tough one for us to overcome because it is based on a strong belief that says out of sight, out of mind and eventually things will get better. Remember that it takes only one bad investment to blow up your whole portfolio. The following points are things you should think about to avoid getting your head stuck in this ostrich approach to trading:

- Create a lot of pain in your mind in "not taking action." Think of what could happen if this stock does not turn around. What will this do to your finances?

- Print charts of stocks you own and draw red lines where support levels are and keep them in an obvious place near your computer so you can't run and hide from the truth.
- If on your last try to manage your risk, you still fail to face the truth and get out of a losing trade, we have no other advice than to seek professional help in managing your portfolio. It would be better to pay one or two percentage points to have a licensed financial adviser do the job than for you to risk your retirement dollars hiding your head in the sand.

## It's Funny Until It Hurts

We had a lot of fun writing this chapter because humor sometimes helps us to remember key points of interest. Poking fun at ourselves every now and then is okay as long as we are not offending anyone in the process. However, if you did take offense to any of the comments we've made regarding our characters, you should take a serious look at yourself, as it may suggest you have a "nonprofit profile."

Although we did base our stories on real people, we were sure not to use their real names. If you happen to have the same name as one of our characters, we assure you this was purely a coincidence.

In our next chapter we are going to talk about how to find a good broker. Once you have found a broker that can help you, be sure to build a relationship with the people you speak with from that firm. After you get to know some of the active trader representatives who handle your account, be sure to ask them if they have ever run into Barry, Betty, or Sal. If they haven't, there is a good chance they've spoken with Margarita, Larry, or Norman. Carl will be blocked from calling them anymore, and Oz and Trish would never call them for help because they will be on vacation. It would be interesting to get their views on the types of traders they speak with each and every day while the markets are open for trading. Chances are they will have crazier stories than we do.

# Going to the Dance

## FINDING YOUR BROKER

---

Single Trader Seeks Broker for LT Relationship
*I'm new to trading so I need someone to hold my hand. Enjoy all types of orders but limits are my favorite! Willing to try trailing stops – I'm crazy that way. Most days find me staring wistfully at the screen – would you leave me for that??? Looking for the broker who will share my dreams without being pushy or demanding. Might even consider options with the right broker. I've only been with banks and they're just too stuffy for my personality. Are you the one? Please don't break my chart! Email only please – spam turns me off.*
*Signed BATR8R in Birmingham*

---

**S**o what does your broker personal ad look like? Have you considered what features and characteristics your broker should have to meet your needs? Or do you think that all brokers are created equal and finding the right one is not much more than a crap shoot? In this chapter, we'll give you some guidelines on finding a broker who can help you execute your trading plan. The following top ten list will help you find the perfect broker mate!

## 1. Accounts

When we talk about account types and considerations, we recognize that the rules and choices vary by location and changes in laws. A retirement account in the United States will have different contribution and distribution restrictions than a similar Canada account. Nevertheless, we want to at least provide some framework for what to look for in your accounts. We will introduce accounts with a review of the following:

- Brokerage
- Retirement
- Custodial
- Ownership considerations

### Brokerage

You need to ensure that the broker you choose can service the types of accounts that you need for your trading and investing plan. The most basic brokerage account will allow you to buy and sell stocks, bonds and mutual funds. Generally, there is a minimum deposit required which varies between brokers. A typical minimum for many firms is $5,000, although some require less for the initial deposit. One of the reasons that brokers require the minimum balance is to provide a buffer in the event that you buy a stock and it drops in price. The broker needs a cushion to absorb the losses; otherwise, the firm is on the hook for the losses.

Adding margin to the account requires a separate application, which must be completed by all account owners. Margin gives you the flexibility to buy stocks with borrowed funds and is also necessary for short selling. You cannot sell short in an account that does not have the margin feature. It's important to note that the margin agreement that you sign gives the broker the right to sell any of your holdings in the account in the event that you experience a maintenance call. The maintenance call is issued when you purchase a stock on margin (borrowed funds) and the stock price drops to a certain level, known as the house maintenance requirement. In this instance, the firm will require the deposit of additional funds to increase the buffer. If they cannot reach you, they have the right to liquidate any of your positions in order to increase the cash balance of the account. We've known traders who thought they could escape this action by ignoring their broker's calls.

### Retirement

Retirement accounts are special accounts that are available in the United States and many other countries which provide advantages for retirement savings. There are many various structures and regulations regarding these accounts so we won't discuss account-specific details. However, most of the retirement accounts have some common characteristics.

Retirement accounts are generally structured to lean toward conservative strategies and investments. For that reason, short selling is forbidden because the potential for unlimited risk is considered unacceptable for a long-term account. Also, most brokerage firms restrict the types of option trades that may be executed within a retirement account. Selling uncovered calls that could place the seller into a short position is a type of trade that would be prohibited. Some types of retirement accounts restrict the choice of investment products, providing only a limited menu of mutual funds from which to choose. Others, such as self-directed accounts, allow you to choose from most available investment products, including individual stocks and options.

Retirement accounts are designed to encourage saving for the long-term and so they generally provide a tax advantage to the account owner. Since tax laws can change at any time, our recommendation is to meet with your broker or tax advisor to determine which specific retirement account best matches your objectives.

### Custodial

Custodial accounts are designed to help you save for the needs of a minor child. The savings may be general in nature or geared toward a specific objective such as education. Once again, the laws and restrictions vary between countries and individual brokers. Much like retirement accounts, custodial accounts provide certain tax advantages and may or may not restrict the types of investments available to you. Custodial accounts often have a lower initial deposit although that usually is attended by limits on annual contributions.

### Ownership Considerations

Ownership of an account is divided into three primary categories: individual, joint, or corporate. An individually owned account is held by one person who makes the trading and investing decisions. The individual owner is the only one authorized to withdraw funds or make changes to the account. A retirement account is a typical example of an account that would be owned by one person. It is possible for an individual owner to designate another individual as an authorized trader but that would not affect the actual ownership of the account.

Jointly owned accounts are typical of brokerage and savings accounts. Often, married partners will open joint accounts that allow both partners to individually access account records, make trading and investing decisions, and withdraw funds. Jointly owned accounts also provide for the efficient transfer of ownership and authority to the surviving partner on the death of one owner.

Corporate accounts may be held by any for-profit or nonprofit organization. These account types are typically held by trading clubs, where the club members pool their funds for trading. Buy and sell decisions are made according to club procedure and the trades are executed within the corporate account. It is common practice to designate certain corporate officers or representatives as having trading and fund withdrawal authority. You can only imagine what the result would be if a trading club allowed all members to access the available funds at any time without accountability. Once the members realized the access they had to free funds, they'd be grabbing at the money like drunken sailors on shore leave.

## 2. Advice and Support

One question that you need to answer in the process of selecting a broker is, "How much help will I need along the way?" Some traders and investors wish to be left completely alone and use their broker as an execution venue only. They don't want advice or any solicitations. There are no-frill, low-cost firms that cater to these individuals. Most traders and investors desire and need some level of assistance and there are brokers who fit in at every level.

The dot-com era saying about bricks and clicks is one consideration in selecting your broker. Does your broker have a retail location where you can walk in and actually speak face to face with your representative? Brokers don't have the numbers of retail locations as banks, and that's why there are still many people who open their trading and investment accounts with a local bank. Some large online brokers have retail offices in major cities. Other online brokers have elected to not open any retail locations and provide all support through call centers. Almost all brokers, with or without retail locations, give you access to representatives by phone. Many also have a premium support group for clients who are active traders or who maintain a large account balance.

For a long time, online brokers would provide transaction-based services only. You could trade, transfer funds, print records, and perform other tasks but they wouldn't offer any guidance on planning or strategies. On the other side of the coin, full-service advisers were especially reluctant to let you make any trades on your own. The investor was left in an either-or situation. Today, many online brokers have varying levels of advice and support. At one end of the spectrum is on-demand assistance for the self-directed trader who only needs some occasional help. Next along the line is the validator, who makes her own decisions but she wants a sanity check from a professional. At the far end of the spectrum is the delegator, who wants someone else to make the buy and sell decisions based on an agreed-upon overall strategy. Many of the full-service, fee-based advisers prefer that the client not trade within the managed account. For that reason, more traders who have professionally managed investment accounts are now opting to open a separate trading account with an online broker.

One key area of support that is often overlooked is technical and trade support. This is particularly crucial as you begin to trade more actively. There are few things more annoying, or more costly, than trading in a fast market and having your trading software freeze or not receiving a trade confirmation quickly enough to let you know where you stand in the position. In times like these, you need to be able to pick up the phone and reach a support representative quickly. If your broker can't deliver timely information backed up by a responsive call team, then it's time for you to find another broker.

## 3. Trading and Investing Products

The basics of the trading and investing products may be found at just about every brokerage firm. Let's start with the basics and then talk about some others.

Most of us think about stocks when we talk trading. Trading stocks is the bread and butter of most retail traders. However, there are other aspects of stock trading besides just pressing the buy and sell button. You should consider whether your broker provides an institutional desk for large lot orders. These representatives will take a large lot order and work it into the market to minimize the impact of your order on the stock price. Also, if you trade penny stocks, or the pink sheets, consider whether your broker will allow you to trade these online. The term *pink sheet* comes from the fact that the prices of these cheap stocks were originally printed on pink paper.

Mutual funds are familiar to most investors today and there are literally thousands to choose from. More firms are now offering a wide selection of no-load, no-transaction-fee mutual funds. You need to look carefully at the loads and expenses associated with mutual funds and ensure that you're not overpaying for underperformance. Index funds are a great way to track the markets with very low fund expenses. Because many mutual funds include a short-term redemption fee, they are considered investment products rather than trading products. Funds are priced once a day at the net asset value (NAV). Your broker should be able to provide you with the NAV and complete fund information for all of the funds they offer. In this category, we also include exchange-traded funds (ETFs). Since ETFs trade the same as stocks, they are available to trade through almost all brokers. However, not all brokers provide you with ETF-specific research tools.

Options are one of the fastest growing segments of the markets today. As a trader, you should be on the lookout for a broker that lets you research and trade options. Unless you are in the most advanced segment of traders, the basic option information will be adequate for your trading. This includes the full option chain with Greeks (how an option price changes) and the ability to place simple and complex option orders. Some of the advanced specialized options brokers offer much more complex trading systems geared exclusively toward the advanced trader. For those who trade at the advanced level, this could be useful. For the majority of the traders who do not, this could lead to analysis paralysis.

Bonds and cash products are important investments that provide stability and growth in your account without the same type and level of risks that come with equity investments. We never recommend trading with your entire portfolio and, therefore, you need other investments to balance your trading activity. A good broker will let you search for bonds, certificates of deposit (CDs), or other high-yield cash securities. Some of these will require that you hold the investment until maturity in order to avoid an early withdrawal penalty.

Looking at some of the more advanced products, you can consider trading futures. Many futures brokers will let you trade futures on multiple exchanges for products such as commodities, currencies, interest rates, metals, market indexes, and energy. Often, a futures account will have a higher minimum initial deposit than a standard brokerage account because of the leverage associated with futures trading. Other products that are available in various locations are contracts for difference (CFDs), spread betting, and forex. You need to be careful to understand the increased risks that may come with the advanced derivative products and choose a broker who will provide support as you may need it.

## 4. Costs and Fees

Everyone looks at commissions so we'll start with this one, even though commissions have dropped to the point that they're almost a nonissue. It wasn't all that long ago that a 1,000 share purchase of a blue-chip stock could set your account back hundreds of dollars from the trade commission. Today, most brokers are hard-pressed to justify a commission above $20 for a stock trade and many are less than $10. Option trades are priced at a base commission plus a per-contract fee. If you trade actively, you should look for a broker who will further discount your commission based on your trading activity. Some brokers also offer a bundle of free trades when you open a new account or deposit additional funds. Any time you bring a value to your broker, you should consider how they might be able to offer you a value in return.

Another fee that is not quite as visible as the commission is the margin interest rate that you pay on margin balances. This is nothing more than the cost of borrowing money from your broker. However, in the same way that you may shop around for the best home mortgage, you should also shop for the best margin rate if you tend to trade with margin. These rates are often pegged to the prevailing interest rate, but just as with commissions, margin rates are often discounted for active traders or high-balance accounts. On the flip side of the margin fee is the yield that is paid on cash balances. You should pay close attention to this because a low yield may act as a surrogate fee if you maintain cash in your account. The return you get on your money is a function of costs and earnings. Low earnings can have just as bad an effect on your account as high costs.

Account fees can quickly add up if you don't pay attention to them. Ask your broker about the charges they impose for certain account types, minimum balances or high transaction activity. You should look for a broker who will consider all of your accounts as a household and not assess fees to each account separately. It's terribly frustrating to have a trading account where you may be trading 50 times a month and paying $10 trade commissions, only to have a separate account where you're paying $20 trade commissions because you don't trade often enough.

You need to consider how various transaction fees are charged to your account and find a broker who can help you minimize these costs. It is becoming more common for brokers to reimburse you for ATM fees when you withdraw funds from your account, even if the ATM machine is not on your home network. Other transaction fees to consider are wiring, checking, option exercise and assignment, stop payment, mail and processing, records and statements, and verification of deposit. As you can see, the menu of fees can be quite extensive, and you need to determine which ones may affect you and which broker keeps these costs down.

## 5. Software

Software for trading and investing is becoming more important as the flow of information has shifted from the realm of the professionals toward the average retail trader like you and me. Market software generally falls into two categories: web-based software and standalone packaged software.

Web-based software is built into the broker's web site and is accessible from any web connection. As a rule, web-based software tends to be simpler than the stand-alone packages since it is used by the majority of traders and investors, particularly those with less experience. There are a few features that you should look for in the web-based software offered by your broker.

First of all, every web application should have some level of charting. This is a must. If your broker doesn't offer basic stock charts, move on. The charting package is all the better if you can add trend lines, moving averages and volume, at the least. It is also nice if you can add some level of customization to the chart such as varying time views and different charting styles. Most web software applications include real-time quotes, as delayed quotes are available to the general public on almost all financial sites. Along with the quotes, you should be able to access various stock statistics such as daily range, volume, current bid/ask and 52-week high. You should also have full access to your account information including balances, transaction history and positions with gain/loss reports.

Web software usually lags stand-alone software from an active trading standpoint. However, for the investor, web software is usually the better choice. Web applications are usually more complete for products such as bonds and mutual funds, for both research and trading. Furthermore, because many of the transaction functions such as banking and bill paying are done through the web, it is easier to integrate all of the account activity through a web-based platform.

Standalone software applications usually come in the form of a Java application or proprietary code that resides on your local computer. These packages are specifically designed to address the needs of the active trader and include more advanced analysis and execution functions than the web applications. There are myriad features within the stand-alone applications, but we'll review some of the more common features to aid you in your decision here.

- *Charts.* A solid charting capability is a must-have for any stand-alone application. The bare minimum features that we would consider for the more advanced software is the three major chart styles (line, bar, candlestick), trend lines, moving averages, volume, scalability, and color/font customization. The latter feature is important because (1) a chart that is easy on your eyes will allow you to read it better, and (2) this feature is so easy to code there's no reason for a broker not to have it.
- *Screening tools.* There are many types of screening tools from preset screens to programmable screens. We prefer to have the flexibility to create our own screens based on criteria that we select. However, any trading platform should include top gainers, top losers, top volume and a high/low list. Remember that selecting a stock is one of the key parts of managing risk, so if you can't screen for your stock, you're starting with an unnecessary level of risk.
- *Option data.* Some people might disagree with us on this point, but we think that you should have access to basic option chain data even if you're not trading the option. As option trading

continues its explosive growth, you'll find that option expiration day, open interest, and other option-specific terms become more important to every trader. Of course, if you are trading options, the full call/put chain, Greeks, volume, and open interest are the least you should expect from your broker.

- *Stock data.* Once the exclusive domain of the professional day trader, the Level 2 screen is now an expected part of the stock data on advanced platforms. This gives you visibility into the price levels other than the high bid and low offer. You also get to see how the stock has traded for the day as well as the current trading ticker. Most of these platforms include direct access, which lets you route your order to any market participant. Even with direct access, we find that the intelligent order routing systems employed by the major brokers are sufficient for most orders.

- *Watch lists.* The Market Guys actually consider this to be a minimum requirement for advanced trading platforms because it supports the stock screening function. Many times, we'll find a stock that is setting up very nicely for a trade but it's not quite at the entry point yet. The best course of action is to place it on a watch list and review it each day until the entry point is reached or it fails to complete the setup, in which case we'll remove it from the watch list.

- *Real-time account and order status.* What can we say here except that you can't manage your trades if you don't know where you stand? You should have instant access to your account equity, buying power, and open positions. Each open position should have real-time profit and loss updates. Perhaps the most important is the order status, letting you know if an order is open, filled, or partially filled. Sometimes the markets move rapidly and you need to take action. It's at these critical times that you need your software to work for you rather than against you.

You may certainly have more features that you consider critical to your trading. That's fine. Our goal in this list is to help you think about the features that we use and that you may want to also consider. Depending on what you trade, your experience level and your time horizon for trading, there are many other tools and features that you'll want to review on a case-by-case basis.

## 6. Order Types

Traders today need the ability to execute trades according to their strategy and market conditions. Your broker should give you the ability to place the following trades as conditions warrant.

### Market

The market order is an order that goes to the market and tells everyone that you want to trade and are not concerned primarily with price. A market buy order will usually fill on the offer or ask price while a market sell will usually fill on the bid price. The market order guarantees execution but not price. A limitation of the market order is that it will only execute while the market is open. Low liquidity and large spreads would make the market order dangerous to use during the pre- and post-market trading hours.

### Limit

The limit order is used when you want to specify a maximum buying price or a minimum selling price for your order. A limit buy order is always placed below the current trading price while a limit sell order is always placed above the current trading price. While the market order guarantees execution but not price, the limit order guarantees price but not execution. If you place a limit buy order below the market and the stock never falls to your limit price, your order will remain open and unfilled. Limit orders may be placed at any time and may be filled while the market is closed since any fill that meets your limit price is a valid trade.

### Stop

The stop order is a little tricky for new traders to understand sometimes but it is really a simple order. The buy stop order is used to buy a stock when the price rises; therefore, the buy stop order is always placed above the current market price. The sell stop order is used to sell a stock when it falls; therefore, the sell stop order is always placed below the current market price. Notice how the limit sell and the buy stop are both above the current trading price while the limit buy and the sell stop are both below the current trading price.

Let's use one example to illustrate the stop order. If you own a stock and you want to sell it if it starts to fall, you would protect your open position with a sell stop. The sell stop will just sit in your account only until the stock drops to the stop price that you specify. When the stock hits your stop price, the sell stop order automatically turns into a market sell order and your position would be closed at the current market price.

It is possible to combine a stop order with a limit order to create a stop limit order. The stop limit order requires that you specify both a stop price as well as a limit price. Let's see how this would work for protecting a stock that you own. Let's say you own a stock that is trading at $50. You decide that you want to sell it if it drops to $47; however, you really don't want to sell it for less than $45. In this case, you would place a sell stop limit order with a stop at $47 and a limit at $45. If the stock drops to $47, the sell stop limit order would automatically convert to a limit sell. Here's the problem, though. If the stock is falling rapidly, it is possible that the stock price could drop below your limit price before your order is filled. In that case, you would own a falling stock without any protection. For that reason, if you're using a stop order to protect an open position, we always recommend that you use a stop rather than a stop limit.

### Trailing Stop

This one is a handy twist to the standard stop order. The biggest limitation to the stop order is that it will protect the stock you own from falling, but it doesn't help you protect your profits. The trailing stop accomplishes both. The trailing stop is a stop order that will continually adjust the stop price in the direction of profits. In other words, if you own a stock and it starts to rise, the trailing stop will rise along with the stock price, thereby increasing the level at which the stop order will execute. The stop order, therefore, trails behind the trading price and will follow it until the stock starts to retreat, at which point the stop order will sell your stock and lock in the majority of the profit.

This is another one that is best understood with real numbers. Suppose you buy a stock for $50 and you want to limit your loss to $2 per share. At the same time, you want to lock in your profits as the stock rises. You could place a $2 trailing stop, which would set the initial stop price at $48. Now assume that the stock price moves from $50 to $54. The stop price would automatically increase to $52 ($54 − $2). Next the stock price increases to a maximum of $57.33. The stop price is now at $55.33. At this point, the stock starts to fall and when it reaches $55.33, the trailing stop turns into a market sell and you exit your trade for a $5.33 profit.

### Contingent

We would not necessarily consider these orders as a hard requirement, but they sure do make trading life easier. A contingent order is any order that will execute when a specified condition is met. For example, let's say that you wanted to buy a stock based on volume rather than price. If the volume of the stock reaches 1 million shares, you want to buy the stock because that would be an indication of rising interest. A contingent order would let you create a market buy order that only executes if and when the daily volume crosses 1 million shares.

Another example would be a sell collar. Suppose you own a stock and you want to sell it for a minor loss if it drops or sell it for a profit if it reaches your price target. You cannot place two active sell orders on one position so you would create a collar. This type of contingent order is called a one-cancels-other (OCO) order. Both of the sell orders would be active, but as soon as either one is executed, the other instantly cancels. That prevents you from executing two sell orders for one position, which would otherwise leave you in a short position.

## 7. Research

While we tend to focus more on the technical analysis as traders, we don't suggest that you give up doing any fundamental research. There are many aspects of the underlying company, sector, industry, or economy that are worth exploring as you prepare for and manage your trades and investments. Fundamental research also is increasingly important as your time horizon lengthens. Of course, a day trader probably wouldn't do any fundamental analysis, but a long-term investor needs to understand the company data more than today's trading data. We've compiled a list of standard research that you might look for from your broker.

- *Earnings data.* Earnings data is one of the highest profile news events that is released by a company. Your broker should provide you with the earnings date, estimates, and all reports and filings related to earnings. This should be fully accessible through your broker's web site when you log in to your account. Many traders pay particular attention to the date that earnings are announced because trading volatility can increase dramatically shortly before and after an earnings announcement.

- *News.* Most brokers will provide news from at least two or three separate news feeds. A useful feature of any news feed is the ability to filter for keywords. If you own IBM stock, it is especially helpful to enter the keyword *IBM* into the filter and see only those headlines that affect your company. Likewise, you may be targeting the energy sector in which case you might filter for keywords such as *energy, OPEC,* or *oil futures.*

- *Company profile.* You should ensure that your broker provides you with the full company profile information including market cap, shares outstanding, short interest, price-to-earnings ratio (P/E), ex-dividend date, and beta. You should also be able to check key ownership by corporate officers and major shareholders. Along with the ownership, it is helpful to see what the insider buying and selling activity looks like. Keep in mind, though, that insider transactions are not real time, they are reported monthly.

  The accounting reports are a standard part of the company profile. These include the balance sheets, income statements, cash flow statements and Securities and Exchange Commission or other regulatory body filings. Once again, keep in mind that the trader should watch price and volume first, because there is often a divergence between the company fundamentals and the price, especially over the short term.

- *Education and training.* We consider this to be part of the research because it is part and parcel with empowering you as the trader or investor. Your broker should not be afraid to enable you to be a more informed client. Many brokers provide online tutorials for their products and services to help you navigate through the choices. The best brokers are those who actually offer education and training classes where you can attend and direct questions to the trainers. If your broker offers these classes, don't underestimate the value that you'll receive from taking your knowledge up a notch.

## 8. Banking

If you want to integrate your trading and investing with your banking, then consider a broker who offers various banking features through your brokerage account. While there can be many advantages from bringing your brokerage and banking accounts together, the biggest drawback for many people is the loss of a local, personal banker. To accommodate that concern, you could maintain a backup savings or checking account at a neighborhood bank with a small portion of your portfolio. Consider the following list when looking for a broker who could take care of your banking requirements.

- *Checking and ATM.* Checking and ATM access are right at the top of the list in the banking checklist. The key details to look for here are the fees associated with various transactions. In order to stay competitive, many brokers are offering unlimited ATM withdrawals from any ATM. As we mentioned earlier, the broker will credit your account for ATM fees incurred when withdrawing funds from an off-network ATM. On the checking side, consider how many checks you write each month and be sure your broker will not charge you for exceeding a monthly check limit.
- *Loans.* Home, car, and boat loans are the current product focus for many brokers. It only makes sense. They're holding your investments, so they've already evaluated your financial situation. As a rule, clients who have trading and investing accounts tend to be a bit more financially established than the average Joe on the street that walks into the neighborhood bank for a car loan. The brokers know that there is a steady revenue stream that comes from issuing high-quality loans so they're going to be courting you when you're looking to borrow money. The shopping list here is the same that you would use for a bank loan. Interest rate and loan terms are what it's all about.
- *Bill pay.* The bill-paying feature is a convenience that many of us choose to not live without anymore. You can pay your bills online through a recurring schedule and not have to worry about stamps, envelopes, and missing payment deadlines. If you haven't used bill pay yet, then look into this when you're checking into brokers.

- *Wiring and fund transfers.* Most people rarely use their broker for wiring funds, but when you need that service, you'll be thankful for a broker who makes the process easy for you. Check into the fees charged for wiring and how your broker processes the wires. Make sure you understand the cutoff time for sending a wire out. Your broker should also be clear to help you with funds tracking when a wire is sent or received.

  More often, when you have multiple accounts with one broker, you'll want to be able to transfer funds quickly between accounts. Your broker should allow you to do this online and provide transfer confirmation immediately. This feature is an integral part of cash management that will enable you to earn the greatest return on your deposited cash. Move funds into checking or trading accounts as you need them, but keep the cash in high-yield cash accounts when the funds are idle.

- *Credit cards.* We're not sure this is a hard requirement for selecting a broker since getting a credit card these days is about as easy as falling off a chair. Nevertheless, many brokers offer a branded credit card or, alternately, a debit card tied to your brokerage account.

## 9. Reports and Records

Most people don't think very much about how good their broker is with reports and records until tax day rolls around. Then you find yourself scrambling for your cost basis, transaction history, or trade confirmation and wonder how you'll ever find the information. Brokers generally provide the information through online access or archive retrieval. The former is usually offered for free or for a nominal fee. The latter requires more handling by the broker and, therefore, you can expect to pay for the service as you request documents. Our suggestion is that you focus on the online reports and records and find a broker who will provide this information without cost.

- *Transaction history.* When did that check that you wrote to the charity clear? What was the date of deposit for the gift check you received for your birthday? How many times did you pay the builder by check? These are the kinds of questions that you want answers to and you want the answers now. Having online access to your account transaction history is a fact of life these days and your broker should accommodate this easily. An added benefit is the ability to search or sort through the transactions. For example, you might want to find all check deposits between July and October. Or you want to reorder the history list so that all of the checks come first, followed by deposits, and so on.

- *Trading activity.* As a trader, you'll need the ability to know exactly what you traded and when. Look for a broker that lets you search through your trading activity for opening and closing prices, date of trade, how many shares were filled at each price level, time of trade, and other information that you would see on your trade confirmation. You'll also want to see a record of orders so that you know which orders filled and which orders expired or were canceled. At the end of the trading year, all of this information should be available in a consolidated report to help you with your tax reporting.

- *Gain/loss.* The gain/loss report is a great way to track your progress on both your trades and investments. The data for this report should be captured automatically for any trades that you place through your broker. As you open a new position, the opening price (or average opening price for multiple fills) is compared against the current market price to let you know your position profit or loss. The report also tallies up all open positions to give you a cumulative profit or loss for the account. If you transfer open positions in to your broker, provide them with the cost basis for your transfer positions and the gain/loss report should be able to track the ongoing performance.

- *Account records.* This is one report that is usually not available online but that's okay because you should rarely have a need for it. The account records include copies of such items as your account applications, powers of attorney, options approval, and written authorizations or instructions. These records are usually required for litigation or estate settlement, for example. While your broker should make these available to you, expect to pay a retrieval and processing fee for each document requested.

- *Data downloading.* There are a number of good third-party software packages on the market now that let you manage your own records and reports. Search for a broker that will let you download your transactions periodically into your own computer. Once you have your hands on the data, you can create your own tax reports or gain/loss reports. We know many traders who include these reports as a part of their trading plan and diary to track their growth and progress. You'll appreciate not having to connect to your broker every time you want to see where you stand.

## 10. Security

Security considerations for selecting a broker generally fall into two categories: fund security and account security. Fund security refers to the safety of your assets held by the broker. This is a function of the health of the brokerage firm overall. Account security deals with issues related to fraud. A breach of either one can be a nightmare for you, so be sure you understand what protection your broker has in place.

### Fund Security

You may have seen the sticker in the corner of the window when you walked into your broker's office. Chances are your broker is a member of one or more of the regulating or insuring bodies. Of course, these organizations will differ among various countries, so we'll discuss the primary bodies within the United States and you can look for the counterpart if you're doing business outside of the United States.

The Federal Deposit Insurance Corporation (FDIC) maintains the stability and public confidence in the U.S. financial system by insuring deposits and examining and supervising financial institutions. Savings, checking, and other deposit accounts, when combined, are generally insured to $100,000 per depositor in each bank the FDIC insures. Deposits held in different categories of ownership—such as single or joint accounts—may be separately insured. Also, the FDIC generally provides separate coverage for retirement accounts, such as individual retirement accounts (IRAs) and Keoghs, insured up to $250,000.

Investors and traders should look for the Securities Investor Protection Corporation (SIPC). When a brokerage firm is closed due to bankruptcy or other financial difficulties and customer assets are missing, the SIPC steps in as quickly as possible and, within certain limits, works to return customers' cash, stock and other securities. Without SIPC, investors at financially troubled brokerage firms might lose their securities or money forever or wait for years while their assets are tied up in court. SIPC has limits of $500,000 per investor with a maximum of $100,000 cash.

One of the self-regulatory organizations (SROs) that oversees the brokerage industry is the National Association of Securities Dealers (NASD). The NASD reviews the activities of nearly 5,100 brokerage firms, about 171,000 branch offices, and more than 663,000 registered brokers. They oversee and regulate trading in equities, corporate bonds, securities futures, and options. The NASD operates the largest securities dispute resolution forum in the world, processing over 4,600 arbitrations and nearly 1,000 mediations a year.

The New York Stock Exchange (NYSE) also has a regulatory body that provides oversight to broker and trading activity. NYSE member organizations hold 98 million customer accounts or 84 percent of the total public customer accounts handled by broker-dealers. Total assets of NYSE member organizations are over $4 trillion.

### Account Security

Account security is not as great a problem as many people perceive it to be. However, that doesn't mean that the opportunity for fraud and account security breaches doesn't exist. Perhaps the greatest risk occurs when traders go to their local coffee shop and log on to their account through a wireless network. Entering your account password in such a setting could put your password into the wrong hands. To address this concern, see if your broker has a secure password key for online access. This simple key generates a random number password, which changes every minute or so. Even if a hacker should get your password in the coffee shop, it would be useless in seconds.

Another useful service offered by many brokers is an account alert system. This will send alerts to your e-mail, cell phone, or personal digital assistant when any transactions or changes occur within your account. Obviously, if an unauthorized individual should gain access to your account, you would be notified when they attempted to do anything.

## You Are in Control

In this fickle game of courting brokers, there's something that you need to keep in mind: You're the one in control. Brokers want your business and when they get it, they don't want to lose you. Dating prospective traders and investors is an expensive proposition for brokers and they want to find clients as cost and time efficiently as possible. Don't assume that the broker holds all the cards and that you must meekly accept whatever service and pay whatever fees are imposed upon you. Define your requirements, do your shopping, and you'll find that Mr. Right Broker is out there for you.

# TAKE ACTION

## Act for Results

# The Trade and Beyond

## WEALTH HAS A PURPOSE

It was in Las Vegas, Nevada, where we were invited to present our Five Points for Trading Success at the Traders Expo held in the Paris Resort Hotel. With standing room only, the room was electrified. The venue had quickly filled to capacity and there was simply no more room left for us to take any more traders who had come to see us that day. We were disappointed that so many had to be turned away but, at the same time, we couldn't help but be excited because, it was then that we knew we had something special to offer. The presentation went well and the crowd responded with many questions and comments, letting us know that we struck a chord. As we were wrapping up our equipment, a lady approached us and introduced herself, thanked us for a great presentation, and asked us if we'd consider writing a book. We listened carefully to her proposal, but as soon as she left the room, we looked at each other, laughed, and said, "Sure, like we have time to write a book."

About six months later, we still had the book idea on our minds, so we contacted our friend from Vegas. We chatted a bit about how this project would come together, and after a number of conversations, we agreed to commit our presentation to paper. We knew that there would be challenges in being able to meet our chapter deadlines, so we devised a plan to write as we traveled. There is no denying that the seminar circuit can be as exciting as it is grueling, and with a schedule as aggressive as ours, there were times when we didn't even know where we were going until we looked at our travel itineraries. So as we visited each country, we made it a point to write along the way. Chapter 1 started in Atlanta, Chapter 2 in Orlando, then on to Frankfurt, Switzerland, London, and Spain. Next stop, Stuttgart, then Stockholm, followed by Chicago before returning back home. As we wrote our final chapters, we found ourselves in Dubai, Hong Kong, and then Taiwan. We finally wound up in Paris in a wonderful little coffee shop off the beaten path to write the last pages of our manuscript. What started out as an almost impossible feat for us wound up becoming one of the most rewarding experiences of our lives. Not quite knowing how we were going to do it, we did manage to complete these 15 chapters in less than three months. With this being our last chapter, we thought it was important for us to tell you some of the reasons why we do what we do and encourage you to take action toward your goals and passions.

## What Is Your Purpose?

We have done our best to deliver what we believe is a plan that can help you create true wealth for yourself. Our goal was to take complicated market strategies and break them down into simple ideas that would be easy to understand and implement. While each chapter has been filled with the "how-to" instructions for creating wealth by using sound trading strategies and risk management principles, we thought it was most important for us to explain some of the "whys" for creating wealth.

We are individuals who believe that our lives have a purpose. Many people think that the reason we do what we do is to show investors how to make money and, although there is some truth to that, our roots go much deeper. In the beginning chapters we talked about greed as an emotion and how it was something that needed to be controlled. As one of the driving forces behind price movement in the market, there is no denying that greed can take on a life of its own. We know that there are many thousands of people who believe that if they were rich the world would think of them as being greedy and with that belief comes guilt. As a result of this guilt, we have met traders who have self-destructed, thinking that it's better for them not to be rich. Instead, they settle for average wages and a life filled with just getting by. Then there are some who believe they don't have the capacity or deserve to be wealthy. These people do what they can to avoid taking any action that might result in success.

There is something you need to know about The Market Guys. Neither of us come from money, and we have both experienced many challenges along the way that have taught us valuable lessons about life. As children we learned from our parents that life is sweet and the challenges we face make it even sweeter. However, the most important thing we have both learned from our parents is that faith is everything—faith in our ability to achieve; faith in people who want to do what's right; faith in our Creator, who has given us the opportunity to touch the lives of others who are less fortunate; and faith in knowing that we all have a purpose in life. It's this faith that brings us, two regular guys who have a passion for teaching and a sweet tooth for life, to a place where we realize that it's not a series of lucky breaks that has brought us to success but rather our purpose in life that has brought us to you.

Take a good look around and you will see millions of regular people working hard to make a living but have somehow forgotten to make a life. It's sad to see so many people just wandering through the years without even a simple plan for retirement. They almost seem okay with just getting by, month to month, paycheck to paycheck, with no regard for their future. Some are happy with the status quo while others are striving to break out, waiting for the time when they can make a difference. We're sure you've heard variations of the 80/20 rule, where 20 percent of the people are doers, who make things happen, and 80 percent are the followers who let things happen. If you think about it, the world needs both doers and followers. The followers are the backbone of society, the driving force behind most world economies, and if it weren't for them, the leaders wouldn't have anyone to lead. The "20-percenters" are movers and shakers who are not afraid to take on some risk in their lives. These are the people who were able to become good leaders because at one time in their lives they were good followers.

But what really separates these two very distinct groups of people? Actually, very little separates them. A 20-percenter might be the five-year-old boy who runs a little bit harder on the football field to score the goal, or the middle-school girl who studies just a little bit longer each day to make the grade. Twenty-percenters could also be the parents who add an hour to their lunch in order to make the school play during the day. These little extra efforts pay high dividends in the world of the doers. And those extra hours for lunch, when invested correctly, leave a lasting impression on the life of a child who sees

Mommy and Daddy clapping for them in the audience while they're singing their song. If these examples are hitting home, then chances are you are a doer who has sampled some of these dividends yourself. It truly is the sweetness of life, and as we get older we see that the examples we set become the standard others will follow.

As parents, we have seen the returns from investing in our kids. They are mirrors who reflect our beliefs and behavior patterns, which is why parents should be careful about how they handle their finances. If we're not careful, we could pass on a legacy of financial disaster to our children and grandchildren. What do you want your legacy to be with your friends and family? What financial legacy will you leave to improve the world around you? These are the same questions we've asked ourselves, and it's the reason why we have written this book.

## Changing the World One Person at a Time

Of course, we show people how to make money in the market, but it's what we do with this money that makes all the difference. If you think you are a doer now, just imagine what kind of a doer you will be once you have accumulated significant wealth in your life. If you were that little boy on the football field who ran a little harder to help your team win the game then chances are you are the man who will go the extra mile to help a homeless person. If you were that middle-school girl who studied to make the grade then there is a good possibility you are the teacher who stays back in class to help that struggling student of yours. If you were one of those parents who took off from work to see your child perform in the school play, then you may be the one who winds up with grandchildren who are leaders of the free world. We teach our children about greatness, but it's our demonstration of faith that convinces them that they, too, can go out and make the world a better place. If you have been to any of our live seminars, you will always hear us talk about the reasons why we do, and it's all about touching greatness.

We were in Stockholm when this idea hit us the hardest. Before we enter any new country we make it a point to study the culture in order to get a better understanding of the people there so we can have an easier time relating to our audience. One of the things we were glad to know is that most Swedes do not buy into the loud infomercials that make promises of millions made overnight, nor do they appreciate anyone making a scene in public, especially when it comes to money. We have never been the ones who make false promises of instant riches. We were in Sweden to talk about how to create wealth in the stock market, and we were doing it on a public stage in the heart of Stockholm. We weren't sure how we were going to be received. Right before we went on stage, back in the dressing room, we made a decision to simply do what we have always done on stage. We spoke for two days teaching charts, trends, risk management, and options. At the end of the two-day seminar, we stood up and told everyone in the theater why we do what we do. What happened next was nothing less than amazing.

One by one, people came to us. Annette spoke of the work she was doing in the business community to help raise money for charity. Maria, our emcee, introduced us to Nordine, a former professional hockey player who retired from the sport to sells bricks. His story was so fascinating that we had to learn more. Nordine was neither a bricklayer nor a construction worker but, in fact, was one of those great people who believe they are here to make a difference. Yes, he sold bricks all right, but not in a way you might expect. He would search for people who lived in small villages that were so poor they didn't even have clean water to drink. Then, once he found these people, he would go back home and sell bricks for them. Every brick he sold carried with it the name of the person who purchased the brick. Once he sold enough bricks, he would go back to those villages and build wells for the people who needed water. Each well cost about $12,000, but the most amazing thing about these wells is that it brought growth to the local economies. Once a well was dug, people would travel to it in order to get drinking water. Once there, they would spend what little money they had on items found in shops scattered around the well. As these small economies grew, roads were eventually built, allowing more people to come. Some of the brick buyers would even come to see the fruit of their generosity, and eventually there would be so many people coming to these towns that it would attract the tourists. Imagine for a moment what would happen if we bought one brick from Nordine with every profitable trade. How many wells could we build? Would that be important to the people in the village?

## What's Your Story?

One at a time they came, one story after the other. Marie talked about a nonprofit organization called Students in Free Enterprise (SIFE), telling stories of students who are aspiring to be the CEOs of their own companies. With business plans in hand, they'd partake in competitions all over the world in order to showcase their talents and ideas. The judges who vote in these competitions are CEOs of major corporations who listen to the candidates present their business plans and hear their dreams of changing the world for good. Imagine how many young minds we could sponsor if we all took only one week of our profits each year and put it toward an organization like SIFE.

Then there was Charlie—a truly amazing man, 26 years young with the wisdom of a 90 year old, who spoke about things he was doing with students to encourage them as young entrepreneurs. For years, these students have heard from the MBAs and lecturers who had all of the degrees and accolades, but Charlie was special. When Charlie spoke, people listened, because they knew he was the real deal. His wisdom came through in every word, and you could see in his eyes the passion for the work he was doing. You see, Charlie considered himself underprivileged as a child. With divorced parents who were unemployed and a father who at one time was homeless, Charlie refers to himself as "The Ghetto Kid." He and his cousin are the only two in his immediate family to have graduated from high school. Today, he speaks to college students to help guide them through the initial stages of setting up a business. Keep in mind that Swedish students are only obligated to go through nine years of primary and secondary school, unlike U.S. students who are obligated to 12 years before going to college. To look at him, you would never know that he is a multimillionaire, yet that was the thing that impressed us most about him. He is a humble man who knows where he has come from but, interestingly enough, he now thinks of himself as being overprivileged. So he spends his days sharing his knowledge and wealth with people he cares about, including his family, and gives back to the world in thanksgiving.

It's overwhelming to see the outpouring of success stories. There are so many stories that there are times when we are up on stage feeling beside ourselves, it's that surreal. Through our travels around the world, we are touching people and people are touching us. If you are one of those people who have it in your heart to give back to the world, then welcome to our club. The energy that keeps us going comes from knowing that in our audience there will be one person who will achieve a level of success that will earn him or her a place in history. Is that person you? Are you the person who is going to go out in the world with the wealth you have created for yourself and make a difference?

If you understand what we have written in this book with regard to profiting in the markets, then you are now armed with a tool that can change the world. It all starts with one person, one story, and one trade. So, as you can see, the Market Guys represent a lot more than showing people how to trade the markets. There is a much bigger picture here. If you want to be a member of the most amazing network in the world, you must first have faith that the plan will work and be willing to act on that plan. Without the action plan, everything just sits there. Everyone swims in a sea of ideas and opportunities but, without action, you never gain ground. One of the most frustrating experiences of all is when you start wondering, "what if." What if I had just acted on that idea years ago and followed through on it? What if I had listened to myself and made that trade? What if that trade allowed me to give back to those who have given to me?

---

### Chatter Box—AJ

I would much rather regret something I have done than to regret something I have not done.

---

## Take Action

After you have followed the four points that we spoke about in the previous chapters, you will see that it brings you to the last point, which is to take action. This is the final step in the "how-to" category, and it's where we get to the place were we are entering the trade. Many people get stuck on this part because it's the point in time where they are actually taking the risk and not just thinking about it. This is also the point where the fear emotion will appear. If this is happening to you, then rest assured—you are in good company. This is why we say, over and over again, expect to lose money from time to time, but make sure you are protecting yourself when a stock moves against you. If you are the person who is going to change the world with your wealth, then you have a lot more riding on the line than the person who is just looking to make a profit in the market.

We are now holding you accountable for your losses. If you do not protect your profits, then how are you going to be able to build that orphanage? If you allow your losses to run, how are you going to help Nordine build those wells? If you are calculated in your strategies, then this step-by-step plan of action will increase your probability of profiting, and you are on your way to success. Remember, enter the trade, and then protect with a stop loss. This is your plan for taking action.

> He who knows not and knows not that he knows not is a fool.
> Avoid him.
> He who knows not and knows that he knows not is a student.
> Teach him.
> He who knows and knows not that he knows is asleep.
> Awaken him.
> He who knows and knows that he knows is wise.
> Follow him.

(Anonymous proverb)

May God bless you,
Rick and AJ
The Market Guys

# Glossary

**ask price**   The price at which a market maker is willing to sell a stock.

**assignment**   A notice that is received by an option writer stating that the option they have sold has been exercised by the purchaser or owner of the option.

**at-the-market**   Describes the action of one who enters an order to buy or sell a stock immediately at the best available current price. A market order guarantees execution but not a price, so be wary of using "market orders" in stocks with low average volume or liquidity. If the bid/ask spread is wide, you may wind up paying a lot more for that stock or option than you originally anticipated.

**at-the-money**   When an option has a strike price that equals the market price of the underlying security. Example: If IBM were trading $95 per share, the $95 call and put would be at-the-money.

**bid and ask (also known as the National Best Bid and Offer, or NBBO)**   The highest and lowest offers for a security in all exchanges and all market makers.

**bid price**   The price at which a market maker is willing to buy a stock.

**breakout**   A price move over an established resistance level or below an established support level that is generally supported by an increase in volume.

**call option**   Gives the owner the right, not the obligation, to buy stock at a specific price over a given period of time.

**cash-secured put selling**   The selling of a put option using cash in the account to cover the purchase of the stock should the put seller be assigned a long position. Selling a put obligates the seller to buy stock from the buyer of the put option. The owner of the put option would exercise the put, which requires the seller of the put to buy stock with the cash that has been held aside in the account for this purpose.

**cost averaging down**   A popular strategy based on a corrupt form of dollar cost averaging. This is where traders buy more of a stock that is trending down in order to lower the cost basis of a losing position.

**derivative**   In finance, a security whose price is dependent on or derived from one or more underlying assets. The derivative itself is merely a contract between two or more parties. Its value is determined by fluctuations in the underlying asset. The most common underlying assets include stocks, bonds, commodities, currencies, interest rates, and market indexes. Most derivatives are characterized by high leverage.

**dollar cost averaging**   This is where investors deposit small amounts of money each month into an account that has been set up to automatically purchase shares in a mutual fund equal to the amount deposited. The goal is to accumulate shares in a retirement portfolio without having to suffer the pain of having to endure extreme price swings brought on by market volatility.

**downtrend**   A time when successive drops in a security price close at levels lower than those achieved in previous moves and when highs occur at levels lower than previous highs.

**exchange-traded fund (ETF)**   A basket of securities that is designed to generally track an index—broad stock or bond market, stock industry sector, or international stock—yet trades like a single stock.

**expiration date**   The day in which the option contract expires. Technically, most option contracts expire on the third Saturday of the expiration month, but what most traders are focused on is the third Friday of the expiration month, with that being the last day the option contracts can be traded.

**Expiration Friday**   The third Friday of the month, representing the last trading day for the options in that calendar month. *Example:* Options that carry the January expiration date will be traded up until the close of the market on the third Friday of the month in January.

**in-the-money**   For a call option, it's when the option's strike price is below the market price of the underlying security. For a put option, it's when the option's strike price is above the market price of the underlying stock. In other words, it's when an option has intrinsic value.

**intrinsic value**   For call options, this is the difference between the underlying stock's price and the strike price of the option. For put options, it's the difference between the strike price and the underlying stock's price. Keep in mind that if the difference is negative, the option has no intrinsic value. Example: If IBM is trading at $95 and you are looking at a call with a strike price of $90, the call will have intrinsic value equal to $5. Compare that to a call with a strike price of $100; the $100 call would have no intrinsic value.

**Long-term equity anticipation securities (LEAPS)**   Publicly traded options contracts with expiration dates that are longer than one year. Structurally, LEAPS are no different than short-term options, but the later expiration dates offer the opportunity for long-term investors or traders to gain exposure to prolonged price changes without needing to use a combination of shorter-term option contracts. The premiums for LEAPS are higher than for standard options in the same stock because the increased expiration date gives the underlying asset more time to make a substantial move and for the investor to make a healthy profit.

**option chain**   A list of option quotes highlighting information such as expiration month, strike prices, trading volume, and so on. The layout is similar to what you might see in a typical spreadsheet.

**out-of-the-money**   For a call, it's when an option's strike price is higher than the market price of the underlying security. For a put, it's when the option strike price is below the market price of the underlying security.

**pending order file**   The place where limit buy and sell orders are held until they are due for a fill. Market makers are very much aware of their pending order file and many times will trade against the order flow brought on by account holders of the broker they trade for.

**premium**   This is the total cost of the option contract, which is nothing more than the sum of the option's intrinsic value and time value. It's important to know that volatility also affects the premium of an option. Higher-volatility stocks have a tendency to trade with higher option premiums because there is a great chance that these option contracts can increase in value over a given period of time. This volatility premium is reflected in the time premium and has no effect on intrinsic value.

**profit taking**   The result of short-term traders placing sell orders in a stock to realize a profit for the trader. This wave of selling results in the stock's moving to lower price levels.

**put options**   Gives the owner the right, not the obligation, to sell stock at a specific price over a given period of time.

**resistance**   The price level at which the selling pressure is strong enough to prevent the stock from rising further. You can think of this as a ceiling where the sellers have convinced the buyers that they are outnumbered, and the buyers move to the sidelines. Like support, this is not an exact price level, and it's best to think of resistance as a price area where supply in the stock has overcome the demand.

**short covering**   The act of purchasing securities in order to close an open short position. This is done by buying the same type and number of securities that were sold short. Most often, traders cover their shorts whenever they speculate that the securities will rise. In order to make a profit, a short seller must cover the shorts by purchasing the security below the original selling price.

**short selling or "shorting"**   A way to profit from the decline in price of a security, such as stock or a bond. To profit from the stock price going down, a short seller can borrow a security and sell it, expecting that it will decrease in value so that they can buy it back at a lower price and keep the difference. Short sellers assume that they will be able to buy the stock at a lower amount than the price at which they sold short. The opposite of going long.

**short squeeze**   A situation in which a lack of supply and an excess demand for a traded stock forces the price upward. This, in turn, forces short sellers into a position where they want out. As short sellers liquidate and buy to cover their positions, the demand increases in the stock and the price rally intensifies.

**sideways trend**   A period of time when prices lay flat or move within a relatively tight range. Also known as a trading range or consolidation pattern, buyers and sellers establish boundaries that represent support and resistance, yet supply and demand are balanced. Investors would see this as a trend less stock.

**simple moving average (SMA)**   The unweighted mean of the previous n data points. For example, a 10-day simple moving average of closing price is the mean of the previous 10 days' closing prices.

**stepping up**   A term used to describe the actions of a person who is moving up his or her limit bid on a buy order. This is a common practice demonstrated by the general public and one that market makers count on after they have taken a long position in their own trading accounts.

**strike price or exercise price**   The stated price per share, for which underlying stock may be purchased (for a call) or sold (for a put) by the option holder upon exercise of the option contract. When you exercise your option, this is the value that you get the shares for. Option strike prices are usually in increments of $2.50 or $5.00.

**support**   Support is the level at which demand for the stock is strong enough to keep the stock from dropping any further. Support levels are usually identified somewhere below where the stock is actually trading and, although it is not an exact price point, we look at support as a general area.

**time value or time premium**   The portion of the option premium that is attributable to the amount of time remaining until the expiration of the option contract. Basically, time value is the value the option has in addition to its intrinsic value.

**trough**   A low point in a business cycle or on a statistical graph.

**uptrend**   A time when successive rallies in a security price close at levels higher than those achieved in previous rallies and when lows occur at levels higher than previous lows.

**underlying asset**   The stock, bond, currency, or other value that an option contract is derived from. All references in this book were made to stocks, which is the underlying asset for all options mentioned in Chapter 10.

**volatility**   The amount of uncertainty or risk about the size of changes in a security's value. A higher volatility means that a security's value can potentially be spread out over a larger range of values. This means that the price of the security can change dramatically over a short time period in either direction. Whereas a lower volatility would mean that a security's value does not fluctuate dramatically, but changes in value at a steady pace over a period of time.

**writer**   The seller of an option contract; one who sells or "writes" the option.

# Index